Revisiting Trustworthiness in Social Interaction

Bringing together trust research, rhetoric, ethnomethodology and conversation analysis, this book formulates an analytical program for conceptualizing and defining trustworthiness as an empirical research object in social interaction.

Revisiting Trustworthiness in Social Interaction examines trustworthiness as a relational and dynamic concept. It reviews sociological and rhetorical approaches to the study of trustworthiness and respecifies it as an interactional phenomenon displayed, tested and negotiated by participants in social interaction. It identifies four participant orientations of trustworthiness that may be foregrounded in peoples' dynamic identity projects, and it defines the phenomena 'character-bound displays' and 'sequential negotiation of character', both indicative of participants' orientation to trustworthiness. In this way, the book turns the theoretical concept of trustworthiness into an empirical object of interaction analysis, pointing to a vast number of interactional indicators, which allow interaction analysts to explore if and how interactants orient to trustworthiness in an encounter. Exemplary cases from both mundane and institutional encounters are analyzed using ethnomethodological multimodal conversation analysis showing how trustworthiness is done, challenged, achieved, negotiated and lost in interaction.

The intended audiences are scholars of conversation analysis, ethnomethodology, rhetoric and the social sciences, especially communication, organizational and leadership studies, and their students.

Mie Femø Nielsen is Professor in the Department of Nordic Studies and Linguistics at the University of Copenhagen, Denmark.

Ann Merrit Rikke Nielsen is a Postdoc in the Department of Nordic Studies and Linguistics at the University of Copenhagen, Denmark.

Routledge Research in Language and Communication

Discourses of Perfection
Representing Cosmetic Procedures and Beauty Products in UK Lifestyle Magazines
Anne-Mette Hermans

The Dialects of British English in Fictional Texts
Edited by Donatella Montini and Irene Ranzato

Discursive Approaches to Socio-political Polarization and Conflict
Edited by Laura Filardo-Llamas; Esperanza Morales-López and Alan Floyd

Bridging the Gap between Conversation Analysis and Poetics
Studies in Talk-In-Interaction and Literature Twenty-Five Years after Jefferson
Edited by Raymond F. Person, Jr., Robin Wooffitt and John P. Rae

The Language of Pick-Up Artists
Online Discourses of the Seduction Industry
Daria Dayter and Sofia Rüdiger

Revisiting Trustworthiness in Social Interaction
Mie Femø Nielsen and Ann Merrit Rikke Nielsen

Communicative Spaces and Media in Bilingual Contexts
Discourses, Synergies and Counterflows in Spanish and English
Edited by Ana Sánchez-Muñoz and Jessica Retis

The Impact of Plain Language on Legal English in the United Kingdom
Christopher Williams

For more information about this series, please visit: www.routledge.com/Routledge-Research-in-Language-and-Communication/book-series/RRLC

Revisiting Trustworthiness in Social Interaction

Mie Femø Nielsen and
Ann Merrit Rikke Nielsen

Routledge
Taylor & Francis Group
NEW YORK AND LONDON

First published 2023
by Routledge
605 Third Avenue, New York, NY 10158

and by Routledge
4 Park Square, Milton Park, Abingdon, Oxon OX14 4RN

Routledge is an imprint of the Taylor & Francis Group, an informa business

Library of Congress Cataloging-in-Publication Data
Names: Femø Nielsen, Mie, author. | Nielsen, Ann Merrit Rikke, author.
Title: Revisiting trustworthiness in social interaction / Mie Femø Nielsen, Ann Merrit Rikke Nielsen.
Description: First Edition. | New York, NY : Routledge, 2023. | Series: Routledge research in language and communication | Includes bibliographical references and index. |
Identifiers: LCCN 2022010965 | ISBN 9781032249568 (hardback) | ISBN 9781032249599 (paperback) | ISBN 9781003280903 (ebook)
Subjects: LCSH: Social interaction—Research. | Reliability. | Conversation analysis.
Classification: LCC HM1111 .F474 2023 | DDC 302—dc23/eng/20220307
LC record available at https://lccn.loc.gov/2022010965

ISBN: 978-1-032-24956-8 (hbk)
ISBN: 978-1-032-24959-9 (pbk)
ISBN: 978-1-003-28090-3 (ebk)

DOI: 10.4324/9781003280903

Typeset in Sabon
by Apex CoVantage, LLC

Contents

1 Introduction

> What a man! I remember he gave me a great piece of direction. There was one scene where I thought my character should speak very deliberately. John just raised his hand and said, "It's okay, Michael, you can speak faster – he's an honest man."
>
> Michael Caine[1]

In this quotation, actor Michael Caine refers to being directed by John Huston when they were shooting the film *The Man Who Would Be King*. The quotation provides an example of how professional actors and directors work with character design based on interactional exchanges. This book explores the specific phenomenon of identity construction via a myriad of miniscule interactional moves, strategies and actions – but it does so with specific regard to trustworthiness as it plays out in real-life settings.

Trustworthiness is one of many aspects that affect the construction of mutual trust. Mutual trust is essential for smooth and successful collaboration in the social systems that people navigate as part of their professional lives and in private settings. Trustworthiness is therefore a concern for all members of society. We believe that interactional construction of trustworthiness is therefore a social action of fundamental importance. That is the concern of this book.

1 Retrieved on 20 November 2018, but no longer active. A similar quote was retrieved on 12 February 2021 at www.sheilaomalley.com/?p=2700.

DOI: 10.4324/9781003280903-1

Trust is a concern for all

Our own way of studying trust and trustworthiness grew out of a large ethnomethodology and conversation analysis (EM/CA)-informed research project on communication in international companies and organizations. The research interest of that project was, at the outset, neither trust nor trustworthiness. Rather, it was the interactional accomplishment of organizational practices such as collaboration, teamwork, management, day-to-day coordination and employee communication. The focus was on the interaction of individuals within these organizations, be they a manager, an employee, a project manager, a research and development consultant or a salesperson in their daily work life. For many years, we have traveled across four continents observing, shadowing and filming meetings and office interactions, collecting email correspondence and documents. We have interviewed countless international employees, managers and self-employed individuals, ranging from a non-governmental organization (NGO) project group in an old historical building in Copenhagen with a stucco ceiling to the senior executives of a major Japanese company in a Tokyo skyscraper. Other examples would be the employees in large cubicle office landscapes of Mumbai, the mediator at a huge and flat windmill plant construction site on the Uruguayan pampas, a small engineering group in compact and noisy office spaces in Kampala, and an information technology (IT) consultant working internationally via his own startup located in a home office in a well-to-do suburb of Buenos Aires. In addition, we have drawn on colleagues' and collaborators' data. Inspired by their work, we ended up working with more than a hundred companies and organizations from thirty-five countries.

What we found to be at the top of everyone's list of concerns was trust: how to trust others, how to determine someone's trustworthiness and how to come off as trustworthy to others. Their interest in these phenomena was not in trust and trustworthiness as purely abstract concepts. Nor was it in the statistical distribution of perceived trust and trustworthiness within certain sociological, demographic or national groups. What they were interested in, rather, was what trustworthiness looked like in practice – that is, in trust and trustworthiness as day-to-day actions negotiated, achieved and sometimes lost through interaction with others. After a while, we began to ask everyone we met about how, specifically, they managed to be able to trust others. What did they do to be considered trustworthy themselves? What were their concerns and practices? Most importantly, how did they see indications of achieved trust and trustworthiness manifested in their interaction with managers, colleagues and various business partners? In parallel, we filmed a wide range of formal and informal meetings – such as weekly updates, team meetings, one-on-one encounters, brainstorming sessions, breakfast meetings, online meetings, cultural training sessions and telehealth consultations. Over two years, we analyzed more than a hundred interviews and collected a large corpus of expressed perceptions concerning what trust and trustworthiness 'looks like' in different types of interaction, as well as more than 120 hours of video ethnographic data containing examples of these practices.

If trustworthiness is a participant's concern and interactional project, it should be possible to trace it in authentic recordings of social interaction. Our ambition was to apply micro-analytic methods to video ethnographic data, in order to be able to identify participants' moves, actions and interactional strategies aimed at achieving, testing, maintaining and negotiating the trustworthiness of themselves and their co-participants in the course of social encounters.

Our ambition became a reality when our massive data collection came to serve as a pilot project for a core group research project.[2] One subproject of this was specifically concerned with the local interactional production of trust and trustworthiness, of which this book now forms part. We have taken great care to expand our video data corpus to include footage of not just more business and health care interaction between professionals, as well as between professionals and laypersons, but also other types of service interaction, such as between municipal service providers and citizens. We will present some of these data as small excerpts in this book, but the vast majority of it has merely been used to guide us in the development of our research questions, to push us in the development of our theoretical models, to force us to test the boundaries and implications of our analyses and to conceptualize trustworthiness empirically.

Exploring trustworthiness from an EM/CA perspective

This book is concerned with how trustworthiness can be explored as an interactional phenomenon within the framework of ethnomethodology (EM) and conversation analysis (CA), with the principle focus on professional settings. Ethnomethodology is a branch of sociology concerned with the study of people's (*ethno-*) methods for doing what they do. Building on Husserl's phenomenology (1970) and the writings of both Parsons (1951) and Goffman (1955, 1959, 1961, 1963), EM was founded in the 1960s by Harold Garfinkel (Garfinkel, 1967, 1996; cf. Heritage, 1984; Lynch, 1994) as the study of the procedures and considerations by which ordinary members of society make sense of the social

2 The Velux Foundations funded the project *Professionals' use of video meetings* in 2017. That project explored what happens when professionals use video-mediated interaction, what challenges they face when doing so, how they compensate for the shortcomings of video mediation and how they accomplish relating to and trusting each other.

world, and of their methods of practical, common-sense understanding and reasoning. Objects of study are the observable and accountable production of social actions, which concertedly constitute local order and meaning. This study implies a re-specification of concepts that are otherwise taken for granted within academic fields such as sociology, psychology and linguistics. Garfinkel points to EM's "fundamental phenomenon" being "every society's locally, endogenously produced, naturally organized, reflexively accountable, ongoing, practical achievement, being everywhere, always, only, exactly and entirely, members' work" (Garfinkel, 1991, p. 11). As a radical turn from conventional sociology, EM made available methods for studying members' methods of practical common-sense reasoning and understanding. This is the lens through which we choose to study trustworthiness: as a member's concern and as a practical, ongoing achievement. Building on EM, conversation analysis is an approach to sequential analysis of talk-in-interaction. It is, much like EM, concerned with the observable and accountable, local and endogenous production of social actions (Sacks *et al.*, 1974; Sacks, 1992, 1985). However, CA's focus is on the sequential organization of situated and social interaction. So whereas EM uses a wide variety of data, including the ones we collected in our pilot project, CA exclusively uses video and audio recordings of naturally occurring interaction as data, as do we in our analyses in this book. These recordings afford analyses of embodied interaction moment by moment, as situated practices produced by members in their social settings. We will elaborate on CA and its methods further in Chapter 4, before applying CA analysis to a range of video ethnographic data.

Focusing on participants' sensorially observable actions, rather than their motives

Image is in the eye of the beholder. For someone to present as trustworthy, someone *else* must find that person worthy of trust. Therefore, trustworthiness is a matter of perception, and this makes the concept of trustworthiness a difficult social phenomenon to study empirically when we are concerned with observable actions. Unsurprisingly, at the outset, EM/CA scholars do not deal with peoples' perceptions, since other people's thoughts are neither observable, accountable nor accessible (Garfinkel, 1963; Heritage, 1995). However, the EM/CA concern is with what participants in interaction are concerned with and oriented to *in situ*. That means, in this context, a participant's concern to be able to trust others and to make others trust them (Garfinkel, 1963).

Each interactional move (or turn at talk) in any given social encounter is shaped by the local context. It also renews/shapes the context for the next action (or turn of talk) in the course of the interaction (Heritage & Clayman, 2010). As interactants we (figuratively speaking) lay out the train tracks while conducting the train. We only have sensorially observable actions and appearances to work with, because we do not have access to thoughts and motives. When members of society interact and experience each other's behavior, they assess one another's character, mood, intentions and so forth – whether or not they prove right in making those assessments. Therefore, if participants in social interaction can draw conclusions about others' trustworthiness from their behavior, so we as analysts should strive to be able to explore, in detail, both the communicative actions and the local social assessments accomplished by participants in social interaction, as they make sense of the social world. As Sacks points out in relation to the members of society, "You cannot find what they're trying to do until you find the kinds of things they work with" (1987, p. 67). The focus of research must be those very "kinds of things" that participants "work with" in their social interaction, not assumptions about their motives, reasons and personalities.

The aim of this book is therefore to explore interactional strategies and moves that may *indicate* trustworthiness as a member's concern in social interaction. We want to establish from the outset that our ambition to study trustworthiness in an EM/CA context should not be mistaken for cognitivism or mentalism. Our research interest is not the mind, mental functions, mental phenomena or thought processes. Our research approach in this project is fundamentally emic and does not draw on introspection. We simply aim to identify interactional behavior that may be observable and interpretable *in the data* as indicators of participants' orientation to their own (or others') trustworthiness *in situ*. We find such a research endeavor to be within the scope of EM/CA methodology, and we have done our best to succeed with this endeavor.

Standing on the shoulders of trust research and rhetoric

Academic fields which have traditionally been concerned with trustworthiness includes the social sciences, especially sociology, economics, political science and psychology; business and management; philosophy; and rhetoric. While we humbly acknowledge the literally thousands of years of research into what constitutes the phenomenon of trustworthiness, what we are seeking to do in this book is to introduce some further understandings of the phenomenon and its conceptualizations in rhetoric and in trust research in both the social sciences and in psychology, as well as ethnomethodological studies of trust and the study of character-like concepts in discursive psychology. We will then move on to elaborate on our own approach to the study of trustworthiness as a social production and as an interactional achievement.

Drawing upon insights from the previously mentioned disciplines and our extensive data collection, and using these as a backdrop, we identified some key aspects of trustworthiness which have guided our study.

We present our theoretical conceptualization of trustworthiness in Chapter 2 and Chapter 3. We introduce our methodology in Chapter 2 and Chapter 4, and then explore trustworthiness empirically, as interactional manifestations oriented to the aforementioned aspects, in Chapter 5–8, before a concluding Chapter 9. Throughout the book, our theoretical conceptualization – as well as our data analysis – is informed by and in dialogue with a review of EM/CA work. In this way, we hope to inspire future work in formal trust research and rhetoric, as well.

2 Doing EM/CA research on inferred social phenomena

In this chapter, we will discuss the classic discrepancies between readily observable and inferred social phenomena. We will argue that it is within the realm of ethnomethodology (EM) and conversation analysis (CA) to explore social phenomena which are neither emic categories nor directly observable (and thus codable) in embodied interaction, yet these phenomena must nonetheless be studied by means of what *is* actually observable, and perhaps even codable. We will also review a couple of classic CA studies which have elegantly and convincingly crossed over into working with research objects of a more abstract character.

Show it in the data

From an EM/CA perspective, it has been said that the only things a researcher can defensibly say something about are those which are observable in the world (Heritage, 1995). We subscribe to that view. In

DOI: 10.4324/9781003280903-2

principle – and it is a strong principle – there is a missing link between observable embodied actions on the one hand and character assessments on the other. That missing link will be dealt with in this chapter.

CA is an inductive method that takes the task of putting 'data first' seriously by appropriately matching types of research questions with data suited to provide the kind of insights necessary for answering such questions. CA is concerned with the identification of interactional practices through which parties to interaction perform and recognize social actions. It aims to disclose their function and organization, as well as the social activities and the social order which they constitute. Key aspects of CA are its emic character, the factor that any analysis always starts with an observation to allow for inductive discovery of the organization of any interaction, and the fundamental premise that all social interaction is endogenously ordered. This orderliness is continuously produced by participants, who are constantly making sense in their interaction, thus co-constructing a world which "is much more finely organized than you could imagine" (Sacks, 1984, p. 414).

Everyone who has spent literally hundreds of hours sitting in on data sessions with Gail Jefferson, Emanuel Schegloff and other founders of this method has been schooled in the basic mantras:

1. "show it in the data"[1], i.e. the proof should really be in the pudding – otherwise, we cannot make a given analytical claim;
2. "if we can hear it, they can hear it"[2], which has been widely used to warrant analytical observations of X potentially being a response to Y;
3. "why that now" (Schegloff & Sacks, 1973, p. 299), which forces the analyst to explore the design of any given action (the "that") in its sequential environment (the "now") before concluding on the meaning of the action (the "why"), i.e.
4. "how they do it before why they do it", since there is
5. "order at all points" (Sacks, 1992, p. I: 484), which is possible because members use the
6. "seen but unnoticed" (Garfinkel, 1967, pp. 37–38) standardized and standardizing background features of everyday scenes as schemes of interpretation, which they reproduce by enacting them. However, that fact should never let the analyst forget that
7. "the context is not a bucket", because each interactional move may indeed be shaped by the global and local context, but also shapes the context (Heritage & Clayman, 2010) for the next action by renewing the potentiality of possible next actions; and

1 We have not been able to trace this quote to a particular publication for citation, and we are therefore left with quoting it verbally from many data sessions, especially those in the 1990s with Gail Jefferson.

2 See footnote 1.

8. participants negotiate intersubjectivity by means of exactly the next-turn proof procedure (Sacks *et al.*, 1974), which consists of looking at how the interactant in the next turn respond to a turn, and how the first speaker responds to the response, i.e. how the meaning is interpreted and negotiated *in situ* by participants themselves.

Working with recordings and transcripts of social interaction in its authentic setting enables the meticulous analysis of multimodal action formation, turn design, sequence organization and the correspondence of talk, body, prosody, mimic, gesture, posture, object handling and physical environment – such as that formulated by Pomerantz and Fehr (1997, 2011) as an analytical program:

Task 1: Select a sequence and examine the opening and closing as achievements.

Task 2: Select a turn within the sequence for close analysis.

Task 2a: Characterize the actions performed in the turn. Consider how the actions fit within the sequences of action.

Task 2b: Describe the methods used to perform the actions. Consider the understandings provided by the use of those methods.

Task 2c: Describe the methods used for taking, keeping and transitioning between turns. Consider the understandings provided by the use of those methods.

Task 2d: Consider the ways in which the interactants enact identities, roles and/or relationships.

Task 3: Select other turns within the sequence and do Tasks 2a–d for each of the turns.

Training students like this obviously makes it clear that there is a weighty heritage involved in that first mantra of showing any analytical claim in the data. So yes, if we aim to study trustworthiness within the realms of EM/CA, using CA as our primary method, restricting the analysis to what is observable in the data is a given.

Nobody is claiming that 'the surface' of discourse is all there is

Sticking to the observable surface is not to be viewed as an obstacle, even if we rightly call it a restriction. It is a rich world of sounds, signs and sensations which we try to grasp by transcribing what we can see and hear. We may perhaps also make a note of what we feel, taste and smell when carrying out the recording, but these notes will always be considered to be secondary data. That said, there is enough left to deal with in the analysis, even when the research interest leans into subjectivity and identity:

> Rather than subjective experience lying outside of, beyond, or behind the 'surface' of talk-in-interaction (cf. Edwards, 2006b), we find it here under active management within talk-in-interaction itself, integrated into the interactional flow of meaningful sounds, signs, words and actions, and yet used precisely for its status – that is, its conventional, semiotic status – as embodied expression, spontaneous, and somewhat beyond words.
>
> (Edwards, 2007, p. 44)

To scholars from disciplines traditionally concerned with studying cognitive processes using primarily elicited data such as self-reports, this might seem like a rather extreme view. Everything is treated 'on the surface', even subjective experience. But that finely ordered, detailed, rich 'surface' of the interaction is the locus of interactants' negotiation of intersubjectivity, identity and social relations. Yet what about that which is not directly observable on 'the surface'? What about motives, agendas and subjectivity, which it is possible to gain an impression of as analyst, but which we cannot precisely point to as being 'shown in the data'? Should we then stick to the 'surface'? Yes and no. An elaborate representation of that balanced view is (also) made by Derek Edwards:

> There is a sense that language, or talk-in-interaction, is to be found only at the surface of things, and that inferences of a different kind need to be made, in order to get at what is going on below the surface. Nobody is claiming that discourse is all there is. However, the rush toward theorizing about context and subjectivity is being done without close attention to what is available on the surface. The surface turns out to be unexpectedly rich (Edwards, 2006b) – I acknowledge my rhetorical use of the counter-dispositional "unexpectedly" – and full of members' orientations to the relevance of the setting, along with the active management of subject-side considerations relevant to what they are saying. In our experience of the physical world, from which we derive the metaphors "surface" and "depth", going below the surface of things merely reveals more surfaces to examine – whether under the sea, beneath the skin or under the skull. As Wittgenstein (1958) cogently argued, and also Garfinkel (1967; cf. Coulter, 1990), and in a different way the perceptual psychologist Gibson (1979), the surface is what members themselves are actually seeing and dealing with. To the extent that subjectivity is part of social life, and relevant to language and social interaction (the practices of intersubjectivity), it has to be made available in mutually understandable ways. There are no private languages. Increasingly, the study of talk-in-interaction reveals the richly detailed and orderly "surface" workings of social interaction, including gesture and voice

> quality as well as lexical language. It is here that we find contextual relevance and (inter)subjectivity under active management in the course of social practices in ways that are essentially, and necessarily, publicly performed, and by dint of that, and *in terms of* that, recordable and analysable.
>
> (Edwards, 2007, pp. 47–48, emphasis in original)

We agree with Edwards that the 'surface' is a construct, albeit a richly detailed one. However, it is the only data available for interaction analysts who are aiming to explore the orderliness of situated interaction. We have worked by that premise for decades (e.g. Nielsen, 2000). Even though many interactants might have been participants in similar interactions with each other throughout their lives, the 'surface' is the only 'data' that is *in situ* available to the interactants or members themselves when they work at making sense of their social world. Still, time and time again, they can manage to make sense of what is not directly observable from what is. Therefore, we as analysts should eventually strive to be able to do that, as well, in order to undertake 'inter-action' analysis properly. This is an important point that we will develop later in this chapter.

Social identity is a research object

Trustworthiness is widely considered to be a character trait (see e.g. Dietz & Den Hartog, 2006). In EM/CA, trustworthiness is not a traditionally studied phenomenon, because character traits are generally not objects of research in this field. As analysts, we cannot determine whether any given participant's sensorially observable action is aimed at constructing, testing or displaying trustworthiness; and we cannot know whether a first speaker is considered trustworthy by a second speaker. Even if such a social assessment is the case (and perhaps also an intended result of another participant's actions), our analysis cannot unravel whether a given interactant's perception is based on the co-participant's locally fitted embodied action, or on something else entirely (such as past experience with or knowledge of the person), when no reference is made to such matters in the data.

However, this does not mean that EM/CA research is not concerned with how members are seen and characterized, both by themselves and by others. A considerable subfield of EM/CA is preoccupied with studying social identity as a local accomplishment, situated and co-constructed in social interaction. The foundation for this has been laid by Sacks' work on social categories, membership categorization devices and category-bound activities (1972a, 1992), as well as by Schegloff's work on descriptions (1972) and Zimmerman's work on 'discourse', 'situated' and 'transportable' identities (1998). More recently, this also includes Stokoe and Edwards on identity categories, and how they become relevant to participants (2009), and Benwell and Stokoe on categorial, operational, relational and unnoticed identities (2011).

'Member's competence' entails doing inferential work

From very early on, Harvey Sacks, one of the founders of CA, pointed to members of society being able to do inferential work based on social categorization, using what he termed *members' competences*. *Members* (i.e. of the society) are Sacks' term for categories of persons (Sacks, 1972b; Schegloff, 2007a, p. 467). Due to their membership of some social order or group, termed by Sacks a 'category', all members possess 'common-sense' knowledge from being active participants in this particular social system. According to Sacks, such knowledge is drawn upon to infer something about someone else. Members use their *members' competence* to make inferences from observing social actions. Creating meaning by inferring it from observations is any ordinary member's concern. Early on, Sacks developed an analytical program, Membership Categorization Analysis (MCA), aimed at investigating just how members go from 'external' observations of other members of the society concerned to inferences about their identity. This offers a method for empirical research into the *in situ* interactional construction of locally relevant identity categories. Sacks also proposed an analytical 'apparatus', the Membership Categorization Device (MCD) (see Sacks, 1989), which can be used to identify what he understood as categories about which ordinary members of society have common-sense knowledge. Part of the MCA program are the rules of economy and consistency, which allow the researcher to organize the categories into *collections* or *sets of categories* which commonsensically go together (Schegloff, 2007a).

There are certain parts of MCA which are particularly interesting for the study of members' inferences, and to which we will return throughout this book. One is Sacks' term *category-bound activities* (Sacks, 1972b). These may be defined as the "kinds of activities or actions or forms of conduct taken by the common-sense or vernacular culture to be specifically characteristic of a category's members" (Schegloff, 2007a, p. 470). Essential to a member's inferential work are the corollaries of two other key concepts proposed by Sacks, those being the 'viewer's maxim' and the 'hearer's maxim'. These maxims state that if a category-bound activity is being done and can be seen/heard by the analyst as being done by a member of a category to which the activity is bound, then it should be seen/heard in this way. This is also a key point to which we will return. We stand with Sacks when he argues that these maxims are oriented to norms, and when he suggests that "[v]iewers use norms to provide some of the orderliness, and proper orderliness, of the activities they observe" (Sacks, 1972a, p. 327). It is also specifically noteworthy for this discussion that Sacks maintained that categories are 'inference-rich' (Sacks, 1992, p. 41): He specified that 'inference-rich' means that "a great deal of the knowledge that members of a society have about the society is stored in terms of these categories" (Sacks, 1989, p. 272). These social categories serve as "the store house and the filing system" of our "common-sense knowledge" about "what people are like [and] how they behave" (Schegloff, 2007b, p. 469). They are built from the lived experience of seen but unnoticed rationales and behavior (Garfinkel, 1967, pp. 37–38), forming the basis of the ongoing inferential work which members of society do when interacting.

Conduct formulations are inferences from conduct

When members of a given social entity interact, they also review each other's actions and label each another's appearance and motives. This is seen in complaint environments – e.g. "he's really touchy about" X, "he was *say*ing it as if you know he wanted me to know that she was *lone:*ly" (Schegloff, 2005, pp. 452, 457). Lexical formulations such as "I dunno why you're being so aggressive" toward what someone has just done have been termed "conduct formulations" (Clift & Pino, 2020: 464).

Conduct formulations are not just formulations of conduct for the sake of it. Local and Walker (2008) point out that when participants make emotional or attitudinal formulations of a co-participant's states (e.g. "you sound happy", "don't sound so depressed"), these formulations have no "regular and systematic correspondences between phonetic detail and the expression of speaker states" (p. 740). Instead, the "phonetic characteristics which might be thought to be associated with affect may better be accounted for with reference to the management of particular sequential-interactional tasks" (p. 723). Conduct formulations are used interactionally to accomplish things other than simply formulating conduct. For instance, they might be used to accomplish getting co-participants to talk about their state (Local & Walker, 2008) or to object to a co-participant's conduct and make accusations (Clift & Pino, 2020). Nevertheless, they are made within the interaction, and they are also made about the interaction by analysts, e.g. in the transcripts (Local & Walker, 2008). Local and Walker argue that "to assert that someone sounds 'happy', 'depressed', 'surprised' etc. without serious analytic work to support the claim, is problematic" (p. 740) and should thus "have consequences for how analysts should proceed in ascribing states to participants in talk" (p. 741), i.e. "avoid making simplistic attributions of speaker states on the basis of the phonetic design of talk" (p. 741).

Nevertheless, such formulations of conduct or character traits are formulated by interactants in order to accomplish something in the interaction, be it merely formulating the conduct or accomplishing other social tasks such as fishing for information (cf. Pomerantz, 1980, on 'my side-telling' of B-events in order to get access to A-events). Those formulations are based on the interactant's perception of the co-participant's prior actions or appearances, i.e. they are inferred. It is therefore not making an unwarranted claim for us to state that inferences from behavior to character or mood or conduct are possible for interactants to make, and are therefore also possible for analysts. This is, in fact, a well-established finding.

Recipient design requires inferential work

From the beginning, CA scholars showed how speakers design their utterances so that they receive structurally aligned responses (Davidson, 1984; Garfinkel & Sacks, 1970; Sacks *et al.*, 1974); that they use 'recipient design', i.e. design their utterances to match their interlocutor's knowledge and preferences (Enfield, 2012; Goodwin, 1979, 1981; Sacks & Schegloff, 1979; Sacks *et al.*, 1974); and that they produce relevant, structurally aligned and type-conforming uptake to (i.e. doing next to) prior contributions (Raymond, 2003; Sacks *et al.*, 1974), perhaps even to the degree of being able to produce collaborative completions (Lerner, 1987/2004; Sacks, 1992). For decades, EM/CA researchers have explored how the interaction order is constituted by participants collaborating in co-constructing activities (e.g. Schegloff, 1986).

This is all very well known to an EM/CA audience. We will, however, point to the implications of this fundamental research, being that participants in interaction cannot produce relevant, situated contributions to the interaction without making inferences about both their co-participants and about information that is not necessarily available to them. Interactants design their turns and actions according to their (tacit) assessment of their co-participant's competences, background knowledge, appearance, state of mind, etc. The term 'recipient design' (Sacks *et al.*, 1974) rests upon the assumption that an interactant is able not only to assess a co-participant's knowledge, attitudes, interests, social circles, etc., but also to use that assessment in the design and delivery of a next turn fitted to the situation and the 'recipient'. The mere concept of recipient design supports our claim that inferential work is used by members to design their talk, and may therefore also – in retrospect – be used by analysts at least to attempt to identify what the inferential work was based on *in situ*.

Participants' interactional projects are recognized in the interaction as such

In social interaction, participants always have something they are "trying to do" (Sacks, 1987, p. 67). This might be an interactional "project" (cf. Schegloff, 2007b, pp. 244–250) such as asking for directions or getting an invitation to a party; institutional 'goals' (cf. Atkinson, 1982; Drew & Heritage, 1992; Heritage & Clayman, 2010) such as making a diagnosis or announcing a decision; or simply planning turn onset (when you start talking) from projection of possible completion points (when your interlocuters are potentially done talking) in a co-participant's talk (cf. Sacks *et al.*, 1974; cf. Levinson, 2012). Their co-participants can undertake the inferential work needed to recognize projects as such, so that they can not only progress, comply, preempt, etc., but fundamentally accomplish intersubjectivity in interacting and negotiating.

Furthermore, Stokoe (2011, 2014) points out that when a first pair part from a familiar type of interaction is played to trainees who are participating in Conversation Analytic Role-play Method (CARM) training, they almost always instantly recognize the utterance as being formatted to do something specific and recognizable. Furthermore, they can come up with possible relevant second pair parts, and probable designs of these, to match what they have just heard. Without the members' ability to recognize an utterance as doing something specific, training programs based on applied interventionist CA (Antaki, 2011), such as CARM (Stokoe, 2014) or the multimodal Video-based Reflection on Team Interaction (ViRTI) (Due & Lange, 2015), would not be feasible. Making observations of social actions and inferring from those observations is therefore indeed a member's concern and accomplishment.

CA studies of inferences from conduct

Making observations of social actions and inferring from those observations is the interaction analyst's concern, too. As analysts, we do not have access to members' social assessments, beyond exploring the observable interactional actions in which they are engaged. Figuratively speaking, there is an invisible line between what is sensorially observable and what may be inferred from such observations. There are, however, fine examples of CA studies of abstract social phenomena which have required some inferential work. We will now review a few of these.

Courtroom interaction

An early example is drawn from Paul Drew's seminal study of courtroom interaction (1978). He convincingly shows how membership knowledge of which neighborhoods are predominantly inhabited by Catholics or Protestants (knowledge stemming from living in Northern Ireland in the 1960s) may be used in court in descriptions of violence in order implicitly to make accusations of responsibility (Drew, 1978). A conversational implicature (Grice, 1975) is created. Such an implied accusation works because the recipients would have to do inferential work in order to recognize the description as an accusation. As Drew puts it:

> The warrant for this mapping procedure lies in interactants' knowledge about the 'religious identity' of certain streets, areas, ends of streets, etc., in the city, knowledge which they may invoke in order to identify persons as members of that religious group to which the street, etc., 'belongs'.
>
> (Drew, 1978, p. 9)

Further, Drew draws on Sacks' work on membership categorization devices (1972b) when he makes a very strong case for how descriptive work as such may be used to make accusations of (e.g. violent) behavior, and that these rely on recipients making inferences:

> The construction of a description is therefore a *conventional* activity, whose performance requires that co-members of a culture employ shared methodic procedures of practical reasoning in collaboratively producing, understanding, and recognizing 'possible descriptions' (as well as any other kind of coherent discourse).
>
> (Drew, 1978, p. 10, emphasis in original)

> Such work can include the production of 'facts', and of descriptions of events, etc., from which the inference that the accused did X (or did X in some special way) can be made. This can involve the accused in a closely ordered task to defeat the accusation, because he may now have to show either that the facts/descriptions, etc., from which the inference that 'he did it', etc., are wrong, or that other inferences may be made from the same facts.
>
> (Drew, 1978, p. 6)

> [. . .] if the descriptions produced in the interaction may be heard, through the properties of membership categorization devices, to do this specific work, then their selection and management is an accountable resource for formulating the interaction as 'doing an accusation'.
>
> (Drew, 1978, p. 19)

We agree with Drew concerning the use of expressions like "deduce" about actions (Drew, 1978, p. 17), "invoke" about knowledge (p. 9), "employ" about "shared methodic procedures of practical reasoning" in "understanding" (p. 10) and making "inferences" about accusations of actions (p. 6). We conclude that these analytical findings are solidly grounded in data. In his work, Drew elaborates on work previously undertaken by Sacks, pointing to the many ways which members use their competences and common-sense knowledge about the social world they inhabit, in order to infer something about other members which is not readily or sensorially available on 'the surface' as part of the local interaction.

Press conferences

Another exemplary study has been conducted by Steven Clayman and John Heritage (2002) on "the phenomenon of adversarialness in question design" (p. 749) in presidential press conferences. The authors identified four basic dimensions of adversarialness: initiative, directness, assertiveness and hostility.

Based on prior research on question design in news interviews (Clayman, 1992, 1988, 2002a, 2002b; Heritage, 2002a, 2002b; Heritage & Greatbatch, 1991; Heritage & Roth, 1995; Macaulay, 1996; Roth, 1998), they distinguished a number of features of such design. This includes question cascades, prevalence of follow-up questions and other-referencing question frames. These serve as indicators of the four dimensions (see Figure 2.1). The questions in press conferences were then coded with regard to their design, and based on this, the degree of adversarialness on the part of different journalists was measured.

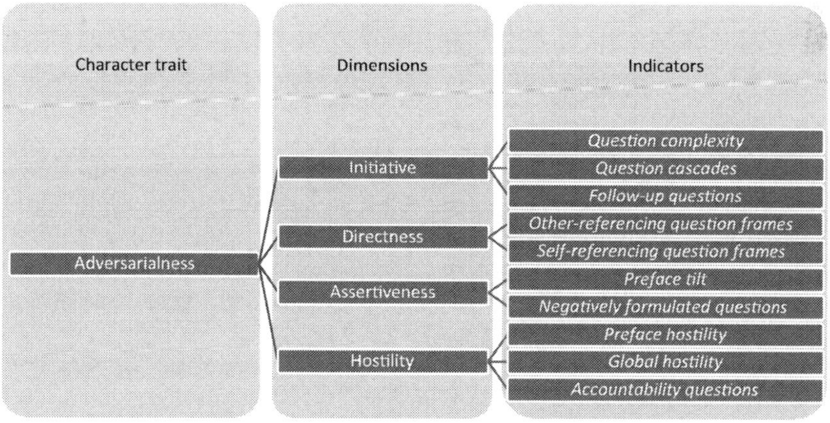

Figure 2.1 An example of a conversation analytic study of a specific character trait, studied by means of dimensions and indicators (Clayman & Heritage, 2002).

The study concluded that "journalists have become much less deferential and more aggressive in their treatment of the U.S. president" (Clayman & Heritage, 2002, p. 749).

This study was followed in 2006 by Clayman, Elliott, Heritage and McDonald's study on the aggressiveness of journalists' questions to public figures. Here a system of analysis was developed based on ten features of question design, functioning "as indicators of four basic dimensions of 'aggressiveness': (1) initiative, (2) directness, (3) assertiveness, and (4) adversarialness" (2006, p. 61).

In 2007, Clayman, Heritage, Elliott and McDonald published yet another study, designed with dependent and independent variables. The dependent variables were "the question analysis system" which decomposes "the phenomenon of aggressive questioning into five outcome measures": initiative, directness, assertiveness, adversarialness and accountability (Clayman *et al.*, 2007, p. 29). Each measure was operationalized in terms of various features of question design, and served as a key indicator.

We consider this collection of studies a milestone in conversation analytic work. They are studies of extreme significance not only with respect to their results, but also their methodology. We also think that the work of Clayman, Heritage *et al.* has important implications for the present study of trustworthiness. Specifically:

1. We agree with Clayman and Heritage that working with "dimensions" of character traits, and breaking such dimensions down to codable actions that may be treated analytically as "indicators" of a "pattern", is a way in which data of interactional forms "can be subjected to systematic scrutiny and analysis" (Clayman & Heritage, 2002, p. 773).
2. Renaming the hyper-category from "adversarialness" in the 2002 study to "aggressiveness" in the 2006 study and "aggressive questioning" in the 2007 study, and adding a fifth indicator of "aggressive questioning" – namely "adversarialness" – in the 2007 study, shows that a taxonomy may very well be developed over time. It also points to the benefits of not withholding publication of results in the shape of taxonomies and models until 'perfection' is achieved. These research strategies are core to the scholarly conversation. We expect our work on the conceptualization of trustworthiness to follow the same path.
3. The basic dimensions of adversarialness or aggressiveness are analytic (etic) categories. Although they are "[b]ased on prior research on question design in news interviews" (Clayman & Heritage, 2002, p. 749), they are not directly identifiable interactional phenomena. Rather, they are inferables. Participants in press conferences may use terms such as "initiative", "hostility" or "directness", but not in the

immediate sequential environment of the press conference questions which were used as data. These studies have a design whereby journalists' questions are the analytical object, and thus do not contain many examples of the presidents' responses. However, this example from a section on hostility (Clayman & Heritage, 2002, pp. 768–769) shows that the category "hostile" is not emic:

(21) [Reagan, 26 July, 1983: pp. 3–4]

JRN: Mr. President, you've mentioned your interest in easing tensions, and you've said you hope the Nicaraguan proposals will have that effect. Now your spokesman has said that the 4000 troops that you're planning to send down there will . . . have standing orders to defend themselves if they're fired upon. How does that help to ease tensions?
RR: . . . this is just a standard order. We don't want war. But I don't think that you prevent war by letting your personnel out there become the victims.
JRN: -> But doesn't this simply increase the chances of war?

4. It is important to notice here that neither the ten features of question design nor the four basic dimensions of aggressiveness to which Clayman *et al.* (2006, p. 561) point are linked to "aggressiveness" *per se* when they stand alone. One of the dimensions is termed "initiative", and is defined as "the extent to which journalists are enterprising rather than passive in their questioning" (p. 565). This is operationalized in questions when journalists "(1) preface their question with statements that construct a context for the question to follow, or (2) ask more than one question within a single turn at talk, or (3) ask a follow-up question" (p. 565). Now, in some contexts, prefacing a question or asking follow-up questions would not in and of themselves be considered aggressive. Prefacing makes a question more difficult to sidestep or resist, and follow-up questions can be used for clarity. But in the context of an oral exam, for example, both question types – while still being indicators of initiative – could indicate obligingness rather than aggressiveness. If a teacher deploys these question designs during an examination, they could very well provide a student with the best opportunity for answering correctly, in depth and with no side-tracking, thus increasing their chances of a good result. However, in the context of presidential news conferences, these features – in combination with the nine other features identified – may be used as (indirect) indicators of aggressiveness. It is, in other words, not the feature itself, but its combination with other features in a specific context, which in this particular study makes this exact feature a valid indicator.

Studies on empathy

A third example of investigations into abstract and character-like constructs is the growing body of CA or EM/CA-type studies of empathy. This includes Ruusuvuori (2005) on empathy in Finnish homeopathic and general practitioner (GP) consultations; Pudlinski (2005) on empathic responses to 'trouble telling' on a United States peer-support help line; Hepburn and Potter (2007) on empathic receipts in calls to a child protection help line; and Ford (2017) on empathy in doctor-patient palliative care consultations in the United Kingdom.

Hepburn and Potter (2007) build their understanding of empathy in interaction on Suchman *et al.*'s (1997) two essential features of empathy in interaction in medical settings. This comes from their model of empathic communication in such settings, namely "the accurate understanding of the patient's feelings by the clinician and the effective communication of that understanding back to the patient so that the patient feels understood" (Suchman *et al.*, 1997, p. 678). Hepburn and Potter, however, break up Suchman *et al.*'s model, setting out to explore "how notions of understanding, accuracy, communication and feeling should be conceptualized" (Hepburn & Potter, 2007, p. 110) and how they make sense as participant issues. In order to do so, they start "with concrete conduct" (p. 99).

Through CA analysis of a corpus of telephone conversations between child protection officers (CPO) and callers, they identify what they term empathic receipts (ER) and define them as being made up of two key elements (p. 109):

1) a formulation of the party's mental state and
2) a marker of the contingency or source of the mental state formulation

They point to ERs typically being identified in environments where the callers display distress by crying, often paired with negative self-judgments and/or unresponsiveness to the CPO's action. The epistemic contingency can be marked in a number of ways, such as constructing the formulation of the mental state as something heard ("I can hear that . . .") or by using a tag question – thus upgrading the caller's right to assess both strategies, which places the epistemic rights with the caller, allowing them to ratify (or not) the formulations.

One example from Hepburn and Potter's analysis shows that while the construction of an ER relies on the two keys elements being present, the understanding of the ER as a display of empathy relies on something more. In this example, an upset caller is reporting a boy trapped in her attic. Contacting the police has been in vain, because they do not believe her. The example is from 12 minutes into the call, and the caller has been crying for much of that time.

Example 2.1 HC Boy in attic (Hepburn & Potter, 2007:106)

Caller:	~I'M ON mahh~ .h↑ihh (0.2) ~I(h)'m des°perate°
	ah really am~ °↑hhu [hh° .hh]
CPO:	[M;'[ppm::.]
Caller:	~Somebody doesn't do something soo:n ah'm
	gonna e-~ (0.2) >.h↑↑ihh< (0.5) ~>↑AH dunno
	waddam gonna do. *I'll die* anyway.< ~
	°a-↑a-° >i[hhuhh<]
CPO:	[↑M m:]::
	(0.4)
Caller:	.H↑↑UIhh
	(0.2)
Caller:	°shih°
	(0.5)
Caller:	°°h↑↑i [:hh°°]
CPO:	[Tk So] maybe life is very very
	f[ri:ghtening.]
Caller:	[~'E doesn't] take- the- the p'lice ...

Hepburn and Potter's analysis points to how the CPO builds on the features of crying displayed by the caller (sobs, sniffs – here transcribed as 'shih' – and volume changes such as °°whispering°°) and the emotion formulations of desperation given in lines 1, 2 and 4–7 in a ~wobbly voice~, when formulating the caller's mental state (frightened) as a result of the features of the world ("life" being "very very frightening"). Further, the authors point out that the inference marker "so" presents the claim as based on what the caller has expressed earlier in the conversation, while the preface "maybe" presents the claim as something that can be rejected or confirmed, leaving the epistemic right with the caller. The CPO's utterance in lines 15–16 thus contains both key elements of an ER.

However, what is here identified as an expression of empathy could potentially – in other contexts – be something completely different. As the authors themselves point out, this ER is identified in a specific sequential context, namely after a long series of "acknowledgement tokens" inflected "with sympathetic intonation" (p. 106). Also, there is no reason to believe that the ER has been delivered in any different intonation. Now, had lines 15–16 been spoken in a completely different setting, say by a teenager talking to a peer, and had it been delivered loudly, in a 'harsh tone' after a series of 'impatiently intonated' minimal responses to the interlocuter's displays of distress, then they would hardly have been recognized as empathetic, but likely as 'crude', 'mocking' or 'insensitive'. What allows the authors to identify this utterance as an ER is not solely their thorough sequential analysis, which enables them to identify the two interactional phenomena, "mental state formulation" (Hepburn & Potter, 2007, p. 109) and "epistemic contingency marker" (Hepburn & Potter, 2007, p. 89), but also the authors' members' competence for recognizing "sympathetic intonation" (Hepburn & Potter, 2007, p. 106) and their understanding of the specific institutional setting in which it takes place. The identification of empathy thus relies on in-depth sequential analysis, contextual understanding and a member's inference of a specific vocal feature being recognizable as displaying sympathy.

Displays of irritation and disappointment in everyday interaction

It is not unusual to see CA studies explore abstract phenomena in even more detail. A very fine example is Couper-Kuhlen's exemplary study of how different prosodic and paralinguistic vocal features (which could be seen as observable 'surface' phenomena) may display "irritation" or "disappointment" (which are 'inferred' phenomena) in response to rejection (Couper-Kuhlen, 2012a, p. 472). Examples of the analytical argumentation for these include the fact that "[t]hese tokens are delivered in a subdued tone of voice, which by comparison with our previously mentioned, similar cases is interpretable as making a display of 'disappointment'" (Couper-Kuhlen, 2012a, p. 470). Also that "[t]he prosody here is once again stylized, creating a gloss that is interpretable in context as exasperation and mild irritation" (p. 471). When the analysis is negative, Couper-Kuhlen states that "[t]he slight pitch upstep on the first syllable of okay prevents the token from sounding 'disappointed.' It is important to note that the study does not claim any strident quality in the tone of voice suggestive of 'irritation'" (p. 470). This analysis seems to build on two things: a skilled technical description of prosody and sequentiality on the one hand, and on the other hand, as was the case in Hepburn and Potter's analysis, a member's competence (in this case acquired as a frequently active participant in conversations of the same sort).

Couper-Kuhlen's work is an example of high-quality CA studies. Other abstract phenomena examined in model CA studies include affiliation (Pomerantz, 1984a; Stivers, 2008; Stivers *et al.*, 2011; Couper-Kuhlen, 2012a; Peräkylä *et al.*, 2015), resistance (Stivers, 2005a, 2005b; Heritage & Sefi, 1992), 'facework' (Lerner, 1996), agency (Enfield &

Kockelman, 2017), identity (Stokoe & Edwards, 2009) and intersubjectivity (Heritage, 1984, 2007).

Concluding discussion

To sum up, we may say that etic categories like 'irritation' or 'disappointment', and character traits and abstract behavioral categories like 'aggressiveness' or 'empathy', are inferred and conceptualized from concrete emic conduct, which comprises participant actions that may serve as indicators of such categories. We will now dissolve the dichotomy of surface vs. inference, since it has served its dual purpose: a) to show that it is not alien to EM/CA to study phenomena inferred from social actions; and b) to employ the empirical restraints and rigor of this field of research to emphasize that sensorially observable phenomena are all there is to observe, regardless of whether the analytical project is to study trustworthiness or something else.

We consider all scholars mentioned in this chapter – from Drew, Heritage and Clayman to Hepburn, Potter and Couper-Kuhlen – to be very competent analysts who display an attention to precision and detail. By highlighting their contributions to EM/CA research, we aim to make a methodological point: namely that through careful analysis, it is possible to identify features – linguistic or paralinguistic – which in one specific context can be seen to display abstract and character-like constructs such as empathy, irritation, and disappointment, but which they would not have displayed had the setting or the sequential environment been a different one. Furthermore, these examples show that it is only through the use of members' competences that these observable features can be identified as local displays of such etic constructs.

As can be seen from these examples, and also from the large pool of studies referenced, it is possible to identify communicative displays which may infer abstract phenomena. If these displays are identifiable – or, as Stivers puts it, if a "clear characterization of what 'counts' as an instance of the target phenomenon" has been analytically established (Stivers, 2015, p. 3) – then it is also possible to code them "in ways that do not sacrifice a CA sensibility" (Stivers, 2015, p. 2). Clayman and Heritage's initial work, from 2002, on journalists' adversarialness, paves the way for not only systematicity and scrutiny, but also quantification and comparison to larger datasets. This is because the indicators are ideally concrete codable actions, even though they are identifiable as indicators only in this specific context, and only in combination with other specific indicators or features.

We argue that trustworthiness can be studied using much the same principle, and that it is an inferred social judgment based on members' observations of what we term *clusters of interactional indicators*. These are things which other members display in social interaction. In this book, we explore what may constitute such clusters, and we return to this point in the next chapter, where we define trustworthiness as an empirically sensorially observable phenomenon in social interaction. We argue that trustworthiness as a socially co-constructed phenomenon may be conceptualized theoretically and studied empirically, using the exact approaches to which we have pointed in the cited studies. Our ambition is to contribute to the pool of research which is, stone by stone, paving the way for similar endeavors in quantifying otherwise hard-to-measure phenomena.

3 Defining trustworthiness as an interactional phenomenon

DOI: 10.4324/9781003280903-3

To define an abstract social phenomenon is far from a neutral process. Indeed, it is the opposite, as the very processes of conceptualizing, defining and operationalizing are processes of constructing the phenomenon as a research object – something which can be studied, discussed and questioned. This chapter deals with those processes. It would be impertinent to clean the slate and ignore the opportunity to stand on the shoulders of thousands of years of research into what constitutes the phenomenon of trustworthiness. Over the centuries, a lot of thought has gone into trustworthiness as a theoretical concept. Even if we aim to study trustworthiness empirically, from an ethnomethodological (EM) and conversation analytic (CA) based approach, these existing studies and theoretical conceptualizations are still important backdrops for our investigation. First, therefore, we will briefly review the most important approaches to the study of trustworthiness, and how it has been conceptualized. Then we will present a series of basic conditions and premises regarding the study of abstract social phenomena such as trustworthiness, which an EM/CA approach to the study of trust and related concepts must encompass. Finally, we will present our definition of trustworthiness as an observable interactional phenomenon.

Approaches to the study of trust and trustworthiness

In this section, we present five overarching approaches to researching trustworthiness. Namely, those found, respectively, in rhetoric; in trust research in the social sciences and in psychology; in discursive psychology (an approach closely related to EM/CA); and finally, in ethnomethodology's work on the concepts of trust and trustworthiness. We have chosen these because we find them relevant in informing our own work on conceptualizing and defining trustworthiness.

Approaches to trustworthiness in rhetoric research

In rhetoric, trustworthiness has represented a core focus for centuries. The foundations for much of the classic rhetorical conceptualization of what it means to be trustworthy were developed by Aristotle when he identified three modes of persuasion used to convince audiences: *logos*, a speaker's means to convince an audience by use of logic or reason; *pathos*, a speaker's means to persuade an audience by appealing to their emotions; and *ethos*, an ethical appeal, a speaker's means to convince the audience of her or his own credibility. Certainly, a rhetorician must "inspire trust in his audience" (Aristotle, 350 BCE/1983, Book 2, Chapter 1).

In the classical period, ethos was a rather encompassing concept. It could include coming from a good family, as well as the entire moral history of the speaker. There has been substantial debate regarding how best to define ethos. The main distinctions concern the location of ethos, its stability and whether it is a descriptive or a normative concept. With respect to the first distinction, ethos has been defined through seven different potential views of – or takes on – where it is located, and these will be presented one by one in what follows.

In classical rhetorics, ethos is either a trait of the speaker or it is a feature of the talk/text. With respect to the former (ethos as a trait of the speaker), ethos is, according to Isocrates and Quintilian, equivalent to 'character'. It is a matter of ethics and morals, an essential identity for the speaker to possess. These thinkers assume a normative approach to ethos, urging speakers to strive to be a "good person", the ideal character. The path to persuade others is to be a good and noble person possessing authority, as Isocrates argued in his speech *Antidosis* around 390 B.C. (Isocrates, 390 BC/1986, p. 254). In fact, one would strive to be a good person in order to be able to persuade others!

With respect to the latter (ethos as a feature of the talk/text), ethos is – according to Aristotle and Cicero – more instrumental, something to signal in speech or text by means of a range of techniques. Cicero viewed ethos as a strategy of choosing the appropriate 'token' of 'character'. He basically argued that ethos is a matter of staging a persona, while Aristotle argued that the speaker should present the speech in a way that made the speaker trustworthy and let the character of the speaker make an impact in order to persuade the audience (Aristotle, 350 BCE/1983).

In modern rhetoric – from the 18th century and until late in the 20th century – ethos is (as in the first view presented previously) primarily positioned with the author. This is so not as a moral imperative, but as a preoccupation with 'source credibility', i.e. "the status and expertise of the author" as a basis for "judging the veracity of what is found in the text" (Warnick, 2007, p. 47f). This leads to a fourth position of ethos, as located in the audience. In this view, ethos is a matter of perception, i.e. the audience's attitude toward the speaker. When it is up to the audience to determine a communicator's ethos, it will consequently be in constant hermeneutic fluctuation. To specify that, McCroskey (1968/1982) has distinguished between 'initial ethos' (before a given social encounter, somewhat comparable to Isocrates' ethos concept), 'derived ethos' (created in the encounter, closer to Aristotle's ethos concept) and 'terminal ethos' (established after the encounter and subsequently forming a new initial encounter with that particular audience). In this fifth take on ethos, we see reflected the impact of specifically classical models of communication (e.g. Lasswell, 1948, on 'Who Says What in Which Channel to Whom With What Effect?').

With this more dynamic approach to ethos comes a view of ethos as a social production, one which resonates with some of the classical views. The word ethos has the form *ēthos*, meaning 'character', and the form *éthos*, meaning 'custom' or 'habit'. The latter form points to ethos being social, and therefore constituted by context, culture and time in history. After all, being a good person is also dependent upon its definition, by and in the social context. This sixth position sees ethos appearing in the socially created space between the speaker and the recipient (LeFevre, 1987). It resides in the tension between individuals and social concerns (Ronald, 1990, p. 38), or alternatively between the speaker's private and public selves (Ronald, 1990, p. 39). Ethos is a production during the encounter of a text (Rancière, 2002), an intertextual phenomenon negotiated across a community and co-created by others across texts and voices (Oddo, 2014).

With the arrival of the World Wide Web (WWW), this social approach to ethos has been taken to new heights of complexity by contemporary rhetorics formulating a so-called online ethos (Burbules, 2001; Hoff-Clausen, 2004, 2008; Miller, 2001; Warnick, 2004, 2007). This is a potential seventh approach. A communicator's online ethos may be co-produced by multiple authors/sources, applying multiple modalities – such as site structure, design look, textual content, textual voice, photo, art, video, etc. Moreover, users formerly known as recipients may be co-authors, and authors may even be invisible or blurry (if no-one is stating authorship), or indefinite (because of intertextual references by means of hyperlinks). As a result of these interactive functions, contributions may immediately be commented upon, reviewed and corrected by readers/users/viewers. As a result of all these technical affordances, ethos is not limited to one author/rhetor, but is rather co-created by a multitude of agents. It is a distributed credibility (Burbules, 2001).

Moreover, these different agents are members of different discourse communities, which are more or less transparent with fluid boundaries (Hoff-Clausen, 2008, p. 213). This not only makes it easily noticeable when a person's credibility is dependent upon the cultural norms of the social system that the particular public belongs to (Warnick, 2004), but also raises the question of whether the trustworthiness of information sources is available for examination or not (Warnick, 2004).

Given that Hoff-Clausen argues that the central question of online ethos is not "who we are willing to believe?" but "who we wish to be in companion with when searching for the truth?" (2008, p. 228), one could argue that an eighth approach exists. This would be a relational approach, since the social element of the situated perception of trustworthiness is probably not confined to online communication. It could also be viewed as an extension of the ethos located in the audience-approach, only with the ethos being negotiated within the audience *as a community*.

Summing up, there are many views of what constitutes trustworthiness conceptualized as ethos, not just within rhetorics where it has been the object of intense research interest for centuries. Contemporary rhetorics view ethos as a social phenomenon. It is seen as dynamic and co-constructed, and trustworthiness is consequently seen as a situated, interactionally distributed, produced and judged credibility of a communicator.

Approaches to trustworthiness in social science trust research

In the multiple strands of trust research which can be found in the social sciences – especially in sociology, economics, political science, and not in the least in organizational and management research – the concept of trust has received substantially more attention than trustworthiness. Trustworthiness is generally accepted to be a separate construct from trust, even though the two concepts are regularly conflated (Mayer *et al.*, 1995; Gillespie, 2015; Hardin, 2001, 2002; Rousseau *et al.*, 1998). This has to do with the close interrelation between these two concepts. As Hardin (2002) points out, the utterance "I believe that you are trustworthy" really means "I believe you are worthy of my trust", or simply, "I trust you" (p. 29). So trustworthiness is generally expected to be a strong predictor of a person's decision to trust someone or something else (also see Mayer *et al.*, 1995, pp. 711, 729).

No field within the social sciences can offer a universally adopted definition of trust (see e.g. Misztal, 1995; Dietz & Den Hartog, 2006; Rousseau *et al.*, 1998; Mayer *et al.*, 1995). It is therefore unsurprising that there is also no absolute agreement as to what exactly trustworthiness constitutes within these fields. However, one broadly expressed view is that trustworthiness is something the trustee *has* (Dietz & Den Hartog, 2006), implying that trustworthiness is to be perceived as a quality or character trait, and thus essentially as a cognitive or psychological phenomenon (Tsankova *et al.*, 2018) or as a moral disposition (James, 2014; cf. Potter, 2002). This view of trustworthiness as something internal to the individual is also in line with Ben-Ner and Halldorson's definition of trustworthiness as "the willingness of a person B to act favorably toward a person A, when A has placed an implicit or explicit demand or expectation for action on B" (Ben-Ner & Halldorsson, 2010, p. 65). Perceived trustworthiness is widely studied as an antecedent of trust (Hardin, 2001, 2002; Mayer *et al.*, 1995). There is also a general agreement across a large part of the social sciences that trustworthiness is only – or primarily – relevant in environments of risk and uncertainty (Hendry, 2002; Molm *et al.*, 2009; cf. Schoorman *et al.*, 2007).

In a more recent strand of research, trustworthiness has been studied as a more dynamic concept. In this, 'trustworthy' has been regarded as something one can chose to be (Potter, 2002), to become (Knudsen, 2001) or to demonstrate (Molm *et al.*, 2009) by acting in "a trustworthy fashion" (Weigert, 2012, p. 176; cf. Wubs-Mrozewicz, 2020). However, the correlation between behavior and perceived trustworthiness (as well as other character-like phenomena) has been pointed out in countless studies in sociology and related disciplines over decades, even though these are often not labeled 'trust research'. One early example is Smith's (1978) study of a woman's account of a person, K, whom she knew and whom over time she came to perceive as mentally ill based on her behavior. In an interview, the woman describes how K's behavior did not make sense neither to her nor to their common friends. K's actions – such as excessive crying over even the smallest things, dropping her classes at university, having difficulties carrying an "intelligent conversation" due to her making "childish inane remarks completely off the point" (p. 29) – made her behavior "recognizable as 'mentally ill type' behavior" (p. 23) to the people who knew her. Linking such concrete examples of micro-behavior not "properly provided for by relevant social rules or definitions of the situation" (p. 23) with social judgments (i.e. not medical diagnoses, but lay persons' perceptions) based on this behavior shows a close correlation between perceived behavior, social norms and judgment of character – including trustworthiness. Being deemed 'mentally ill' by your peers may be seen as a label of untrustworthiness in their eyes, at least with respect to competence, predictability and stability.

In summary, there is a diversity of views on what constitutes trustworthiness within social science trust research, but equally, it has not been the object of much research interest. Indeed, it has predominantly been studied within an essentialist paradigm, either as an identity or personality trait, or a perception from others based on what is (deliberately) demonstrated.

Approaches to trustworthiness in psychology

In psychology, much as in the social sciences, much of the research focus has been on trust rather than on trustworthiness (Erikson, 1950/1993; Rempel *et al.*, 1985; Evans & Krueger, 2009; Simpson, 2007; cf. Kiyonari *et al.*, 2006). A considerable overlap can also be found with parts of the social sciences, especially economics (Evans & Krueger, 2009). Also, as in the social sciences, the two concepts of trust and trustworthiness are often conflated (Evans & Krueger, 2009). In traditional branches of psychology – such as behavioral, cognitive, developmental and clinical psychology – there is agreement neither on the nature of trustworthiness nor on whether it is a cognitive, a behavioral or an emotional concept, or a combination of all three. Trustworthiness has largely been conceptualized and examined as a perceived individual character trait (Tsankova *et al.*, 2018; Everett *et al.*, 2016; Rotter, 1980; Delgado *et al.*, 2005). People's perceptions of others' trustworthiness are studied as stemming from what people perceive as different outlets of these traits such as facial attractiveness (Anne *et al.*, 1993; Memon *et al.*, 2003; Vine & Bull, 2003), static facial properties (e.g. Todorov *et al.*, 2008; cf. Shen & Ferguson, 2021) and expressions of emotion (Todorov & Oosterhof, 2011), as well as more social concepts as kinship and group membership (e.g. DeBruine, 2002, 2005).

One way in which scholars have determined and studied trustworthiness in psychological research is via polygraph tests. Lying is thought to be associated with increased arousal. Specifically designed to measure arousal, a polygraph is thought to be able to determine something about the truthfulness of a specific statement, and therefore in principle about the truthfulness – and by proxy the trustworthiness – of the person taking the test. For a discussion of this, see Memon *et al.*, 2003. Another way the study of trustworthiness has been approached is via trust games (Burks *et al.*, 2003; Gunnthorsdottir *et al.*, 2002; Ben-Ner & Halldorsson, 2010; Everett *et al.*, 2016; Evans & Krueger, 2009). Here the Machiavellian scale (Geis *et al.*, 2013) is often used as a measurement. For a critique and discussion of this, see Ben-Ner and Halldorsson (2010).

In psychology, trustworthiness is associated with credibility and truthfulness (König & Jucks, 2019; Lui & Standing, 1989; MacMartin, 1999; Memon *et al.*, 2003). Experimental studies point to a close link between credibility-enhancing circumstances, or a person's credibility-enhancing behavior, and how trustworthy they are perceived to be by others (cf. Memon *et al.*, 2003). Likewise, when people display what is in some strands of psychological research considered to be a marker of lying, such as blinking, or indicating affective stances, such as guilt (Griesel & Yuille, 2007), these are studied as items which lower credibility, and thus trustworthiness.

In summary, in psychology, trustworthiness (or lack thereof) has largely been seen as a character trait. Much interest has been shown in the psychology of lying and deceiving, which is why most research has been devoted to the study of what influences perceptions of credibility, and how its lack may be disclosed.

Approaches to aspects of trustworthiness in discursive psychology

Discursive psychology (DP) is a branch of critical social psychology closely linked to EM/CA by applying conversation analysis and broadly drawing on ethnomethodology, as well as the later Wittgenstein and some elements of Foucauldian thinking (Hepburn & Wiggins, 2007; Wiggins, 2017; Barnes & Moss, 2007). Although trustworthiness *per se* has not been studied in a DP context, some concepts related to both trusting and trustworthiness have received substantial interest, and it is therefore appropriate to mention them here. Much discursive psychology is concerned with direct studies of people's activities, and in that it offers an alternative to the individualism and cognitivism found in more traditional forms of psychology (Hepburn, 2002; Hepburn & Wiggins, 2007; Wiggins, 2017). In the latter, as well as in everyday lay discourse, when people ascribe person types or 'personality' traits to someone, these are treated as regarding the person's cognitive functions and therefore their intentions and dispositions (Alexander & Stokoe, 2020). Contrarily, DP studies psychological concepts as socially managed and consequential in interaction, and is therefore concerned with the rhetorical production of a 'rich surface' (Edwards, 2006b) of talk in which diverse social worlds are constructed and created (Potter & Wetherell, 1987, p. 1). In DP, personality traits, character traits or dispositions, are examined as social practices. Multiple psychological topics (such as attitudes, emotion, identity and intention) have been studied and re-specified as discursive actions, rather than as mental processes.

Trustworthiness is not among the concepts which have been re-specified in this tradition, but there has been a keen interest to explore the discursive construction and negotiation of related phenomena, such as stake and interest (Edwards & Potter, 1992; Edwards, 2007). Also, the characters and characteristics of persons have been studied as phenomena invoked and mobilized in everyday interaction – e.g. via characterological formulations (Alexander & Stokoe, 2020), understood as descriptions which formulate a person's "tendencies, dispositions, moral nature, desires, and intentions" (Edwards, 2006a, p. 498), or as self-characterization via reported 'private thoughts' as a particular embodiment of cognitive process (Barnes & Moss, 2007). For instance, studies have examined how formulating events may be used to construct the accountability and dispositional character of someone (Edwards, 1994), how formulating actions as regular or exceptional may serve to construct a person's accountability within a moral order (Edwards, 1995) and how social categories and categorial descriptions may be used to accomplish identity construction for others (Stokoe, 2009).

Much work within discursive psychology has been concerned with exploring the linguistic details of fact construction and credibility (de) construction. A study of twelve written judicial decisions in Canadian sexual abuse trials (MacMartin, 1999) has explored the discursive practices used to construct or undermine the facticity of accounts and/or the credibility of complainants and witnesses. These include modalized formats versus unhedged assertions in the description of events, and using three-part lists and couplets in evaluations of the credibility of an agent. The extensive analysis also showed that there is no one-to-one relation between such rhetorical strategies and the perception of credibility:

> Reference to inconsistencies in complainants' allegations of abuse constitute a basis for doubt that judges orient to in their evaluations of credibility. . . . Inconsistencies across a complainant's various statements can also be categorized as signs of authentic, expected memory loss over time. Judges may work up the lack of interest of complainants.
>
> (MacMartin, 1999, p. 172)

Some recent DP studies have been concerned with abstract and character-like constructs closely associated with trustworthiness, such as Hepburn and Potter's study of empathy (2007), Iversen's study of believability and credibility in the context of negotiation of knowledge and its moral implications (2014), and the connection between the perceived credibility of politicians, their self-presentation and their referencing to factual evidence (Burke & Demasi, 2019).

In summary, discursive psychology has had a long-lasting and substantial research interest in studying the *in situ* construction of the credibility of facts, descriptions and agents, and the discursive construction of stake and interest in character-like constructs – but since trustworthiness *per se* has not been the object of DP research, no DP conceptualizations of trustworthiness can be found.

Approaching trustworthiness within EM/CA

Trustworthiness has hitherto not been an object of research within EM/CA (see Chapter 1, p. 3 and the entire Chapter 2). In the next chapter, we will both discuss why this is so and defend why it should and could be just that. However, the ethnomethodological foundation for the study of human interaction indeed concerns mutual trust and intersubjectivity.

In his seminal paper on trust as a "Condition for Stable Concerted Actions" (1963), Garfinkel famously took a different approach to trust than the one found among his contemporaries (cf. Watson, 2009; Turowetz & Rawls, 2020). Although Garfinkel's paper is sometimes considered proto-ethnomethodological (cf. Lynch, 1994; Watson, 2009), his reflections on, and definition of, trust from 1963 still form the basis of all later research on trust within EM/CA. Via the systematic disruption of games such as tic-tac-toe, as well as by "breaching" or distorting people's ordinary social routines, Garfinkel was able to point out two sets of rules. These were, respectively, the "basic" (or constitutive) and the "normative". The former were essentially what people must mutually commit to and understand to form the basic conditions of any constitutive practice. Based on this, Garfinkel "conceived the phenomenon of trust" and its definition as compliance to "the 'constitutive order of events'" (p. 190). Garfinkel saw how participants orient to environments perceived as normal and, if these are disturbed, react with frustration, anger, fear, bewilderment, etc. Also, participants will try to normalize, or at least make sense of the unexpected breach of normality, by treating it like a joke, a deliberate provocation, etc. These are all signs that the "trust conditions", understood as a minimum of equality and reciprocity (Garfinkel, 1963; cf. Turowetz & Rawls, 2020), are not present. To Garfinkel, trust then comprises participants' common adherence to a sensible order of mutually produced events or, as the title of his paper reads, "A Condition for Stable Concerted Actions" (1963).

Whereas trust in classic psychological or social science trust research is often defined in relation to risk, Garfinkel's understanding of trust was as "a presumptive element in *all* concerted action irrespective of its 'risky' character" (Watson, 2009, p. 484, emphasis in original). If we consider trust as a basic constitutive condition underlying all human interaction, not just trust but also trustworthiness must be in play in all interaction. That is, not just in what is traditionally perceived as high-risk contexts, although these may be perspicuous settings for investigating trust, particularly the breaches of it (cf. Watson, 2009, p. 492 ff.).

As we covered in Chapter 2, conversation analysts have, since the beginning, explored how interactants question concepts related to trustworthiness, such as the agendas of others (cf. "I gather you also want to try to sell me some insurance", Schenkein, 1978, p. 60, 65) and the validity of claims made in the interaction (cf. "Are you shitting me?", Goodwin, 2003). Also, CA research has recently been devoted to the study of the abstract concepts of authority, as displayed in social interaction (e.g. Heritage, 2005; Stevanovic & Peräkylä, 2012; M. F. Nielsen, forthcoming-a), and epistemics, i.e. how interactants show and negotiate their mutual degrees of, quality of and claims to knowledge about, a certain referent (Heritage & Raymond, 2005, 2012; Raymond & Heritage, 2006; Mondada, 2011; Stivers *et al.*, 2011; Heritage, 2012a, 2012b). These are also concepts related to trustworthiness. However, the basic concept of trustworthiness has not been a research object as such.

This last section, as well as all of those previously mentioned, serves to demonstrate that both contemporary rhetoric, certain parts of the social sciences and psychological trust research all increasingly embrace the idea that social phenomena in general (and trustworthiness and related constructs in particular) can be approached as dynamic social co-creations rather than inherent personality ideals or character traits. This is true also in discursive psychology, and not in the least in CA.

A theoretical conceptualization of trustworthiness

In rhetoric, in the social sciences and in psychology, scholars have strived to conceptualize and – at least in the case of the latter two – also operationalize trustworthiness. Some key points from these conceptualizations are briefly reviewed in this section, before going on to discuss an EM/CA perspective on trustworthiness as a concept and presenting our theoretical conceptualization of trustworthiness.

Rhetoric work on conceptualizing trustworthiness

In rhetoric research, ethos is the concept by which trustworthiness is conceptualized. Aristotle saw trustworthiness as a matter of possessing a high ethos based on relevant competences and wisdom/good sense (*phronesis*), moral character/virtue/being a good moral person (*areté*), and goodwill toward the audience (*eunoia*) (Aristotle, 350 BCE/1983). It is a separate and decades-long (if not centuries-long) debate as to which and how many virtues should be considered when exploring ethos, and if they all add up to trustworthiness, or if that is just one of many components. We will not cover the entire discussion here, but we are inspired by how virtues are repeatedly suggested as constituents for ethos and, consequently, for trustworthiness. Some empirical researchers (e.g. O'Keefe, 1990), inspired by Aristotle, do not use trustworthiness and ethos as synonyms, but rather propose audience perceptions of ethos as being a matter of 'expertise', 'trustworthiness' and 'liking'. Also, part of the discussion is about whether and how to distinguish 'credibility' from 'charisma' and 'one of us-ness' (cf. Hansen & Kock, 2003). Recent work has argued that external factors such as institutional affiliation contribute to a person's trustworthiness (McCroskey, 2001).

We would particularly like to mention one example of a conceptualization here. Klaus Kjøller, not a rhetorician but a linguist and philosopher with a long interest in rhetoric and political communication, has conceptualized ethos (1991a) as a question of scoring well in relation to four different virtues: 'honesty', 'idealism/altruism', 'competence' and 'identity'. The latter was subsequently (2007) renamed 'stability'. Three of these ('honesty', 'idealism/altruism', 'identity/stability') he groups under the category 'trustworthiness', thus making a distinction between ethos and trustworthiness. Furthermore, he has argued that these virtues may be (1991a) thought of as credit balances. That is, if people think a politician is lying (thus over-drafting 'honesty'), e.g. about using tax payers' money for personal matters, he may remedy or balance this by 'borrowing' from other virtues such as 'competence' ("I did not understand the reimbursement rules" or "I mistakenly used the wrong credit card"). This may perhaps be done in combination with 'idealism' ("The reason why this misjudgment happened is because I work so many hours for the sake of the public and was overworked") and/or 'identity' ("This is the first time; I never do such things; this is not me"). The purpose of such repair work is to gain a good credit score back, and a long time of showing yourself to be virtuous with respect to all four parameters will build the goodwill necessary for effective explanatory work like this when facing accusations from others. The worst virtue to have in bad standing, Kjøller claims, is honesty, because if people think you are lying, they will likely not believe the repair work you attempt to do when bringing the other virtues into play.

Conceptualizing trustworthiness in social science trust research

In the social sciences trust, and thus also trustworthiness, is often linked to – or defined in relation to – risk (see e.g. Coleman, 1990; Cook &

Santana, 2017; Gambetta, 1988). Trustworthiness as a concept is often seen as highly relational (as there always has to be someone to be trusted (or not) by someone else for it to come into play). It is also dispositional, and linked to the trustee's attributes and past actions (Hardin, 2002) and therefore credibility (Mayer *et al.*, 1995). However, conceptualizations also include trustworthiness as a *willingness* (Ben-Ner & Halldorsson, 2010), *motivation* (Hardin, 2002; Mayer *et al.*, 1995), or *moral obligation* (Potter, 2002) to act favorably toward someone else. In their extensive review of trust conceptualizations and definitions, Dietz and Den Hartog (2006) point to ability, benevolence, integrity and predictability as the four most commonly mentioned characteristics linked to trust belief, and thus by proxy to trustworthiness. Mayer *et al.*'s (1995) seminal paper on trust focuses on ability, benevolence and integrity as the key components of trustworthiness, but many other attributes such as consistency, loyalty, openness, fairness and receptivity have also been highlighted as possible indicators or components of trustworthiness (see e.g. Butler, 1991).

Conceptualizing trustworthiness in psychology

In most psychological research, trustworthiness is studied as a personality trait inherent to the individual and perceivable by others via different indicators. Schiemann points to trustworthiness being "formed by the trustee's ability, integrity and benevolence" (Schiemann *et al.*, 2019, p. 166). Precisely the trustee's ability, in the form of competence, is frequently mentioned as a condition for trustworthiness (Hendry, 2002; James, 2014; Jones, 2012), as are altruism and fairness (Kiyonari *et al.*, 2006). In norm-based theories of trust, trustworthiness is percieved as – and therefore studied as – the result of peoples' "desire to follow social norms" (Evans & Krueger, 2009, p. 1009; cf. Krueger *et al.*, 2008). This involves conceptualizing trustworthiness as an internal motivation.

In much psychological research, someone's perception of others' trustworthiness is understood as heavily reliant on first impressions of, e.g. facial features (Willis & Todorov, 2006; Tsankova *et al.*, 2018). According to some branches of research, "particular combinations of facial features and texture are generally perceived as trustworthy or untrustworthy", thus constituting a "stereotype" (Tsankova *et al.*, 2018, p. 32). Also "dynamic facial properties", including expressions of emotion (Tsankova *et al.*, 2018, p. 32; Todorov, 2011) and the temporal characteristics with which the expression appears (e.g. Krumhuber *et al.*, 2007), as well as the perception of group membership and kinship (e.g. DeBruine, 2002, 2005), is proposed as playing a part in forming ones impression of others' trustworthiness. However, these strands of research show a remarkable lack of reliable definitions or conceptualizations of trustworthiness.

Trust and trustworthiness in ethnomethodology

Before presenting our conceptualization of trustworthiness, we would like to take a moment to pause in order to look at the etymology of the word. Trustworthy literally means 'worthy of trust'. So when we study trustworthiness, our research object is 'that something' which makes someone worthy of trust in the eyes of someone else, and not trust as a concept *per se*. Even so, what we understand by trust forms the basis of – and becomes a determining factor in – our understanding of and approach to trustworthiness. Therefore, we would like to take a brief look at trust from an ethnomethodological perspective.

According to Garfinkel, a trustworthy person is one who manages "the discrepancies with respect to these attributions [of attitudes of daily life] in such a fashion as to maintain a public show of respect for them" (Garfinkel, 1963, p. 238), or someone who displays 'common sense'. In our study, we also look at 'public show' of trustworthiness – that is, for local orientation to both self and other as being 'worthy of trust'. We do so not just in 'perspicuous settings', such as police interrogations or courtroom interactions, but also in more mundane – albeit still primarily institutional – settings.

Following Garfinkel's 'trust' paper, the concepts have been studied, re-specified and conceptualized in several studies within the field of ethnomethodology. Rawls and David (2005) argue that, in a modern differentiated society, Garfinkel's notion of trust as constitutive becomes highly relevant. They see situated practices (rather than, for example, moral obligations or values) as determining "what is appropriate or trustworthy". This means that, to be considered trustworthy, people must "demonstrate competence in detailed situated ways" or else be "ostracized and find themselves either alone or segregated from others, physically, socially and legally" (474). Also rooted in Garfinkel's conceptualization of trust, Clifton has studied trust as something which "is achieved as an emic participants' first-order accomplishment" (Clifton, 2012, p. 107). He points to how trustworthiness can be displayed via epistemic primacy. Recently, Turowetz and Rawls have studied the development of Garfinkel's trust argument "that a minimum of equality and reciprocity he called 'Trust Conditions' is a prerequisite for sense-making in interaction" (2020, p. 1). They trace this by examining fourteen unpublished Ph.D. proposals of Garfinkel's. González-Martínez and Mlynář also present an "ethnomethodological re-specification of trust as an observable phenomenon of order involving continuous practical work, *in situ* and in real time" (2019, p. 608; also see González-Martínez, 2001), or what they term "practical trust".

Across all these very different approaches to trust research, we see a pattern of similar conceptualizations forming. This is something which we find interesting, as well as consoling. Some of them are not far from the one we will present in what follows, even if the points of departure – in the shape of research methodology, let alone research paradigms – are very different.

Our work on conceptualizing components of trustworthiness

Drawing on data from our extensive pilot project on international business interaction and our project on professionals' video-mediated encounters, we have worked to develop a synthesis of our research object. The previously presented review of rhetoric, social science, discursive psychology and psychology research on trustworthiness, as well as ethnomethodological re-specifications of trust, has informed our study, and has led us to identify what we choose to term 'orientations'. It has been a long journey to distill our work into four orientations to trustworthiness as a theoretical concept. These are the following.

- Orientation to truth and honesty.
- Orientation to stake and interest.
- Orientation to ability and knowledge.
- Orientation to consistency and predictability.

The conceptualization of these four orientations is one of the key outcomes of our study, and we use them in this and the following chapters to guide both our empirical conceptualization in Chapters 5–8, and our presentation of our results. Initially, however, we will shed light on how we drew on our backdrop, and how we were inspired by work on trustworthiness in these research traditions.

From rhetoric research, we have been inspired by the ethos concept and centuries of debate on what constitutes it and its sources, contexts and performances. Also, we have adopted the idea of conceptualizing trustworthiness into virtues, which are basically subcategories of ethos. This has led us to apply a grounded theory approach to our study. It has resulted in us working with a hierarchy of categories in the shape of orientations, components, indicators and clusters of indicators. From rhetoric research, we have also derived one of our orientations, competence, which dates back to Aristotle and is repeated by all the rhetoric scholars we know of who have been working with ethos and virtues. We do not use the concept of ethos, and we are not exploring basic sources of trustworthiness, although we have come to agree that stability is a central component of trustworthiness even though that it operates at a different level.

From social science trust research, we are inspired by the components of ability and predictability. However, we do not agree with the typically applied methodology used to explore them (Nielsen & Nielsen, in review). Consequently, we have chosen another research design.

From psychology, we have inherited a focus on truth, honesty and (lack of) deception, although we do not explore the latter *per se*. We acknowledge that trustworthiness is commonly perceived and treated by people as a character trait, and we agree that interactants are concerned with their own and others' perceived credibility. We do not, however, agree with the majority of the methodologies used in psychology to explore trustworthiness, and we have chosen another research design.

From discursive psychology, we have adopted research interests in stake and interest as key to trustworthiness, as well as a focus on how agents, facts and events are constructed as trustworthy (or not) by means of a large variety of linguistic strategies. Trustworthiness is something which is practiced – and continuously oriented to – by interactants.

From EM/CA, we have adopted our methodology for exploring trustworthiness, even if our research object is so far from most EM/CA work that we felt the need to devote many pages to arguing for the relevance, appropriateness and feasibility of conducting such a research project within the methodological frames of EM/CA. We are also inspired by EM work on trust as a continuous participant concern which is the object of local negotiation, and by CA work on authority and the role that epistemics can play.

Our four orientations have long been underway. When we apply a text edition philological approach to our own document files from all the drafts produced in the process, we see that, in the course of the years that this project has been underway, we have worked with a number of different categories, different category definitions, different category levels, hierarchies and taxonomies, different names and contents, and different notions of what to include in the categorial work and what to exclude. In fact, this has proved to be an iterative process very true to the principles of grounded research and collection-based CA, because the category work evolved as we went back and forth from working on our data, reading prior studies and returning to our theoretical conceptualizations with our empirical observations in mind. We literally spent years on this work, and indeed hoped to reach our conclusions in easier and faster ways. Although we came from very different starting points, and took a long winding road toward agreeing on our four orientations, they correlate surprisingly well with the original work of Klaus Kjøller (1991a, 1991b)), which for many years we found truly inspiring. Even so, the components that make up our orientations are defined differently, and they are definitely applied to social interaction and put to use in ways that only an EM/CA approach would enable. However, even if we did end up in the same neighborhood, it only goes to show that our four orientations may stand the test of time and scrutiny from other scholars taking other routes to similar destinations.

So much for the theoretical backdrop for our work. We have still not presented our definition of trustworthiness, nor have we elaborated on the analytical use of the four orientations, or even why we call them that in the first place. Also, we have yet to present our conceptualization of trustworthiness as an empirical research object. But before we are able to do so, we must first present our basic research premises for approaching trustworthiness as an empirically observable phenomenon in social interaction, from an EM/CA perspective.

Basic premises in our approach to trustworthiness as an empirical concept

In order to use EM/CA as an approach to the study of trustworthiness, and by proxy of trust and trusting, some conditions and basic premises need to be clarified about how we understand these abstract social phenomena within the EM/CA framework.

Trustworthiness is an identity project for interactants

We understand trustworthiness as a local, dynamic identity project for participants in social interaction (cf. Antaki & Widdicombe, 1998). Using their competences, members navigate the 'hidden' taken-for-granted details of how identities are cooperatively achieved in interaction (Garfinkel, 1964, 1967; cf. Turowetz & Rawls, 2020). In so doing, they accomplish more or less trustworthy identities, so that they come off as highly trustworthy, somewhat trustworthy or not trustworthy at all to other members *in situ*. As already mentioned, our interest is not in members' social judgments as such, but in the interactional moves and strategies that members base these judgments on, and which may therefore also enable us as analysts to come to terms with their practical interactional work when they accomplish 'being trustworthy' or discern if others come off as trustworthy or not. As we also discussed in Chapter 2, we may see interactants explicitly attribute personality traits to each other, but it is essential to bear in mind that, even when they do this, it may also be part of other social agendas. Explicit attributions of trustworthiness formatted as conduct formulations or assessments, for example, is therefore just one of many ways in which members orient to trustworthiness as a local concern. It matters to participants to be perceived as honest, competent, precise, altruistic, and so forth – that is, as trustworthy – and it often matters to them that others do so, too. How this can be accomplished through interactional work is the focus of the rest of this book.

Participant orientations comprise the analytical object

When we discuss participants' interactional projects to accomplish being seen as trustworthy, or observing others' trustworthiness, we use the expression that they 'orient to' some component of trustworthiness – for example, knowledge or predictability. In an EM/CA context, the term 'orientation' has been used frequently in EM/CA studies, at least since Garfinkel (e.g. 1967). But it has not been specified methodologically. (See, however, Nielsen & Toft, in review). It is used (e.g. Goodwin, 1979; Schegloff, 1972) to describe participants' embodied strategies to demonstrate what they find/make locally relevant to them, or to the interaction. However, "[w]hereas many authors have written about 'participants' orientations', 'member's categories' and so on, the actual discursive practices involved in 'attending to', 'making relevant', 'indexing' or 'orienting to' . . . remain unspecified" (Stokoe & Smithson, 2001, p. 248). We will not delve further into this particular discussion here, but use Nielsen & Toft's definition of orientation:

> We define "participant orientation" as an action, an etic category to describe participants' situated embodied (i.e., verbal, visual, facial, gestural, postural) moves that may display (to the analyst as well as to co-participants) their attention to some social, physical or procedural target in a scene in order to monitor, display availability to, and/or participate in it; in order to make topics, issues, incidents, objects or norms locally relevant to co-participants; or in order to pinpoint their orientation or shift of orientation. The orientation may be full or divided, foregrounded or backgrounded, single or multiple, upgraded with layered modalities in use or not, with change-of-orientation markers deployed or not, interactionally coordinated or not.
>
> (in review, p. 8–9)

In this book, we use the term 'orientation' to indicate the interactional work that interactants do to make locally relevant one or more of the components of trustworthiness in the interaction.

Social actions, moves and interactional strategies are codable

The interactional actions, moves and strategies orienting to our suggested components of trustworthiness (either their own, or that of others) must be identified and analytically defined and described to the degree to which we can recognize them in data, in order to show where and how participants orient to trustworthiness. This is also an important step on the way to a possible future operationalization of trustworthiness, should it be found to be relevant to develop a scale for measuring one or more components of trustworthiness in a large-scale research project. What are codable, we should note, are all parts of the sequential negotiation of trustworthiness. This includes the questioning of others' trustworthiness by orienting to a perceived lack of (or flaw in) others' character, regardless of which component(s) of trustworthiness the questioning regards, as well as the individuals' orientation to their own trustworthiness.

Interactional actions, moves and strategies are situated in a sequential context

Depending upon the situation, interactional actions and moves must be coded as different things, since the work they and the orientation they display may be very different, depending on both the sequential context and local discourse and the situated identities. Basic CA premises must apply if they are to be seen as indicators of trustworthiness. In other words, the interactional construction and negotiation of trustworthiness are both context-specific and role-specific.

Social character as an identity project is subject to dynamic negotiation

We find that contemporary rhetoric's dynamic view of ethos corresponds with the conversation analytic notion of social actions being context-shaped and context-shaping (Heritage & Clayman, 2010). It makes sense to study trustworthiness as it develops over the course of an encounter. Character-oriented actions may shift from one turn to the next, and from situation to situation; hence, the emic concern for predictability and consistency as a separate virtue and orientation.

Local identity projects may be foregrounded and backgrounded

Many so-called character traits are communicated all the time, but not all matter for that context or for those participants. To complicate things further, not all character traits that do matter in a given interactional context are displayed in that context. Some traits are presumed by co-participants, since they are social constructs of perception. If we presume that our colleagues are honest, over time, we do not expect them to display such a trait, and we do not test them to see whether they are. In these situations, honesty is backgrounded. If a character trait is displayed explicitly, such as by being demonstrated (Schegloff, 1972; Heritage 2007), it becomes a local identity project – that is, it is foregrounded. Note, for instance, Schegloff (1972) on how a display of competence may express an understanding of not being trusted to be competent, and Heritage and Clayman (2010) on how displays of genuineness, such as accounting for the intention or motivation for calling, are foregrounded in 911 emergency calls.

Looking for noticeable absence, misplacement and breaches of norms

From the beginning, CA scholars showed how speakers design their utterances so that they would receive structurally aligned responses

(Davidson, 1984; Schegloff & Sacks, 1973; Sacks *et al.*, 1974). They use 'recipient design', that is, to design their utterances to match their interlocutor's knowledge and preferences (Enfield, 2012; Goodwin, 1979, 1981; Sacks & Schegloff, 1979; Sacks *et al.*, 1974). They also produce relevant, structurally aligned and type-conforming uptake by performing next to prior contributions (Raymond, 2003; Sacks *et al.*, 1974), perhaps even to the extent of being able to produce collaborative completions (Lerner, 1987/2004; Sacks, 1992). For decades, EM/CA researchers have explored how the interaction order is constituted by participants collaborating in co-constructing activities (e.g. Schegloff, 1986).

These features of social interaction are so basic that abiding by such tacit norms of the interaction order has nothing to do with being trustworthy *per se*. However, breaching these norms might be perceived as a lack of trustworthiness – for example, producing misaligned, misplaced, unfitted, or delayed utterances; avoiding or improperly maintaining eye contact; and/or speaking too loudly, too quickly, too softly, too slowly or too carefully. Regarding a behavior as suspicious requires expectations of a normality which are guided by the norms as to what constitutes just that (cf. Garfinkel, 1963; Jefferson, 2004a; Sacks, 1984).[1] Recipiency is important to trustworthiness, because a lack of recipient-designed communicative acts may be used to create a lack of transparency to agenda/interests, truth, and ability. By being, for example, 'fluffy', or too technical, it is possible to disguise discrepancies or hide vital information.

Defining trustworthiness as a social phenomenon

We have now presented both our theoretical conceptualization and our research agenda for an empirical conceptualization of trustworthiness as an interactional phenomenon informed by decades of EM/CA studies of social interaction. These two have guided our work on an empirical conceptualization, which can be found in Chapters 5–8.

Before moving on, we need to reflect a little more on the very concept of conceptualization. A conceptualization is a process of clarifying or developing concepts which involves, or has as its end goal, the construction of clear, concise definitions. In this book, we use both the terms 'theoretical conceptualization' and 'empirical conceptualization'. We find, however, that neither the definitions, nor the use of, nor the relations between, theoretical and empirical conceptualizations are very clear in the literature – where we see the terms used quite differently (see e.g. Wood *et al.*, 2008; Cordeiro *et al.*, 2017; Maltby, 2010; Resnick *et al.*, 2005). We understand a theoretical conceptualization as the process of defining a concept theoretically based on existing studies, and theories

1 This is a fundamental concern when studying trust in interaction, and consequently, looking for indications of mistrust is an easier undertaking (Nielsen, 2016a, 2022).

as well as empirical analysis; whereas the empirical conceptualization involves empirically deriving a definition of the concept, drawing both upon the theoretical conceptualization and upon direct analysis of data.

As stated previously, our work resulted in a theoretical conceptualization of trustworthiness as consisting of four etic orientations. These orientations were developed in an iterative, abductive process, whereby our empirical conceptualization informed our theoretical conceptualization. The purpose of conceptualizing trustworthiness empirically was to formulate a definition of trustworthiness as a social, interactional phenomenon. The definition of trustworthiness set out in what follows as a research object in social interaction is therefore a result of the entire process, including our analyses in Chapters 5–8. We have, however, chosen to present it here for reasons of pedagogy and transparency. Knowing the exact character of the research object increases readability and informs our readers of one of the key results of our study, thereby making the four empirical chapters both more accessible and more meaningful.

We define trustworthiness[2] as a research object in social interaction as:

> A perceptual outcome (i.e. a social construct) achieved in dynamic interactional negotiation of identity, realized by person A's observable interactional actions, moves, and strategies that manifest orientations to one or more components of trustworthiness (those being truth and honesty, stake and interest, ability and knowledge, and/or consistency and predictability) in interaction with person B; which may be identifiable and codable, which may appear in clusters of displays, or be noticeably absent or misplaced, and which may therefore foreground one or more components.

As is evident, this definition includes more than our research object. We are not looking at the perceptual outcome or what is achieved, but only on what observable interactional actions, moves and strategies may serve to orient to a component of trustworthiness. This raises the question of how we will identify these, which we will discuss in what follows.

Identifying orientation to trustworthiness in social interaction

As stated in Chapter 2, character is an inferred (emic as well as etic) category. Only participants' actions, moves and strategies are observable, and can therefore be explored. In our empirical work on identifying

2 We use the term 'trustworthiness' instead of the otherwise widely used term 'credibility' because we find that they are not synonyms, and that the former encompasses more than the latter.

participants' orientation to trustworthiness, we treat in our analyses one or more of their codable actions, moves and strategies which may be heard or be seen as orienting to components of trustworthiness, which are (in principle) also codable occurrences.

We saw two basic types of participants' interactional orientations, those being either to influence (others' perception of their) own trustworthiness; or else to test, negotiate or explore the perceived trustworthiness (or not) of others. We have already established that interactional actions, moves and strategies orienting to our suggested components of trustworthiness must be identified in their sequential environment in order to determine if they are indicators of orientation to trustworthiness or not. These indicators sometimes stand alone, and sometimes can be found in what we term *clusters* of indicators. In the following, we will introduce different types of indicators constituting codable actions and moves. Some of these we see as functioning through what we term *character-bound displays* (CBDs) – that is, clusters of codable actions and moves orienting to one or more components of trustworthiness, or a specific type of cluster which we term *sequential negotiation of character* (SNOC). Both will be elaborated in what follows.

Social actions may be character-bound displays (CBDs)

In many situations, actions are oriented to as displays of character traits. This can be seen in utterances such as, "Did you eat all the cake? How greedy of you!" We argue that participants orient themselves to both their own and others' actions and moves, taking them as displays of character traits when they find this locally relevant. We are interested in the displays that invoke such interpersonal (mostly tacit) conclusions. Parallel to Sacks' notion of 'category-bound activities' that we introduced in the preceding chapter, we define the concept of 'character-bound displays' (CBDs) as interactional strategies, actions and moves which might activate a perception of a certain character. That is, they can be seen as or heard that way (cf. Sacks, 1972a) by the interlocutor. We therefore argue that it is possible to use those same members' competences – which Sacks pointed to members using in their membership categorization of each other – in order to recognize specific (clusters of) displays oriented to making a character trait relevant.

Character-bound displays may have different sequential positions

CBDs can either be self-initiated or other-initiated, by somehow being made locally relevant through other participants' actions or utterances. In case of the former, a participant orients to one or more of the four components of trustworthiness either in a first pair part, or by other kinds of first move. One example could be someone regularly being late to meetings. Upon entering, they produce an unprompted account for this action. In the case of the latter, someone else uses moves, strategies or actions to orient to a participant's lack of trustworthiness by somehow orienting to one or more of the components which is lacking – thereby eliciting a CBD from this participant. Not all actions which could be taken as indicative of untrustworthiness are necessarily codable as such. Being late for a meeting is not, in itself, indicative of a lack of trustworthiness, and others may not perceive it as such. We therefore do not see this action as a codable action, unless it is treated so by the participants *in situ*.

Character may be sequentially negotiated (SNOC)

Furthermore, character may be sequentially negotiated. To expand on the aforementioned perpetual latecomer entering a meeting: they could be met by another participant who demonstrably looks at the clock (an embodied uptake to the physical action of arriving late) – thus eliciting an account formatted as an excuse, an explanation or another type of exoneration (Antaki, 1994) from the latecomer. If the latecomer, in their account, orients to one or more of the components of trustworthiness, they have produced a prompted (or other-initiated) CBD. This confirms their understanding of the uptake as a call for some display of character with regard to (in this case) stability and predictability, or knowledge and ability even, and thus an orientation to trustworthiness. We term this a *sequential negotiation of character* (SNOC). This can take many formats and involve many modalities.

We argue that it is possible to use members' competences to recognize specific displays oriented to making one's own character trait relevant (cf. Sacks' hearer's maxim and viewer's maxim). This is so regardless of whether these are self-initiated or prompted by others' action(s), thus being a SNOC. Furthermore, we argue that actions orienting to someone else's lack or flaw with regard to one or more of the four components of trustworthiness is a codable action that can be recognized as part of a SNOC, regardless of whether the response given can be identified as being a CBD.

Recognizing clusters of indicators is a member's competence

Considering the situated character of what can be inferred from character-bound displays, it is important to underline that the identification of clusters of indicators is a member's concern and accomplishment. The analyst may (using their member's competence) detect the interactant's separate moves, actions and strategies in orienting to their own or others' competence, interest or other components of trustworthiness (as well as the lack thereof) when studying a stretch of talk. Likewise, it can be detected how these separate displays might form a pattern or cluster. Consequently, in order to 'falsify' the analysis, accumulated EM/CA research – as well as the member's competence – may be used to look for displays which may counter the identified potential pattern.

In summary, participants can orient either to their own or others' (lack of) trustworthiness – the former producing a character-bound display (CBD, e.g. as a stand-alone action), and the latter by prompting, eliciting or otherwise calling for a CBD in a sequential negotiation of character (SNOC). We argue that this sequential organization does not only apply to the social negotiation of trustworthiness but to the social negotiation of all kinds of character.

Character-bound displays (CBDs) do not equal character

Although we treat character-bound displays as observable indicators of invisible character traits, we by no means stipulate a one-to-one correlation between CBDs and character. First of all, a particular display may be interpreted in many ways. Speaking quickly may indicate all sorts of things, among them character traits. Moreover, they are not a matter of stand-alone micro-casting. They may be acknowledged as well as rejected in the participants' responses; they are interactionally negotiated by means of action and uptake. So, although we treat CBDs as observable indicators of invisible character traits, it is clear that it cannot be known whether these displays reflect honesty, competence, lack of self-interest, etc., or whether, as part of a fraud or a scam, they are simply being imitated in order to create a trustworthy persona. Both Michael Caine playing John Ford's honest man (cf. Chapter 1) and the scoundrel are competent members of society, and both know how to display orientation to trustworthiness. That does not mean that all members of society are trustworthy. Frauds and tricksters may use the same displays as a genuine person. The motivation and intention underlying these displays may remain unknown to the analyst and to co-participants in the encounter. Consequently, what we are studying when pointing out CBDs is not how trustworthy people are (that is, whether someone is honest, competent or will keep their promise) but how the ongoing co-construction of trustworthiness as an interactional phenomenon is achieved *in situ*. We will return to this, and provide examples, in the analysis of our data in Chapters 5–8.

Summary

In this chapter, we have presented several research approaches to – and conceptualizations of – trustworthiness, before presenting our own theoretical conceptualization of trustworthiness. We have also introduced the basic EM/CA premises which guide our study of trustworthiness as a social phenomenon identifiable as a research object for interaction analysis. Finally, we have presented our take on the identification of interactional indicators of trustworthiness.

In the next part of this book, we will empirically conceptualize and analyze the interactional negotiation of trustworthiness in an EM/CA context. In that part, the four orientations will be unpacked, and we will suggest local micro-level manifestations of participant behavior as examples of participants' displays of orientation to aspects of trustworthiness. First, however, we will briefly present our methodology and data.

4 Methodology

Depending on the line of research, trustworthiness has been studied in different ways from a purely theoretical construct to an empirical phenomenon studied using a variety of empirical data and methods of analysis. In this chapter, we will initially and very briefly present some methodological insights into how trustworthiness is studied in, respectively, rhetoric and classic trust research in the social sciences and psychology. We will then present our methodology by elaborating on the basic mantras and premises of EM/CA, which were outlined in Chapter 2.

Methodology for studying trustworthiness in rhetoric

The tradition for studying trustworthiness in rhetoric has grown out of studies of public oratory. Therefore, many studies are text studies that make sense if the scholar subscribes to ethos as an appeal in the 'text'. This is because it is a descriptive approach to ethos, entailing communicative strategies to be identified and described (e.g. Black, 1965; Richards, 1930). However, if the scholar subscribes to ethos as the identity of the speaker, it is a normative approach to ethos; and empirically, an 'ideal character' cannot be seen or studied directly, but speakers striving to achieve an ideal might be identifiable by means of textual choices. In rhetoric, trustworthiness also has a profound theoretical focus (e.g. Burke, 1966; Perelman, 1982). Contemporary approaches make it relevant to combine textual studies with interviews (cf. Cheney, 1991), or server log analysis with protocol analysis. McCroskey (1968) has therefore pointed

DOI: 10.4324/9781003280903-4

out that when recipients or informants relate to trustworthiness, they use terms like 'competence' and 'character' but when they describe trustworthiness in others, they use terms such as 'composure', 'sociability', and 'extroversion'. This supports our argument in the direction of conceptualizing trustworthiness as a hierarchy of categories, and distinguishing methodologically between participant behavior and perception.

Methodology for studying trustworthiness broadly in trust research

Although interest in trustworthiness has been nowhere near as intense as interest in trust itself, it has been studied within different branches of the social sciences and in psychology, both as a purely theoretical construct and as an empirical phenomenon. People's perceptions of trustworthiness have been studied via ethnographic methods, especially self-reporting approaches such as interviews or surveys (Mayer *et al.*, 1995; Lyon *et al.*, 2015). Attempts to measure trustworthiness have been made either via direct measurement, primarily using the Machiavellian scale (Christie & Geis, 1970), or indirectly as a prerequisite for trust (see e.g. Dietz & Den Hartog, 2006; Gillespie, 2015; Mayer & Davis, 1999). Trustworthiness has also been studied in experimental lab settings using trust games, in which observed behavior serves as an indicator of a trustor's beliefs about the trustworthiness of others (Barr, 2003; Berg *et al.*, 1995; Lewicki & Brinsfield, 2015; Ortmann *et al.*, 2000; Wilson, 2017).

Both self-reporting and experimentation have been widely criticized with regard to validity. This is due to factors such as social desirability bias, respondents' strong preferences for agreement with the researcher's question and confirmation bias. Examples of this can be found in a large study of the 'perceived credibility' of witnesses, suspects or victims in the criminal justice system, and the factors that influence the accuracy of evidence (Memon *et al.*, 2003, p. xi). Here the authors report how DePaulo *et al.* (2003) and Vrij (2000) have reviewed more than a hundred studies of nonverbal and verbal indicators of deception – so-called micro-expressions (see Ekman, 2009) – as well as things such as a high pitch of voice, unstructured speech production, quantity of detail, spontaneous corrections and claims to a lack of memory. Both reviews concluded that "a typical nonverbal response during deception does not exist" (Memon *et al.*, 2003, p. 11), but that there are "strong stereotypical" beliefs among "observers, including professional lie catchers", that such micro-expressions exist, e.g. that liars look away or make grooming gestures (Memon *et al.*, 2003, p. 16). So strong, in fact, that a popular television series (*Lie to Me*) has been made revolving around these factors and the scholar who proposed them. The problem is that truth-tellers show the same behavior, because they may also get nervous while being interrogated (for example) – not because they are lying, but because they are afraid that they will not be believed by, e.g. the police (Bond & Fahey, 1987; Ofshe & Leo, 1997; Memon *et al.*, 2003, pp. 16, 29). This is a well-known phenomenon called the 'Othello error' (Ekman, 1992). Also, there are no strong indications in any of these studies of either the existence of deception indicators or the lack hereof, since: "Deception research has almost exclusively been conducted in university laboratories, where the participants (mostly college students) tell the truth or lie for the sake of the experiment" (Memon *et al.*, 2003, p. 16). Moreover, even if permissions were given to use video recordings of real-life cases, such as police interviews with suspects, this would require that it would be possible to establish a "ground truth" in order to distinguish truth-tellers from liars, which is difficult (Memon *et al.*, 2003, p. 17).

It is outside the scope of this book to go more into detail regarding the many common validity-issues in traditional trust research, but see Nielsen & Nielsen, in review; Antaki & Rapley, 1996; Fan *et al.*, 2006; Houtkoop-Steenstra & Antaki, 1997; Potter & Hepburn, 2005, 2012; Sudman & Bradburn, 1974.

In research concerned with the biological bases of trust, trustworthiness is studied in experiments whereby, for example, a set of human faces are first shown to a control group, who are asked to scale these after perceived trustworthiness, before the same faces are used as stimuli during MRI scans of the observers (e.g. Engell *et al.*, 2007).

Trust and trustworthiness have also been examined in organizational studies using discourse analysis methods (Wang, 2016; Candlin & Crichton, 2013). The latter methodology is the one that comes closest to what is proposed in this book, since it provides some insights into what being 'trustworthy' looks like in a highly institutionalized context. But unlike EM/CA, these methods do not take into account the endogenous orderliness produced by social interaction, which is a core premise in EM/CA.

Aside from the latter, neither these types of data nor the methodologies used to analyze them offer much insight into how trustworthiness is demonstrated in real-life settings, nor what trustworthy behavior looks like *in situ* (cf. Watson, 2009; Nielsen & Nielsen, in review). In our approach, we therefore do not so much draw on the methodology from classic psychological or social sciences research in trustworthiness, as we depart from it in our methodological approach to the study of trustworthiness as a dynamic, interactional achievement. The latter will be presented in what follows.

Our methodology

As we have already stated, our methodological approach to studying trustworthiness is conversation analysis (CA) (Sacks *et al.*, 1974; Schegloff, 2007a; Drew & Heritage, 2006; Sidnell & Stivers, 2012). CA is an interdisciplinary field of study founded in ethnomethodology (EM) (see

Chapter 2) (Garfinkel, 1967; Heritage, 1984, 1995) and concerned with understanding how people accomplish and understand social actions, and how they make sense of the social world when interacting with others. This section is far from a thorough introduction to CA methodology, as that is way beyond the scope of this book, let alone this chapter. For in-depth introductions to CA, we would point to Drew and Heritage (2006), Pomerantz and Fehr (2011), Lerner *et al.* (2017) and Sidnell and Stivers (2012), among others. With that said, a few of the most fundamental concepts deployed and explored in the next chapters will necessarily be presented here.

CA is a strictly empirical approach, and data are always recordings (preferably video) of naturally occurring interactions (sometimes labeled 'in the wild') in whatever setting is of interest. Examples are from the most mundane family dinner table conversations right through to institutional interaction from, for example, health care, courtroom or service encounters. These recordings are analyzed using a set of distinctive analytic techniques and methods aimed at explicating the social phenomena, rather than explaining them. A list of the most fundamental mantras of CA was presented in Chapter 2, including CA's inherently inductive and emic character. This means that any analysis always starts with an 'unmotivated' observation of the data, and that for any analytic claim that researchers make, they should be able to 'show in the data' – that is, point to where and how in the recordings the phenomena of interest can be observed.

CA is the study of social interaction turn by turn, as these interactions unfold in their sequential environment (Sacks *et al.*, 1974). In CA, the goal is to identify and describe in detail the many interactional practices (Heritage, 2011) which participants in interaction use to accomplish different actions (Schegloff, 2007b; Levinson, 2012), such as offering, claiming, explaining, apologizing, etc., and also how a turn, or number of turns, is recognizable as accomplishing just that particular action. CA research is concerned with identifying and explicating the norms, practices and actions that members of society themselves recognize, and orient to, both as resources for their organization of conduct and for making sense of the world (Pomerantz & Fehr, 2011). These orientations can be seen as displayed in the ongoing interaction as it progresses turn by turn. In CA, they are explored via detailed micro-analysis of the participants' talk and embodied actions, including such features as word selection, intonation contours, exact positioning of inhalations, the length of silences, positioning of overlapping talk, direction of eye gazes, temporal development of hand gestures and torquing of upper body, to mention just some.

Some of the key domains or *loci* (cf. Drew & Heritage, 1992; Schegloff, 2007a; Wilkinson & Kitzinger, 2008) of sequential micro-analysis which we explore through analysis in this book are:

- turn-taking organization (Sacks *et al.*, 1974);
- sequence organization (Schegloff, 2007a; Schegloff & Sacks, 1973);
- action formation (Goodwin, 1979, 1981; Heritage, 2013; Schegloff, 2007a; Zimmerman, 1998) and ascription (Levinson, 2012);
- category-bound activities (Sacks, 1972a, 1972b) and predicates (Watson, 1978, 1983; Psathas, 1999);
- reference work (Schegloff, 1972; Drew, 1978; Edwards, 2007);
- self- and other-repair (Schegloff *et al.*, 1977; Drew, 1997);
- preferred vs dispreferred responses (Pomerantz, 1984a).

Further, we apply conversation analytic concepts such as:

- reciprocity and alignment (Zimmerman, 1998; Peräkylä *et al.*, 2015; Pomerantz, 1984a; Stivers *et al.*, 2011);
- recipient design (Sacks *et al.*, 1974);
- next-turn proof procedure (Sacks *et al.*, 1974);
- the text linguistic concept presupposition (Harder & Kock, 1976; Levinson, 1983; Russell, 1905/1956; Strawson, 1950);
- accounting and explaining (Antaki, 1994);
- misplacement marking and unfitted responses (Drew, 2003);
- precision and relevance (Drew, 2003; Schegloff, 1972);
- online commentary (Heritage & Stivers, 1999; Mangione-Smith *et al.*, 2003);
- epistemics (Heritage, 2012a, 2012b, 2013; Heritage & Raymond, 2012; Raymond, 2018);
- deontics (Stevanovic, 2011; Stevanovic & Peräkylä, 2012).

CA's inductive and emic character is also visible in that what is tended to in CA is not what the analyst wants to study *a priori*, but rather what is made locally relevant in interaction by the participants. For doing so, participants deploy a great variety of interactional moves, strategies and actions. In this way, it is not just mutual understanding and intelligibility that is accomplished, but also an orientation to making subject matters, problems, questions, social phenomena, conflicts, etc., locally relevant. It is through the identification and analysis of these in the next four chapters that we point to how orientation to the four components of trustworthiness is achieved in excerpts from naturally occurring interaction.

Analytical focus

The analysis part of this book, in each of the chapters on the four orientations, will explore different manifestations of various participant orientations to these in (primarily) professional settings. The purpose of these analyses is to test both our theoretical conceptualization and the analytical program. All orientations may be present in all stretches of talk-in-interaction, but in each case, we will focus on the foregrounded orientations made locally relevant by the participants as they orient to them. We study trustworthiness as an interactional phenomenon via the observable *in situ* indicators of identity work within all four identified participant orientations (to truth and transparency, stake and interest, ability and competence, and consistency and predictability). Therefore, sequential analysis of action and uptake, interactional moves and strategies are the best tools we have available to study identity work – and therefore, a concept like trustworthiness, as well.

Ethnomethodology (EM) and particularly CA has been criticized for using primarily recordings of naturally occurring interaction as data, which means missing out on insights about participants – such as macro-sociological variables (age, gender, socio-economic status) and institutional position and context. CA specifically is also criticized for not utilizing data from, for example, interviews or other self-reports in its analyses. However, many – if not most – CA studies consider institutional roles and the deontic and epistemic status that these roles entail, as well as age and gender. Even so, this method is less suited to saying something about, for example, how different socio-economic groups perceive trustworthiness; or, on a macro-social scale, how a population's perception of the trustworthiness of groups of people or institutions is developed, why that is so, and how that affects the dynamics or economy of a society. Furthermore, from an EM/CA perspective, *why* people trust or find someone trustworthy is not knowledge which can be obtained; all we claim to be able to see is *how*.

Data

Our data in this book are video and audio recorded encounters from a vast number of settings. We have collected some data as part of our project on communication in international companies and organizations (1993–2016) and also the Velux-funded project on professionals' use of video meetings (2017–2021). Much data have been collected by EM/CA researchers and analyzed in CA literature over the last 60 years. Hardly any of these latter data were analyzed with the study of trust or trustworthiness in mind. But we use some of them here to illustrate/demonstrate that aspects of the participants' orientation to the four components of trustworthiness can be found more or less foregrounded in a large number of settings across time and place. Most of the encounters analyzed in this book are between professionals or between professionals and laypersons (Drew & Heritage, 1992). The specific characteristics of institutional data have received considerable analytic attention in CA over the past three decades. However, in this context, the institutional character is not key, and we will neither reference nor explicitly draw on this line of research. All data are analyzed from a CA perspective, and when possible, from a multimodal perspective (Deppermann, 2013; Goodwin, 2000; Mondada, 2014) in their sequential environment. Our own data are transcribed according to the principles developed by Jefferson (2004b), and data from previously printed works are reproduced as they were originally. All participants in the data are anonymized with respect to names and appearances of themselves and their companies. In the few cases when participants are recognizable, we have obtained their written consent.

Having introduced our methodology, which is congruent with, and rooted in, the basic premises we presented for our empirical program in the previous chapter, we will now present our study. In the next part of the book, in four separate chapters, we will explore participants' orientations to the four components of trustworthiness.

5 Orientation to truth and honesty

There is a reason why witnesses in court are asked to give the sworn testimony to tell 'the truth, the whole truth and nothing but the truth'. Bearing honest witness is anchored in truth, but the truth may be selective (hence 'the whole truth'), and it may be polluted, distorted or relativized (hence 'nothing but the truth'). This is probably also the reason why the formulation 'this is my truth' is now frequently found in the public debate. It often seems like versions of a representation of reality, 'alternative facts' – or even lies – are more appealing to people who would rather tell themselves any of these than acknowledge unpleasant truths. So, matters of truth and honesty are complex, and we cannot and would not get to the bottom of that in even the largest book. Our focus is not on

DOI: 10.4324/9781003280903-5

what is truthful *per se*, but on how interactants orient to truth and honesty in their social interactions. Basically, people do not trust you if they know you lie. Truth is the opposite of a lie, but telling a truth is, in and of itself, not enough to be trustworthy. One truthful piece of information can easily come from a dishonest person who is concealing or leaving out other relevant facts. Therefore, honesty is important, as well. It relates to fairness and adherence to facts, even though they may not benefit you. Truth and honesty are crucial – even fundamental – to trustworthiness. They often function as a precondition or prerequisite for the other components. Once you are caught lying, the road back to being perceived as trustworthy is hard and long, no matter if you appear capable, knowledgeable, consistent and transparent as to what is at stake.

The truth – and versions of it – are continuously negotiated between interactants. Honesty may be expressed in many ways and with many different outcomes. In this chapter, we will explore participants' orientation to truth and honesty. In terms of trustworthiness, this component is about being perceived as someone pursuing openness, transparency and access to all information relevant to both self and others. Being perceived as truthful and honest, even – or especially – when the truth is not in your favor, is widely regarded as the key parameter of being trustworthy. It may involve interactants neither hiding nor distorting important facts, nor holding back vital information that would have made a difference for other participants had they known, nor leaving others in the dark concerning what is going on, regardless of it being in the interactants' favor or not. These are all aspects of the orientation to truth and honesty. Likewise, being devoted to getting to the bottom of things, attention to detail and precision, and not being 'for sale' are dimensions of this orientation, as are representing reality without distorting it and choosing to give only relevant information rather than all information.

We will never know the truth, let alone the whole truth. That is not the purpose of this chapter. The purpose of all our analyses in this and the next three chapters is to test our theoretical conceptualization, as well as the analytical program, and empirically to conceptualize trustworthiness as an interactional research object. Initially, it is paramount to state that all orientations may be present in all stretches of talk-in-interaction. But, in each case, we will focus on the orientations foregrounded in the interaction by the participants. Furthermore, we cannot look for what cannot be seen. Neither the participants nor the analysts have access to what is *not* said – what information is distorted, left out, or even hidden: this is not available data. What we can observe, and therefore code, are actions and information which participants volunteer, information relevant for the other participants – the matter at hand or future actions, decisions, etc., including when they orient to something in need of clarification, correction, pursuit, and so on.

The truth

This section is not about the truth. It is about participants orienting to telling or eliciting the truth. We consider the default setting to be interactants living their lives, including the moments when they exchange facts and information for a range of different purposes, and are not treating that exchange as anything out of the ordinary. Since this is so simple, it is easy to overlook. As such, we have to make this assumption without evidence. If we cannot know what the truth is, we also cannot know if people are telling the truth. However, we can see what people treat as true and truthful in the moment.

Accepting things as the truth

Much everyday interaction regards the stating, asking for, giving, receiving or negotiating of facts and information. This is found in myriads of settings – from everyday mundane interactions to courtroom proceedings, health care consultations and business meetings. Facts are, just like truth and knowledge, an interactional achievement brought about via negotiation. This interactional negotiation has been studied in EM, particularly in discursive psychology, by Potter (1996), for example.

In the following exchange, four colleagues are cleaning up after a meeting, and they are talking about how it is not sustainable to buy a new pack of butter each week, when in fact they only use a third of it.

Example 5.1 We buy one each Friday

25 Le: vi ↑køber jo en hver fredag,
we ↑buy PT(y'know) one each Friday,
26 Mi: ja det rigtig
yeah that's right
27 Le: og så bruger vi en tredjedel af den.
and then use we a third part of it.
and then we use a third of it.
28 og så:
and the:n
29 In: ja, man ka oss købe kvarte smør,
yes, one could also buy quarter (packets of) butter,
30 det ku væ:r man sku begynd på det,
that could be: one should begin on that,
perhaps one should begin doing that,
31 Le: det ku man oss
that could one also
one could do that yes
32 In: fordi ø:h
because e:h

```
33 Le:    ja det rigtig, kvarte eller halve,
          yeah that's right, quarter or half,
34        de koster kun sy- seks kroner
          they cost only sev- six crowns
```

When Lene is stating the innocent fact that they buy a new pack of butter each Friday, nobody questions whether that is the truth. On the contrary, they are using that as a received fact to progress their exchange. Michael is acknowledging it (l. 26), not as if to say "that is correct", but more along the lines of, "yeah, you're right; I didn't think of that until you said it". Also, when Lene goes on to say that they only use a third of it, nobody questions that, either. Again, somebody (now Inge) builds on this to suggest that they buy quarter packs instead (l. 29). When Lene backs her suggestion, she can even provide the price (l. 34).

We offer this very trivial example because it shows how people usually treat what their co-participants say as the truth. They do not question each other, or the information provided. They progress the talk, and by being able to process trivial matters quickly, they will have more time for more complex issues, like their work. If we could not live our lives like that, we would go insane. From looking at Lene's, Inge's, and Michael's short exchange, it is likely that they also consider each other trustworthy in other more complex matters. We will use this as a benchmark example of lack of orientation to truth and honesty.

Negotiating the quality or truthfulness of facts and information

One way in which interlocutors orient to answering honestly is by disclosing what they know and do not know by means of formulaic constructions, such as "as far as I know" or "to the best of my knowledge". These can be codable moves indicative of this orientation – something which has been explored in a separate line of research, especially within pragmatics (e.g. Andersen, 1986; Schiffrin, 1987)[1]. One example of codable moves orientating to both truth and honesty is evaluating or disclosing the (lack) of quality of their own knowledge.

Another way of orienting to truth and honesty is asking questions about the quality or truthfulness of specific facts or what is presented as knowledge. This may in itself serve to evaluate or disclose the (lack) of quality of one's own knowledge, or that of others.

The following example is from a legal context, where extra attention is being paid to the scrutiny of whether statements will hold up in court. That is, whether they will be considered formally true and trustworthy.

1 Closely related to this is the negotiation of epistemic authority, or the right to "know" (see Chapter 7, p. 103). This is often found in the same sequential environments as the orientation towards truth and honesty.

Example 5.2 Not to my knowledge (Bilmes, 2012, p. 1634)

1. L: Y'mean no examples have ever happened?
2. J: Not no none to my knowledge.
3. L: How yo gonna prove it in a district court. (10) Y- balls in your court. How
4. are you gonna prove it in a district court I repeat.

Here, two participants are evaluating the strength of a case in court. In the first line, L is producing a clarifying follow-up question ("Y'mean no") to J's prior statements (not shown here). J is confirming this with reference to the quality of her own knowledge (l. 2). J's response resembles a B-side, as opposed to an A-side (cf. Labov & Fanshel, 1977; Pomerantz, 1980; Heritage, 2012a) presentation of facts: by letting the possibility remain open as to whether it may have happened. But J is not aware of any such instances, and thus, only having B-side (limited) knowledge, modifies the quality of the statement. It is not a clear no, but a no as far as she can know and thus a truthful no. J is then (l. 3) made accountable for how to 'prove' the truthfulness of this knowledge in court. So, the uptake in l. 3 is exactly treating l. 2 as a weak rejection of the possibility. This reaction is very unlike the participants' reaction to L's casual presentation of a fact in Example 5.1. L is thereby showing a strong orientation to the truthfulness, or not, of J's statement. We can see this whole sequence as a sequential negotiation of trustworthiness, where all three moves are orienting to truth, but only l. 2 is a character-bound display.

The whole truth

Orienting to truth and honesty often means recounting more than just the simple facts, because there may be other relevant facts to include. In this section, we will explore ways in which participants orient to the whole truth as well as honesty.

Creating openness and transparency and giving access to information

A separate pool of EM/CA studies has explored interactional strategies devoted to creating openness and transparency in decision-making and other processes. Codable actions indicative of this are, for instance, explaining and arguing (Antaki, 1994; Huisman, 2001), online commentary (Heritage & Stivers, 1999), or making references to procedure (Nielsen *et al.*, 2012) – all in sequential contexts when these strategies and moves can be beneficial for the co-participants.

In the following excerpt from the opening of a geriatric case conference in which a patient (PA) is discharged from the hospital, the doctor (DO) creates transparency with regard to the institutional process that they are part of right now. Also present is the patient's adult daughter (DA), a municipal representative, and other health care personnel not shown in this example. The doctor initiates the case conference in the following manner.

Example 5.3 Why you were hospitalized (S.B.Nielsen, 2007; Nielsen et al., 2012)

```
1 → DO:  nu er vi her alle sammen så nu ↑starter jeg med a
         we're all here now so I'll ↑begin by
2 →      fortælle lidt (.) om ↑hvorfor du blev indlagt på
         telling a bit (.) about why you were hospitalized
3 →      sygehuset (.) hvad jeg kan læse mig til i journalen.
         (.) what I can read from the file.
4        (0.5)
5 →      og hvad der er sket undervejs (0.2) mens du har
         and what has happened along the way (0.2) while you've
6 →      ↑været her.
         ↑been here.
7        (0.9)
8 → DO:  så ((navn på kommunal repræsentant)) (.) fra
         so ((name of municipal representative)) (.) from
9 →      hjemmeplejen oss, (.) får en ide om
         the home help service also, (.) gets an idea about
10 PA:   ja.=
         yes.=
11 → DO: =hva der=↑hva det handler om ikk?
         =what there=what this is about right?
```

By telling what is going to happen step by step in the meeting (l. 1–6), and why (l. 8–11), the doctor provides information and creates process transparency for the patient and her daughter. By creating such transparency, the professional gives the laypersons a basis for making the decisions they are about to make together with the professionals (e.g. whether to move to a retirement home or not). This establishes the trustworthiness of 'the system' within the process. The introduction also serves to explain why the next utterances will not be recipient targeted to the patient (who probably already knows why she was hospitalized) but to the municipal representative. It is a double transparency-creating act: "I am telling you what is going to happen, and also telling you why I am telling it". The confirming uptake from the patient in l. 10, rather than in the long pause in l. 7, shows that DO's reasoning makes sense for the patient. We see the doctor's whole turn at talk as a codable action designed to create trust in the process, and hence the system. By performing that very action, the doctor also creates an identity as meeting chair, and uses that position to create transparency. As the turn may serve to activate the perception of a certain character as someone oriented to transparency, it works as a character-bound display.

A counterexample would be a person asking a lot of questions about process or procedure, until the co-participant finally has to ask, "Don't you trust me?" The reason why we see multiple questions about process or procedure as an indication of lack of trust, or an attempt to point out lack of trustworthiness on behalf of the counterpart, is that such questions make relevant the issue of "where is this going?" Attention to openness and transparency therefore very much overlaps with an orientation to stake and interest. In such cases, the codable actions may very well be part of a sequential negotiation of character (SNOC).

Explaining and giving detail are also interactional moves which can be oriented to transparency, to giving access to all relevant information (Antaki, 1994), and thus to truth and honesty. An example of this can be seen in Example 5.4, where a young Greek woman and her older relative are at a Danish municipality service center to exchange the younger woman's Greek driver's license for a Danish one. Her older relative (Ci1) is there to help, as she speaks Danish fluently. In the example below, she explains the matter at hand to the municipality employee (Emp), while providing a translation of the original driver's license.

Example 5.4 Because it's a scooter license

10	Ci1:	men jeg tænkte os på hun har det her (.)
		but i also thought about she has this (.)
11		jeg har fået det oversat (.5) fra:
		i've had it translated (.5) fro:m
12		**(2)**
13		hvad det svarer til (.)
		what it corresponds to (.)
14		altså jeg tænkte på om det kunne komme der
		that is i thought if that could get there
15		fordi det er knallertkørekort hun [har]
		because it's a scooter license she [has]
17	Emp:	**[hmhm]**
18	Ci1:	og så jeg har fået det oversat til dansk(.4) i det hele
		and i've had it translated to danish(.4) in the full
19		(.) altså hendes og der er os'
		(.). that is her and there is also
20		(1.5) ø:h (.) m regning med der er betalt
		(1.5) e:h (.) with the bill which is paid
21		da han er ø:h (inaudible)
		since he is ø:h (inaudible)
22		du ved fra den græske ø::h
		you know from the greek e::hm
23	Emp:	ja
		yes
24	Ci1:	ø:h ambassade altså ø:h (.6)
		e:hm embassy that is e:hm (.6)
25		der han oversætter den (.)
		there he translates it (.)

While showing Emp the translation papers from the Greek Embassy and pointing to the relevant places in them, Ci1 explains in detail the matter at hand: how she had the license translated (l. 11), that it's a scooter license (l. 15), that every part of it is translated (l. 18), that it's her relative's license (not her own) (l. 19), that the translation has been paid for (l. 20) and that the translator is from the Greek Embassy (l. 21–22 and 24–25) – which is one of the institutions legally able to translate official documents. We see Ci1's whole turn at talk as containing a series of codable actions: first volunteering facts and providing information (l. 11–13), her request (l. 14) and her account for this request (l. 15), followed by more volunteered information (l. 18–20) and an explanation slot (l. 21–22 and 24–25) which she has carved out for herself, and where she explains why this information is relevant. This way, the citizen works to create openness and transparency regarding the character of the document and the process she has gone through to get it right. Her interaction with the employee constitutes a (not problematized) SNOC. We see this series of actions as designed to create trust, both in the papers she is about to present and in her own truthfulness and honesty. The employee's uptake (l. 17, 23) confirms the relevancy of the steps taken in that process. Because of that uptake, this stretch of talk not only represents a series of character-bound displays, but also a SNOC.

Doing being honest by volunteering unflattering facts and information

Volunteering facts, details, and information that is less flattering (or even incriminating for the person, and perhaps not strictly necessary) is also a strong orientation to honesty. An example of this can be found in Example 5.5, where a health care worker (HCW) at a live-in rehabilitation center is conferring about the state of a patient with the patient's general practitioner (GP) (DOC) via video conference. The GP is unable to come to the center, and therefore relies on the information given by the HCW in his long-distance treatment of the patient. In this example, the HCW discloses some information about what has happened with the patient which is, strictly speaking, unnecessary for further treatment, and at the same time not flattering for the personnel involved.

Example 5.5 Suddenly a crash sounds again

1 HCW: han har(.8)flere gange i går
he has(.8)multiple times yesterday
2 (.9)
3 været faldet
fallen
4 (1.0)
5 fordi han rejser sig.
because he gets up.

6 (1.4)
7 DOC: han rejser sig af sig selv? fra stolen=
he gets up by himself? from the chair=
8 HCW: =ja (.).hhh så har han siddet i >lænestolen
=yes (.).hhh then he has been sitting in the >easy chair
9 han har selv rejst sig fra kørestolen
he has gotten up from the wheelchair by himself
10 og gået over i lænestolen og det var gået fint<
and gone to the easy chair and that had gone fine<
11 .hhh vi ser det ske og når at løbe op tilham men når ikke
.hhh we see it happen and manage to run to him but does not have time
12 at afværge det. ø:h men det går egentlig fint nok(.)
to stop him. e:h but it actually goes well enough (.)
13 så går der ikke andet end ti minutter så hører vi et rabalder
then no more than ten minutes later we hear a crash
14 .hhh så har han forsøgt at gå hen til sengen
.hhh then he has tried to go to his bed
15 .hhh men så har han taget fat i sengebordet
.hhh but he has taken hold of the bedside table
16 med pladen ud og støttet sig til den
with the extension board out and supported himself with that
17 og det kan man jo ligesom ik øh:m
and that you evidently cannot do eh:m
18 så han han faldt ned øhm (.) der var ik andet
so he he fell down ehm there (.) was nothing else
19 at se end et lille afskrab på øh på ø:h albuen virker ok
to see except a small rash on eh on e:h the elbow seems all right
20 er ikke smerteklagende eller noget som helst
is not complaining about pain or anything
21 .hhh så får vi hjulpet ham op i seng for det var det han gerne ville
.hhh so we get him helped into bed because that was what he wanted
22 (1.6)
23 og da han har været i sengen i et kvarter (.)
and when he has been in bed for fifteen minutes (.)
24 pludselig lyder der et rabalder igen
suddenly sounds a crash again
25 for så er han stået op? (.7) af sengen
because then he has gone out? (.7) of the bed

In this excerpt, the HCW recounts no less than three incidents when the patient has done something potentially harmful to himself, and which the personnel did not manage to prevent. Initially, the HCW says that the patient fell several times yesterday (l. 1–3) due to him getting up, which is something he cannot do safely because he has untreated Parkinsonism and other health issues. She then goes on to explain how these falls were possible: that they were due to the inability of the nurses and other personnel to respond quickly enough to prevent the falls (l. 11–12) – or them not being around to intervene, not even when they knew it had happened several times that day. This information is given to the GP as part of the HCW's request for advice regarding the patient's medication, although it was not necessary for her to disclose this in order to ask for – or get – the advice. It is therefore a strong orientation from her to being perceived as honest, and also to displaying her trust in the GP's reaction. In this case, the doctor gives the health care worker plenty of time to tell her story, and he does not pose follow-up questions to get to the bottom of things, making it apparent that he does not need to. The lack of uptake to her codable action indicates that he trusts her enough to not let it turn into a SNOC.

Related to this volunteering of information (flattering or not) is the ready answering of questions, thereby admitting potentially problematic behavior or knowledge.

Another practice strongly indicating a participant's orientation to truth is the participant displaying, or offering to display, their own lack of knowledge, insight or competence regarding a locally relevant matter – since this honesty could potentially pose not just a threat of losing face (cf. Goffman, 1955), but could also alter the person's epistemic stance.[2] The more the participant has at stake by disclosing or volunteering information (also see Chapter 6 on stake and interest), the more honesty is oriented to *in situ*.

Orienting to detail and precision

Orientation to detail and precision is a suborientation of truth and honesty which is backed by a strong line of CA research with plenty of examples. They include journalists questioning presidents (Clayman *et al.*, 2006, 2007; Clayman & Heritage, 2002), the pursuit of adequate answers in broadcast journalism (Romaniuk, 2013), revealing politicians' stands on salient issues so as to ensure that the public knows the relevant details (Clayman & Loeb, 2018), cross-examining witnesses in a courtroom interaction (Atkinson & Drew, 1979) and police interrogations (Edwards, 2006a; Edwards & Stokoe, 2011).

2 One longer example of the latter can be seen in the analysis of Example 7.3 and Example 7.9 in Chapter 7, on knowledge and ability. That example clearly shows – as many others will in the next three chapters – that displays of truth and honesty are closely intertwined with – and crucial for – the other orientations.

Detailing facts and insisting on precision are practices used by participants (Jefferson, 1974) to determine whether something is believable or not. The following is an example of interactional behavior missing in Example 5.1 at the beginning of this chapter. It is an exchange from a traffic court (Drew, 2003, p. 919) between a prosecution counsel (PC) and a defendant (D) accused of speeding.

Example 5.6 Doing doubting factual statements (Drew, 2003, p. 919)

```
1  PC:   And then you uh: uh, when you approached the fifty five mile
2         per hour sign what, what speed were you going?
3  D:    Forty five when I approached it.
4  PC:   And what speed were you going when you passed it?
5  D:    Fifty five.
6  PC:   Exactly fifty five?
7  D:    Somewhere in that vicinity.
8  PC:   Well did you look at your speedometer?
9  D:    Yes, I know I was under fifty five.
10 PC:   Well do you remember what you were going?
11 D:    No I don't
```

In this example, we see the PC questioning the facts ("Exactly fifty-five?"), questioning the basis of the report ("Well did you look at your speedometer?"), suggesting skeptical inferences or conclusions (l. 10), and not progressing to other matters but lingering around the credibility of "fifty-five" (compare the progress from l. 3–4. with l. 5–11, which does not convince us that l. 12 will move on to other matters). These are all moves orienting to detail and precision. We can see the entire exchange as a SNOC, and the defendant's moves in l. 5, 7 and 9 as character-bound displays that orient to the truth and quality of the facts, and hence to the trustworthiness of the speaker. Here, PC focuses on detail and precision in order to determine the trustworthiness of D's statement, and thus of D himself.

When the trustworthiness of a participant is at stake, and the implications are important, no detail seems too small to be significant, as the following exchange from a rape trial (Drew, 2003, p. 921), where the alleged victim is cross-examined as a witness (W) by the defense counsel (DC), will show:

Example 5.7 Correcting details (Drew, 2003, p. 921)

```
1  DC:   An' during that eve:ning (0.6) uh: didn't Mister (defendant's
2         name) come over (to) sit with you.
3         (0.8)
4  W:    Sat at our table.
5         (1.1)
6  DC:   Didn't he sit next to you?
7         (0.6)
```

```
W:     No (.) he sat across from me.
       (0.3)
DC:    Acro:ss from you?
       (0.7)
DC:    D'e (never) sa:t next to you:
       (0.3)
W:     No?
```

Here, we see the witness substitute a version of the alleged rapist sitting "with" her with a version of him sitting "at" the "table" where she sat with her friends, noting that he did not sit "next to" her but "across from" her. Such details may matter, not for matters of deixis and geography, but because of their potential implications. Was she collaborating in the establishment of special expectations, or was she indeed raped later? If no hard evidence is brought to bear in such a courtroom trial, the trustworthiness of the speaker may be the determining factor of the case. The smallest details may therefore be treated with intense scrutiny. Again, we may see this entire exchange as a sequential negotiation of the character of the witness.

Pursuing response in cases of reluctance and minimalism

An aspect of orienting to precision and detail is being devoted to getting to the bottom of things by pursuing clarity and detail, not hiding more or less important facts, getting all information out, and not holding back any information that would have made a difference for other participants had they known about it. Codable actions include self- and other-initiated self- or other-repair (Schegloff *et al.*, 1977) done to pursue detail or further information, as well as volunteering information.

In the preceding paragraphs, we have explored participants' moves and strategies devoted to getting to the bottom of things. The opposite situation – when relevant information is not volunteered – is treated by interactants by means of asking questions and pursuing answers in order to obtain elaboration or further information. Answering minimally may create an explanation slot (Antaki, 1994) which makes it evident that something is missing or insufficient, not enough; that the respondent is not finished responding; or that space for telling a long story is being made. Reluctance to answer questions, or giving evasive answers without accounting for this, can be seen as giving 'less than the whole truth'. Pursuing something more – be it detail, transparency, or further information – makes it locally relevant that only partial truths or irrelevant facts have been provided, and that these are not 'enough' for a person to be perceived as honest. These pursuits are therefore orientations to breaches of trustworthiness (cf. Atkinson & Drew, 1979).

An example of this can be seen in the following (Example 5.8), taken from the same data as 5.5. Here we see Emp pursuing a clarification of detail, despite having been given abundant information. Just before the excerpt begins, Ci1 has asked (using an if-formatted interrogative) whether the scooter license could also be on the new Danish license.

Example 5.8 That is a thirty scooter, right?

33 Emp: det kommer der på det danske ja
it will be on the Danish one yeah
34 Ci1: ja=
yes=
35 Emp: =at hun må både køre bil og knallert
=that she is allowed to drive both car and scooter
36 Ci1: ja (.) det var det jeg
yes (.) that was what I
37 Emp: det kommer der
that will be there
38 Ci1: det er derfor jeg har taget det her med så I
that is why I've brought this over here so you(pl.)
39 og så få det oversat fordi det var på græsk
and then get it translated because it was in Greek
40 .hhh og så stod der jo her eh:m (.)
.hhh and then it said (adv.) here eh:m (.)
41 .hhh altså det betyder på græsk knallert du ved=
.hhh that is it means in Greek scooter you know=
42 Emp: =ja
=yes
43 Ci1: det sådan nogen knallerter der så:::
it's those kinds of scooters there so:::
44 Emp: altså en tredive knallert ik os
that is a thirty scooter right

In the previous example, information had been plentiful, and the Emp has just confirmed in l. 33 and 35 that the Danish license will be for both the car and the scooter. Still, Ci1 keeps explaining the translation of the word scooter (l. 38–41, 43). Also, the one specific piece of information locally relevant for Emp, in order for her to be able to order the new license – that is, the type of scooter – is missing, making Emp ask for confirmation that what was in question was in fact "a thirty scooter", (l. 44), i.e. the Danish standard scooter, which is allowed to go up to a maximum of 30 km/h. This way, Emp orients to not yet having received all relevant information, in spite of all the detailing – thereby, by her uptake, sequentially negotiating the trustworthiness of the citizen's explanation.

Also, something might be technically true but far from the exact or 'whole' truth. An example from Sacks can be seen in Example 5.9 following.

Example 5.9 Didn't you smack her one? (Sacks, 1992, p. 113)

(1) *A*: Yeah, then what happened?
(2) *B*: Okay, in the meantime she [wife of B] says, "Don't ask the child nothing." Well, she stepped between me and the child, and I got up to walk out the door. When she stepped between me and the

child, I went to move her out of the way. And then about that time her sister had called the police. I don't know how she . . . what she . . .

(3) *A*: Didn't you smack her one?
(4) *B*: No.
(5) *A*: You're not telling me the story, Mr B.
(6) *B*: Well, you see when you say smack you mean hit.
(7) *A*: Yeah, you shoved her. Is that it?
(8) *B*: Yeah, I shoved her.

This example from Sacks is from a telephone conversation between a social agency staff member (A), which B has called because of some marital troubles. A has no prior knowledge of B, or vice versa. Still, from l. 2, A is able to infer that something more must have happened, since B's sister-in-law, according to him, had called the police. A takes a guess in l. 3, asking B "Didn't you smack her one?" As Sacks points out, B does not treat this guess as something out of the ordinary; he simply denies it. It could have stopped here. Technically, the answer could be true. What B described was "moving her out of the way". However, B is not content, and in l. 5, he essentially accuses A of lying. B's carefully worded reply focuses on the exact word used by A, and what it means ("when you say smack, you mean hit"). So, A tries again in l. 7, now getting what happened and using a word that B can accept as a description of his prior action, namely "shoved". In this lecture, Sacks is concerned with "seeing lies" (p. 114) and making sense of a person's utterances using what he calls "The Inference-Making Machine" (p. 113pp). We will not go into more detail here, but will return to the problem of detecting lies later in this chapter. We may see the entire exchange as a sequential negotiation of B's trustworthiness, designed to clarify whether he told 'the whole truth', or perhaps only part of it.

Relevance

What the important facts are – or what the vital information is – for the participants depends upon context. This means that any telling or displaying of information regarding something relevant can potentially be a codable move, strategy or action indicative of an orientation to truth and honesty, depending on the situation. The question of local, situational relevance is therefore very important. Coming across as trustworthy by orienting to truth and honesty is a matter concerned with the character and extent of the information or facts provided in relation to the local situation, and the epistemic status of the participants. A key line of research within pragmatics concerns relevance (e.g. Grice, 1975; Sperber & Wilson, 1986).

In an EM/CA context, one example of dealing with the question of local relevance is to be found in Schegloff's paper on place formulation

(Schegloff, 1972). Here he points out that a truthful and correct formulation of the location of something (e.g. Manhattan) may be irrelevant, or even confusing or misleading, if it is not context-relevant and recipient-designed. (In this case, if the object to be located was a set of notes in an office, 'Manhattan' would not be a useful place formulation). Also, Drew attends to the matter of "relevant precision" (Drew, 2003, p. 917) in his study of the "associations between precision, exaggeration, and truth or lying" (Drew, 2003, p. 937). Drew argues that the

> practices through which claims are revealed to have been insufficiently precise, overstated, or exaggerated shade into matters of the *perceived truth* and *credibility* of claims, and hence concern the micro-politics of alternative and competing versions of events, both in ordinary interaction and also in public affairs.
>
> (Drew, 2003, p. 937, emphasis in original)

Drew quotes Shapin's (1994) study on the social history of truth, whereby he traces the emergence of truth as a social institution and notes:

> When we assess the truth of a claim to factual knowledge, we typically take a view on whether or not it is a representation that corresponds to the world. That assessment embeds some notion of adequate precision: How exact is that correspondence supposed to be? . . . [P]ractical decisions about precision and variation in factual reports are moral judgements . . . which embed norms about the degree of exactness and certainty *it is right* to expect of competent and sincere human reports. . . . Precision judgements, consequently, always have a normative character.
>
> (Shapin, 1994, pp. 310–311, emphasis in original; here referred after Drew, 2003, p. 937)

This explicit combination of assessments of truth and (normative) assessments of "adequate precision" Drew sees as exemplified and captured in "the following conversational remark, made after a claim by the speaker has been called an exaggeration: 'DON'T SAY that I'm exa . . . – just say I'm a liar'" (from Schegloff, 1979, p. 275) (Drew, 2003, p. 937).

We agree with these observations and analyses, and point to giving both too much or too little information relative to what is locally relevant, for both the matter at hand and the recipient, as possibly being oriented to not telling "the whole truth and nothing but the truth". Possible codable actions include repeated self-initiated explanation slots (Antaki, 1994, p. 79ff), misplacement-marked utterances (e.g. "by the way", Schegloff & Sacks, 1973), careful wording regarding specific topics, misfitted questions or responses – all in environments where specific information is relevant. In the following section, we elaborate on this and provide some examples.

Nothing but the truth

The flip side of truth is, of course, lies, and an important aspect of orientation to honesty is detecting whether something is a lie. Again, we are not interested in truth versus lies, but rather in participant orientations to something being true and honest versus a lie. In the last section of this chapter, we will explore participants' orientation to lies.

Being fishy by giving too much information, detail and precision

"Only lies have detail", states Conan Doyle's famous detective in the BBC television series *Sherlock*. Although this is essentially a layperson's misconception (cf. Goldman-Eisler, 1968; Memon *et al.*, 2006), being buried in facts and seemingly unnecessary details by someone who is evidently strongly oriented to facts and precision – and to appearing truthful and ultimately trustworthy – can actually have the opposite effect. It can undermine the trustworthiness of the participant. As we mentioned in Chapter 3, breaches of any tacit norms within the interaction order – including the production of misaligned, misplaced, unfitted or delayed utterances, or speaking too loudly, too quickly or too carefully compared with what would be the norm (cf. Garfinkel, 1963; Jefferson, 2004a; Sacks, 1984) might, in certain environments, be perceived as fishy, or even as a marker of potential untrustworthiness. Even so, it is important to recognize that there is no one-on-one relationship between the previously mentioned interactional moves or formats and being trustworthy or not. It remains a question of the interpretation of indicators.

However, as we have repeatedly pointed out, the very orientation to truth and honesty may be exploited to effect disguise, and to create a false appearance of being trustworthy. It is difficult to fool others if one does not seem to be trustworthy. This is also the reason why our EM/CA approach to trustworthiness can never be used to assess whether people really are trustworthy – only whether they orient to being perceived as trustworthy or not.

In the analysis of the following example, we will point out how a massive orientation to truth, precision, transparency and detail, as well as knowledge and ability, make up what we call a cluster of indicators allowing us to point to this as an example of a participant's orientation to trustworthiness. Excerpts from this example have been analyzed throughout this chapter (Examples 5.4 and 5.8), but here we will analyze it in its entirety. The example is from a face-to-face encounter between a citizen's service employee and two citizens (Figure 5.1). As mentioned earlier, the reason for the citizens' visit to the municipality service center is that the younger citizen (Ci2) wants to exchange her Greek driver's license for a Danish one, while her older relative (Ci1) is there to help because she speaks Danish. Exchanging licenses is a fairly standard procedure between European Union (EU) countries. The applicant must bring

Figure 5.1 Two citizens are meeting with a citizen's service employee (Emp, to the right of the computer) at the municipal service center. One is a Danish resident, Ci1, sitting with a large scarf and her glasses on her head. Her younger family member, Ci2, is sitting to her right (lower left corner of the photo). Ci2 has recently moved from Greece to take up temporary residence in Denmark. Ci2 has a Greek driver's license, which she wants to exchange for a Danish one.

to a citizen service center an appropriate photo, the original license, their passport, and a translation of the foreign license by a police-approved translator. From there, it will be forwarded to the police, who will issue the new license. In this excerpt, Ci1 is holding out the translation (so that the service employee can see it) and pointing in it from l. 6, before handing it to her during the silence in l. 19.

In our analysis of this very long excerpt, our main foci will be on Ci1 and her many character-bound displays orienting to truth and honesty, and Emp's orientation to relevance and detail.

The excerpt begins just after Emp has had a long conversation on the phone regarding various other matters. While Emp was speaking on the phone, Ci1 and Ci2 talked in low voices in Greek, while leaning in to each other. Emp was speaking with Ci2 in English, right before the phone call.

Example 5.10 So I was just gonna have him translate it

```
1  Emp:  I'm sorry
2  Ci1:  .hh må jeg lige forklar dig noget først .hh
```
.hh can I just explain you something first. hh
```
3        ø:hm hvad hedder de:t hun har jo det der [græske]
         kørekort
```
e:hm what is i:t. she has that [Greek] driver's license

4 Emp: [hm]
5 Cil: .hh og så
.hh. and then
6 jeg vil bare lige sige fordi i grækenland
I just wanted to say that because in Greece
7 er det blevet lavet sådan nu at man men men (.3)
it's been made so now that you but but (.3)
8 mt ja det kan jo så være lige meget
mt yeah that doesn't really matter anyway
9 .hh øh hvad hedder det nu (.)
.hh ehm what is it (.)
10 men jeg tænkte os på hun har det her (.)
but I also thought about she has this (.)
11 jeg har fået det oversat (.5) fra:
I've had it translated (.5) fro:m
12 **(2)**
13 hvad det svarer til (.)
what it corresponds to (.)
14 altså jeg tænkte på om det kunne komme der
that is I thought if that could get there
15 fordi det er knallertkørekort hun [har]
because it's a scooter license she [has]
16 Emp: [hmhm]
17 og så jeg har fået det oversat til dansk(.4) i det hele
and I've had it translated to danish(.4) in the full
18 (.) altså hendes og der er os'
(.) that is hers and there is also
19 (1.5) ø:h (.) m regning med der er betalt
(1.5) e:h (.) with the bill which is paid
20 da han er ø:h (inaudible)
since he is ø:h (inaudible)
21 du ved fra den græske ø::h
you know from the Greek e::hm
22 Emp: ja
yes
23 Cil: ø:h ambassade altså ø:h (.6)
e:hm embassy that is e:hm (.6)
24 der han oversætter den (.)
there he translates it (.)
25 Emp: hm
hm
26 **(2,4)**
27 Cil: og så ville jeg bare ha han oversatte det
and so I was just gonna have him translate it
28 så I ku se at det <u>er</u>
so you(pl)could see that this <u>is</u>
29 (.) altså til den der (.) knallert om det så kunne
(.) that is for this (.) scooter if that then could
30 komme på på det nye
get on on the new one

31 .hhh eh der hvor der står at øh::m (.) ø::h (.)
.hhh eh there where it says that eh::m (.) e::hm (.)
32 Emp: det kommer der på det danske ja
it will be on the Danish one yeah
33 Ci1: ja=
yes=
34 Emp: =at hun må både køre bil og knallert
=that she is allowed to drive both car and scooter
35 Ci1: ja (.) det var det jeg
yes (.) that was what I
36 Emp: det kommer der
that will be there
37 Ci1: det er derfor jeg har taget det her med så I
that is why I've brought this over here so you(pl.)
38 og så få det oversat fordi det var på græsk
and then get it translated because it was in Greek
39 .hhh og så stod der jo her eh:m (.)
.hhh and then it said (adv.) here eh:m (.)
40 .hhh altså det betyder på græsk knallert du ved=
.hhh that is it means in Greek scooter you know=
41 Emp: =ja
=yes
42 Ci1: det sådan nogen knallerter der så:::
it's those kinds of scooters there so:::
43 Emp: altså en tredive knallert ik os
that is a thirty scooter right
44 Ci1: e:h j:o altså (.) halvtreds eller jeg ved ik
e:h ye:ah that is like (.) fifty or I don't know
45 Emp: hm
hm
46 Ci2: halvtreds (.) halvtreds
fifty. (.) fifty
47 Ci1: ja og det er halvtreds ø:h
yes and it is fifty e:hm
48 Emp: men det er i hvert fald politiet under alle omstændigheder
but under any circumstances it's the police
49 der tager stilling til (.4) hvad det
who decides (.4) what it is
50 kom[mer til at svare til i danmark]ik'
gon[na correspond to in Denmark] right
51 Ci1: [mer til at svare til (unintelligeble)]
[na correspond to (unintelligeble)]
52 ja
yes

After ending her phone call, Emp apologizes in English (for taking the call during their encounter). Ci2 does not respond, and Ci1 self-selects: bending forwards and holding the translation of the license so that Emp can see it. Ci1 sets up an explanation slot for herself (l. 2) and goes on to produce a very long account regarding the translation she is about to hand over, while pointing at different places in it. The account initially lasts almost a minute (l. 3–32), and during this period, Ci1 carves out self-initiated explanation slots again and again – such as "I just wanted to say" (l. 6), "but I also thought about" (l. 10), and "that is, I thought if" (l. 14), thus volunteering facts and information. Via self-correction, or repairs, she also orients to local relevance (l. 7–8) as well as precision (l. 23–24). All these pre-explanations lead up to a self-initiated request in l. 29: "This (.) scooter if that then could get on the new one", meaning Ci2's new license. At the possible completion point (PCP) after this turn constructional unit (TCU), Ci1 self-selects again and continues her explanation (l. 31), now concerning where, on the new license, the scooter permission should be. However, after she searches for words and pauses, Emp takes up her request, confirming that both the car and the scooter "will be on the Danish" license (l. 32 and 34).

Ci1's initial account is oriented to coming across as both knowledgeable (with regard to the legal demand that one should bring a translation, and that this should come from the embassy), competent, and also able to act appropriately (by procuring the translation and bringing it to the relevant authority), as well as being well-prepared. (Ci1 explicitly displays having relevant and accurate knowledge, including background knowledge on the rules in Greece [l. 6–7].) But as is often the case, we do not just see knowledge and capability being oriented to; she is also oriented to truth. As she self-repairs (Schegloff *et al.*, 1977; Jefferson, 1974) and searches for the exact words, she seems to strive together for precision, detail and relevance. The detailed and substantial information and the careful delivery both display an orientation to transparency, correctness, quality and, thus, the truthfulness of her account. However, the account also contains a good deal of detailed information which is not directly relevant for Emp, such as the translator's precise identity, that the bill has been paid, and the specific wording of the vehicle type in the translation.

After Emp confirms that the scooter will be on the new license (l. 2 and 33), Ci1 once again self-selects. She continues to explain (l. 35 and 37–42), now elaborating on her reason for bringing the translation ("because it was in Greek" l. 38), pointing to the translation of the word "scooter" while using the adverb "jo" (l. 39). The use of this adverb implies that this is common and taken-for-granted knowledge. In l. 40, Ci1 finishes her turn with "you know", again implying common knowledge and understanding, and Emp confirms this. However, Ci1 continues to specify and elaborate: "it's those kinds of scooters there" (l. 42) while pointing within the document. This receives an uptake from Emp, who now produces a request for clarification, "that is a thirty scooter, right", referring to the Danish speed limits of 30 km/h for regular scooters. The tag "right" has a preference for a positive answer. Ci1 hesitates with a slightly prolonged e:h before carefully confirming with a prolonged "ye:ah". This is, however, followed by the adverb "altså", often used to project a clarification or correction of what has just been uttered. Then, following a micro-pause, Ci1 now states, with a frown, "fifty or I don't know". After a minimal response from Emp, Ci2 self-selects and speaks for the first time: turning her head and touching Ci1's arm while looking at her, she confirms Ci1's correction twice, with a stressed "fifty, fifty" (l. 46), and she does so in Danish. Looking at Ci2, Ci1 aligns with her in l. 47 ("yes"), before looking back at Emp, addressing her with "and it is fifty". This little intermezzo shows that getting the license confirmed for 50 km/h scooters is a very important project. At this point, Emp explicitly disclaims both epistemic and deontic authority regarding the matter by stating that "under any circumstances", it is "the police who decide what it is gon[na correspond to in Denmark", thereby transferring the entire subject from being an administrative matter to being a police decision.

Interestingly, Ci1's accounts are strongly designed to provide precise, detailed facts and information, thereby displaying orientation to truthfulness, and also to knowledge and ability (see Chapter 7). She is foregrounding that orientation. Ci1's accounts in this excerpt contain numerous character-bound displays and other interactional moves orienting to components of trustworthiness, such as precision and detail, which together form a cluster of indicators. These show her to be oriented to doing being trustworthy *in situ*. However, neither the level of detail nor the type of information she provides display *relevant* precision – it is contrarily too much and too detailed compared to what is necessary for the Emp to perform such a standard administrative matter. Also, Ci1 avoids explicitly mentioning the crucial detail: the type of scooter which is of interest, and instead she resorts to ambiguity with respect to the license being for more than one type of vehicle, without explicitly stating which types, in her evasive trail-off "I don't know" in l. 44. We cannot know her motivation, but this is not in line with an overall truth-orientation. By underspecifying (Bergmann, 1992; Nielsen, 2012), she is distorting facts and withholding vital information that the Emp may need. In so doing, Ci1 is hiding an agenda: that Ci2 will lose her right to drive her "fifty scooter" back in Greece if she does not get her Greek scooter license exchanged for a Danish motorcycle license. After this exchange, Ci2 decides to cancel her application for exchanging her Greek license to a Danish one. We see the entire exchange as a sequential negotiation of trustworthiness with a cluster of codable actions and uptakes that serve to foreground the orientation to truth and honesty.

The example shows how several orientations can be found in the same stretch of talk, intertwining and facilitating each other. It also shows that when a cluster of indicators orients 'too much' to something, while transparency is avoided at crucial points, the identity project 'doing being trustworthy' is side-tracked. The ambiguity in Ci1's interactional moves creates a potential perception of her as not trustworthy. During her account it becomes increasingly possible to see and hear her that way (cf. Sacks, 1972a; Schegloff, 2007a).

Miscrediting others' versions

Part of the orientation to truth and honesty – or the lack of both – is miscrediting other versions of the world. This can be done interactionally, by constructing a degree of skepticism to other people's version of events, as pointed out by Pomerantz (1988). This may include juxtaposing a statement with 'facts' to the contrary, presenting a visual document of a statement as perceptibly weak or suspicious, presenting contradictory statements from the same speaker or by reporting 'facts' that imply different and inconsistent versions of events.

In the following excerpt from a Danish news interview, we see the interviewer (IR) begin by animating a statement from earlier that day from the interviewee himself (IE). This was when he, as the bank director, announced the acquisition of another bank. He does this before shifting to animating the Danish Consumer Council, an NGO working for consumer rights:

Example 5.11 But the Consumer Council, they say the opposite

1 IR: (1.0). h du har i dag givet udtryk for at drivkraften bag
(1.0). h today you have expressed that the driving force behind
2 fusionen er at tjene penge til aktionærerne
the merger is to make money for the shareholders
3 .h ↑hvorfor ikke la fusionen komme °kunderne° til gode.
.h ↑why not let the merger benefit the °customers°.
4 (0.2)
5 IE: det kommer den også ↓til.
it will do that ↓too.
6 (0.4)
7 det blir en bedre virksomhed og gode virksomheder de har oss':
it becomes a better company and good companies they also have:
8 (0.3) gode tilbud til ↓kunderne.
(0.3) good offers for their ↓customers.
9 (0.4)
10 IR: men: nu hører >>vi jo altså Forbrugerrådet<< dih .h mener det modsatte
but: now we hear >>that ADV the Consumer Council<< they. h say the opposite
11 de tror ikk' på at det her kommer til at gavne fo forbrugerne.
they don't believe that this is going to benefit the cu customers.

Here the IR shifts footing from animating (Goffman, 1981; Clayman, 1992) first the IE himself (l. 1–2), on how the merger benefits the shareholders, then the Consumer Council (l. 10–11) on the merger not benefiting the customers. The IR is maintaining his formal neutrality while constructing an environment of skepticism. In his uptake at l. 10–11, he flat-out counters the IE's response in l. 5–8, using his shift of footing to question the IE's trustworthiness, and treating the Consumer Council as the authority on the truth of the merger.

Sometimes participants are very explicit in verbalizing the lack of trustworthiness of others' versions. This is the case in the following example (5.12, see p. 79), whereby a prominent newspaper chief editor (S) is interviewed about his decision to publish an entire book as a section of the newspaper (with the author's alleged consent). The book was written by an EU commissioner, and then at the last minute before publication, publication was withdrawn due to external pressure not to reveal confidential information. The chief editor (S) argues that the decision was legal, legitimate and in the interests of the public. It was not a matter of stealing a manuscript from the publishing house for reasons of sensationalism and profit. Such an accusation is pure fantasizing, he claims. The interviewer (J) confronts that directly in his uptake:

When the journalist (J) says, "you SO::und like the persecuted'innoce[nce" (l. 16), he confronts the defense that the S makes (l. 8 and 11) and follows it up with "t]hat you cannot=expect [people t]o believe?", (l. 16–17), explicitly voicing his skepticism, which he extends to something general (people). His follow-up laugh (l. 22), when S insists on being innocent (l. 20–21), further escalates the confrontation. J is essentially coming very close to directly accusing S of lying. We see the entire exchange as a sequential negotiation of S's trustworthiness – whether he is speaking the truth or not, whether he was acting in good faith or not, whether he is a thief or not.

Miscrediting others' versions of the world, and therefore making them appear less than truthful – or not truthful at all – can serve both to test or to reduce the trustworthiness of some and to bolster that of others – including one's own – by comparison.

Detecting lies: misplacement markers and unfitted responses

Taking an interest in detecting lies is not a new endeavor in EM/CA. What makes untruths and lies recognizable as such is briefly attended to by Drew (2003), and in a more in-depth manner by Komter. The latter points to strategies such as pointing to, and identifying, the lack of a 'good' explanation, and contrasting someone's story with alternative versions which provide 'logical' explanations (2003). Still, as Komter also underlines, detecting lies is difficult, because

> a suspect can concoct a believable story by the same methods that people use to expose a lie, relying on commonsense knowledge

about 'normal' behavior and plausible stories (cf. Garfinkel, 1967, pp. 76–103; Sacks, 1995, Part 1, pp. 113–125). Thus, if a suspect is lying, there may be no way of knowing, for liars are engaged in presenting their stories as correct, and recipients of possible lies know that (cf. Sacks, 1995, Part 1, p. 255).

(Komter, 2003, p. 434)

Example 5.12 You sound like the persecuted innocence

```
1   J:  nå[::. .hh ve du hva'?, det der- det der IKK'] er fantasteri.
        we[::ll .hh you know wha'? that there- what is NOT'] fantasy
2   S:  [undskyld jeg sir det de:t' REN fantasteri.]
        [sorry to say it that there is PURE fantasy.]
3   J:  det er jo at [det ↑li::ge] er kommet frem
        that is (adv)that [it ju::st] came out
4       at der faktisk er en politisag i gang
        that there is in fact a police investigation going on
5       (.2) ø:::h mod dig=IKKE ma[n ˙hh]
        (.2) e:::h against you=RIGHT the[y .hh]
6   S:                                [*jo:w-m]
                                      [*ye:a-b]
7   J:  man vil nu gå ind i STRA::f↑FEloven, (.)
        they will apply CRI::mInal ↑Law, (.)
8   S:  ma[nipul-]
        Ma[nipul-]
9   J:  [vi taler o]m en KRrimi↓nel han↑ling, man vil gå
        ind i straf↑fe↓loven
        [we are talking a]bout a ↓CRiminal a↑ct, they will
        apply crim↑inal ↓law
10      .hhh og forfølge dighh.
        .hhh and persecute youhh.
11  S:  manipulatio::nerne fortsætter. .hhh=
        the manipulatio::ns continues. .hhh=
12  J:  =.h*nå::h?,=
        =.h*so::?,=
13  S:  =la' os li::ge holde fa[st i,
        =let's just hold on t[o that,
14  J:                         [du'n forfulgt'uskyldighed er [du,
                  [you are a persecuted'innocence that's what
        [you are
15  S:                                                      [hva sir du?,
        [sorry?,
16  J:  du f- du LY::der som om den forfulgt'uskyldig[hed,
        d]et ka du da ikke=
        you p- you SO::und like the persecuted'innoce[nce   t]hat
        you cannot=
17  S:                                [jamn::,]
                                      [bu::t,]
18  J:  =forvente [at man s]ka' tro?,
        =expect   [people t]o believe?,
```

19 S: [jam-]
[but-]
20 S: jamn hør nu her, »JEG VED IKK' HVAD DET ER VE MIG SOM GØR AT DU IKK TROR DET?»
but listen now, I DONT KNOW WHAT IT IS ABOUT ME THAT MAKE YOU NOT BELIEVE IT?
21 S: alså det jeg ↓ER [DA faktisk] en °uhu-uskyl- ø::h en uskyldighed°
Well it i AM [adv. actually] an °imo-inno- e::h an innocence°
22 J: [hehe˙hhh]
[hehe.hhh]
23 i ↓denne her ↓sammenhæng, [.hhh V]I HAR=GJORT ↓DANskerne en ↓tje:neste?,
in ↓this ↓case [.hhh w]e have done a ↓service to the Danish ↓people

Even so, orienting to whether someone is telling the truth is observable in interaction. In the following example, we can see a clear example of an attempt at 'lie-detecting'. The exchange is from a police interrogation in which a young man (YM), already well known by the police, is interviewed about the theft of frozen groceries from a nursery school. At one point, the young man is asked where in the institution the freezer was, and he replies:

Example 5.13 Police interrogation

1 (.)
2 YM: den stod u:dei ø:h KØ:Knet.
it stod ou:tin e:h the KI:Tchen.
3 P1: ja (.) så er det DIG
yes (.) then it is YOU
4 der har været der
that have been there
5 YM: ja
yeah
6 (2.0)
7 P1: var du a↑lene
were you a↑lone
8 (1.0)
9 YM: næ:=jeg har været alene dernede=
na:=I have been alone down there=
10 =jeg kan ik huske der har været
=I can't remember there have been
11 nogle med dernede=
anyone with me down there=
12 P1: =DET' LØGN
=THAT'S A LIE
13 (1.0)
14 der står heri at du er sammen med to
it says here that you are together with two

15 andre.
others.
16 (2.5)
17 vil du SELV ↑læse det
will you yourSELF ↑read it
do you want to read it your↑SELF
18 (2.0)
19 YM: ja jeg veda godt læ:s det¿
yeah I canPT PT re:ad it¿
yeah okay I can read it alright
20 P1: .ha
21 (3.0)
22 hvem er de to ↑andre
who are the two ↑others
23 (1.0)
24 YM: det kan jeg ikke huske
that can I not remember
I can't remember that
25 ja:r mener jeg var alene.
I: believe I was alone.
26 (.)
27 P1: du lyver¿
you lie¿
28 (.)
29 YM: °jeg lyver¿°
°I lie¿ °
30 (.)
31 P1: DET VED DU GODT
THAT KNOW YOU WELL
YOU KNOW THAT VERY WELL
32 (1.0)

In l. 1–6, the police officer established that since the young man knows where the freezer was, he had evidently been there. Not a strong case, one should say, since a freezer located in a kitchen is not unusual for a daycare institution. But the young man acknowledges it (l. 5–6). The project for the police officer from l. 7 and onwards is to get the young man to confess that he was not alone when breaking and entering the kindergarten. The interview goes on like this after l. 32 until the young man explains why he cannot present the names of his friends as accomplices. So, the police officer eventually gets the confession that he is after from the young man.

Until that point, what makes the police officer so sure (l. 12) that the young man is lying? We do not know if it might be partly due to prior experience or structural reasons, but what we can see in the data is that some of the young man's utterances are not perfectly fitted responses. When the police officer asks in l. 7, "Were you alone?", a strong response from the young man would have been, "Yes, I was" or "Yes of course", or something prompt and categorial like that – a confirmation with high affinity. Instead, there is a delay of one second (l. 8) and then a weak "No", the prolonged "Na:", quickly followed by the statement, "I have been alone down there". This is followed by the latched-on (cf. Sacks *et al.*, 1974, p. 731; Jefferson, 1973) "I can't remember there have been any with me down there". Substituting "I have been alone" with "I can't remember there have been anyone with me down there" serves as a downgrading not only of his statement, but also of his epistemic authority. The young man produces a somewhat complicated answer to fit the question "Were you together with someone?" instead of a simple and clear confirmation of being alone (to protect his friends). He also produces a weak rejection (of the implied accusation), hesitates, redesigns his turn project and produces a statement that he then immediately voluntarily abandons in favor of a weaker statement. It all adds up to a dispreferred response (cf. Pomerantz, 1984a). This is one which the police officer, as a competent member of society, recognizes as being off, most likely a lie (l. 12) – which indeed it turns out to be.

We see the entire exchange as a sequential negotiation of trustworthiness. The codable actions here are the combination of an unfitted response, a dispreferred response, redesign and a volunteered downgrading statement displaying less epistemic authority than was first assumed. It is a compound, a cluster of indicators, which together gives the impression of lying. We see YM's l. 10–11 and l. 25 as character-bound displays designed to negotiate the affinity of his utterances.

We do not have a list of indicators of lying, and perhaps such a list is not only difficult (or even impossible) to make, but also not necessary. We will conclude this section by quoting from a study of deception and detecting lies:

> All deception studies published to date have been laboratory studies. In such studies people lied only for the sake of the experiment, consequently the stakes were usually low. Although research has shown that most spontaneous lies told in real life are trivial, such studies tell us little about lies where the stakes are high (such as police/suspect interviews). In Study 1, we discuss the behaviour of an actual suspect while he was interviewed by the police in a murder case. Although the man initially denied knowing and killing the victim, substantial evidence obtained by the police showed that he was lying. On the basis of this evidence, the man confessed to killing the victim and was later convicted for murder. To our knowledge there has been no other study published that has analysed the behaviour of a liar in such a high-stake realistic setting. The analysis revealed several cues to deception. In Study 2, we exposed 65 police officers to six fragments (three truthful and three deceptive) of the interview with the murderer and asked them to indicate after each fragment whether the man was lying or not. *The findings revealed that the participants were better at detecting truths (70% accuracy) than lies (57% accuracy).* We also found

> *individual differences among observers, with those holding popular stereotypical views on deceptive behaviour, such as "liars look away" and "liars fidget" performing least effectively as lie catchers.*
> (Vrij & Mann, 2001, p. 187; our italics)

We are convinced that much more research will be done on detecting lies and deception. Our research endeavor is not that, but rather to explore participants' interactional negotiations of local trustworthiness, including the component of orientation to truth and honesty, irrespective of whether what is being negotiated is really the truth or a lie.

Summing up the orientation to truth and honesty

The orientation to truth and honesty is an overarching one. It can be – and often is – found to be a facilitator or foundation for the other orientations presented in Chapters 6–8. Truth and honesty are fundamental for these orientations and what makes them relevant as displays of trustworthiness. In this chapter, we have reviewed studies of different aspects of interactants' orientations to truth and honesty. We have argued their relevance for exploring participants' orientation to trustworthiness. To summarize, we see the following codable actions, moves and interactional strategies as potentially – but not exclusively – displaying interactants' orientations to truth and honesty.

- Orienting to the quality and truthfulness of facts and information by means of codable actions and moves, such as formulaic constructions like "as far as I know", and by asking questions about the quality or truthfulness of specific facts or information.
- Orienting to openness and transparency regarding information and processes via codable actions or strategies; for example, explaining and arguing (Antaki, 1994; Huisman, 2001), online commentary (Heritage & Stivers, 1999), making references to procedure (Nielsen *et al.*, 2012) or providing details, thus bolstering trustworthiness.
- Orienting to lack of transparency and openness via codable actions such as asking questions about processes, events and facts.
- Orienting to honesty and openness via codable actions such as volunteering seemingly unnecessary facts, information or detail, regardless of whether or not these flatter and benefit oneself.
- Orienting to detail and precision by pursuing answers or responses when they are lacking or not sufficient, and by asking for clarification; or conversely by detailing facts and correcting oneself to assure precision, via codable actions or strategies such as self-initiated self-correction (Jefferson, 1974), explaining and elaborating; or via other-initiated other-correction (Schegloff *et al.*, 1977), asking follow-up questions aimed at explaining detail and achieving precision.

- Orienting to honesty by pursuing relevant precision (Drew, 2003) via codable actions and moves such as giving locally relevant and recipient-designed information, or by pursuing relevant and adequate information important to the task at hand.
- Orienting to honesty, or lack thereof, by miscrediting others' versions by, for example, stating conflicting facts, citing experts saying otherwise, and drawing on 'common sense' and on what is generally accepted as true.
- Orienting to honesty by doing 'lie-detecting', paying attention to codable actions such as unfitted or dispreferred responses, redesign, self-repair and a downgraded statement displaying low epistemic authority.

The codable actions, moves and strategies which we have identified as possibly displaying interactants' orientations to truth and honesty do not necessarily accomplish trustworthiness or the opposite *per se*. This is because they are context-sensitive, and may be used interactionally to accomplish other social goals, as well, but we see them as possible indicators of a local orientation to trustworthiness when the local sequential environment makes it relevant to do so, especially when they appear in clusters of indicators.

6 Orientation to stake and interest

Motives matter when we are considering the trustworthiness of others. The old saying "if it sounds too good to be true, it probably is" is often used to discern who really benefits from a grand offer. An honest fool "with a heart of gold" might not be trusted with a fortune, but can be trusted not to secretly feather their own nest by deliberately hiding information. The same cannot be said about a lawyer who purposely chooses to disclose only a selected portion of facts, or who undermines the credibility of their opponent by questioning the opponent's motives with the purpose of placing their own client in a more favorable light. The lawyer has an interest in doing so, because they have something at stake. Whenever someone has something at stake, the issue of trustworthiness is imminent.

Therefore, the second participant orientation we propose is to stake and interest. Interactionally, this requires transparency[1] about one's own agendas, motives and dispositions, or lack thereof. This orientation may deal with balance between different concerns. It may be manifested as

1 This overlaps with suborientations of the orientation to truth and honesty, which was the focus in the prior chapter. Here, however, the focus is not on truth and honesty *per se*, but rather on the fact that efforts to create openness and transparency are in this case facilitating an orientation to disclosing one's stake and interest in the subject at hand.

DOI: 10.4324/9781003280903-6

interactional strategies and moves to secure fairness and neutrality, and to disclose any bias – or even better, to demonstrate that there is none. It may also deal with interactants' local negotiation of their respective 'benefactive status' and their verbalized attempts to live up to the expectations of others. Something at stake being managed may be observable when participants are dealing with transgressions and misconducts, e.g. by complaining or arguing. Additionally, it may be manifested as concern for others, and what is at stake for them, e.g. by not threatening their face (cf. Goffman, 1955) or integrity. We explore these facets of the orientation to stake and interest in this chapter.

The key to the orientation highlighted in this chapter is what is *at stake*[2] for someone with respect to something. The notions of 'stake', 'management of stake', 'stake-inoculations', etc., have been introduced to EM/CA studies from discursive psychology (e.g. Edwards & Potter, 1992; Potter, 1996, 1998; Edwards, 2000, 2003, 2005, 2006a, 2006b, 2007; Antaki, 2003). Jonathan Potter is – as far as we know – the only EM/CA scholar to date who has used the term "orientation to stake" (2004, p. 215), and Derek Edwards and Jonathan Potter have defined participants' "stake and interest" (Edwards & Potter, 1992, p. 117) as "a particular kind of dispositional consideration relevant to factual claims" (Edwards, 2007, p. 46). Stake relates to motives and subjectivities of various kinds (prejudice, ulterior motives and agenda) and it is integral to action formation[3] in preempting accusations of lack of objectivity, credibility and reliability (cf. Edwards, 2007, p. 46).

From an EM/CA perspective, the orientation to stake and interest has in effect been studied in several lines of research. These have targeted suborientations or subcategories which may be considered orientation to stake and interest, depending on the local sequential context. In what follows, we will review some of these subcategories to demonstrate what orientation to stake and interest relates to interactionally, and present examples of where and how manifestations of subcategories of orientation to stake and interest may be observable as codable moves, actions and interactional strategies that serve to negotiate trustworthiness.

2 Stake management should not be mistaken for stakeholder management (Freeman & Reed, 1983; Preston & Sapienza, 1990) – a strong and vibrant subdiscipline in economics, project management, strategic communication, issues management and public relations. Here, a stakeholder is defined as "any group or individual who can affect or is affected by the achievement of the organization's objectives" (Freeman, 1984, p. 46). The core meaning of the term 'stake' is therefore the same, but the theoretical and methodological approach is very different from these disciplines.

3 Action formation is defined as the way "the resources of the language, the body, the environment of the interaction, and position in the interaction [is] fashioned into conformations designed to be, and to be recognized by recipients as, particular action[s]" (Schegloff, 2007b, p. xiv).

Is something always at stake?

When we were working to identify a baseline example for this chapter, we made many detours which did not prove fruitful in the end. This was because it always seemed that there might be something, potentially, at stake for at least one of the participants – if nothing else, then maintaining mutual relation. The following is an extract from an international phone meeting between several locations. However, we do not see any orientation to stake or interest here, as the meeting chair (l. 1) located in Chennai asks another participant Peter where he is located.

Example 6.1 I am in Copenhagen approximately three feet from Anders

```
Ra   [Peter, (.)] which part of the world are you in.
     (0.5)
Pe   well, I: am in Copenhagen
     approximately: (.) three feet from An↑ders
     (1.8)
Ly   ((smiles))
M?   arHH,
Ra?  eh he he,
Ra   well then a good morning
Ra   ↑to [you]
M?       [hah]
Pe   ha ↑thank you
Ly   ((smiles))
```

This participant (Pe) responds by telling that he is in Copenhagen (l. 3), in the same meeting room as one of the other participants (l. 4). The phone meeting is filmed from the Mumbai office, where Lynn (Ly) is located. This is why we see her smile as a response to l. 4 and 12. Not much is going on in these turns of talk here, and what is disclosed (that Anders is three feet away) could probably have been hidden or unmentioned (l. 3–4) without causing any trouble. In fact, it is disclosed as a joke (l. 4) and received as such (l. 6–8). There does not yet seem to be any agenda, project or interest for the participants to orient to. There is nothing that shows us, as analysts, that the participants do not, *in situ*, consider each other trustworthy. They might have severe issues. We do not know that. But there is nothing to give an impression of any lack of trust or trustworthiness, as it cannot be seen oriented to by any of the participants.

Stance, neutrality and subjectivity

As we have seen in Chapter 2, subjectivity is not to be seen as 'outside' a given interaction, but as intersubjectivity within social interactions. Also, as we discussed in Chapter 2 and Chapter 4, speakers *orient* to whatever has sequentially gone before in the interaction, and to what might come after. This mutual understanding – or intersubjectivity – is created through the production of actions and next actions, demonstrating what Heritage terms "the sequential architecture of intersubjectivity" (Heritage, 2005, p. 105). The participants' stance with regard to whatever their co-participants or they themselves are saying, or with regard to their relative rights in a certain domain, are moment-by-moment linguistic expressions. They are made observable in this sequential architecture. Or, as Edwards puts it:

> Through [their] manner of vocal delivery, speakers display subjectivity or stance with regard to what they are saying.
>
> (Edwards, 2007, p. 39)

It is therefore in the expression and negotiation of stance and subjectivity that the participants' orientation to stake – both their own and others – can be identified, and that their neutrality – or their lack of it – can be seen to be displayed.

In social encounters, participants locally negotiate their speaker neutrality (Clayman, 1988). An example of a codable action serving this purpose is the use of 'footing shift', whereby interactants may bring others' concerns or voices to light, while avoiding any affiliation with the viewpoint that they report (Clayman, 1992, p. 173). This can be seen in "person A accuses you of B; what is your response to that?" Another example is the use of extreme-case formulations (cf. Pomerantz, 1986) to manage "various kinds of 'investment' on the part of the speaker (e.g. commitment, certainty, caring, determination, a critical or positive attitude, etc.)" (Edwards, 2000, p. 347), while still maintaining neutrality (such as in "let us proceed as if [extreme Y]").

When speakers negotiate subjectivity through displays of neutrality, or the opposite, the use and design of (respectively) object-side or subject-side accounts, descriptions, explanations and assessments are examples of codable actions. As pointed out by Edwards, "subjective or 'subject side' accounts are ones that reflect a speaker's 'stake and interest' in a topic" (Edwards, 2007, p. 31; see also Edwards & Potter, 1992). These subject-side actions display the interactants' personal preferences, dislikes, opinions, etc. As such, they are codable actions. When "working up the subjective status of an account, generally somebody else's account, its objectivity is undermined" (p. 31). This is evident from the following example, taken from Edwards and Potter's early discussions of stake and interest (1992, p. 117). The following is an excerpt from when 'call girl' Mandy Rice-Davies was asked by Counsel James Burge about her knowledge of a prominent party in the case of Lord Astor's denial of having sexual relations with her.

Example 6.2 Well he would, wouldn't he? (from Edwards & Potter, 1992, p. 117)

```
Counsel:       Are you aware that Lord Astor denies any
               impropriety in his relationship with you?
                 (0.8)
Rice-Davies:   Well he would wouldn't he
Jury, etc.:    ((prolonged laughter))
```

Rice-Davies does not treat Astor's denial as being objective, but rather as a reflection of his stake and interest: Her answer in the form of a well-prefaced, negated interrogative comes to function as a rhetorical question appealing to the common sense of the jury and others present. Her repeated use of the modal verb "would" clearly serves to miscredit Astor's intentions. This way she works up the subject-side of his account, thereby pointing out that he would have obvious motives to lie. Without openly accusing him of lying, or herself proving otherwise, she effectively miscredits him – and thereby questions his trustworthiness (cf. Edwards, 2007). When working up the subjective status of one's own account, and depending on what is foregrounded, this 'undermining of subjectivity' can work as a display of honesty,[4] thus overlapping with that particular orientation – especially if the subject-side action reveals something not in one's own favor.

Another example of orientation to trustworthiness, or the lack of it, by use of subject-side assessment is found in the following example. This example is from a meeting between four representatives from two international collaborating companies. In the data, the participants call one company "outcome owners" and the other "process owners", since the latter company serves as vendor to the former. The example is from one process owner employee's response to an unpleasant and surprising revelation made by one of the outcome owners regarding "the second part" of a project.

Example 6.3 We are taken by surprise that that is even part of the agenda

```
284 EMP2 ↑the ↑discussion out on the second part→
285      that either (.)
286      willingly not acknowledging it→
287      o:r a:re honestly taken by surprise→
288      that that's even part of the agenda↘
```

4 Revealing *any* unpopular, unpleasant, incriminating or otherwise negative fact about an aspect of oneself may serve to display honesty, but it may also imitate honesty in order to accomplish other social goals. Regardless of motive, the orientation to honesty is observable in the data as codable actions. See also Chapter 5 on orientation to truth and honesty.

Here we see how an unpopular, face-threatening subject-side assessment is produced by the process owners (here represented by EMP2). From the exchange, we clearly see that what is "even part of the agenda" (some aspects of "the second part") is treated as a crucial concern, as one participant openly attempts to assess the other's motives. Here this is done by counterposing the options 'deliberate malicious action' ("willingly not acknowledging") and 'being honestly not aware of' ("honestly taken by surprise"). The wording of the latter frames the former option as an accusation of dishonesty on the part of the outcome owners. These two opposites are presented as candidate rationales which add up to the process owner's subject-side assessment of the trustworthiness – or not – of the outcome owners. It can be seen as an attempt at eliciting either a confirmation (of the latter option) or an exonerative account (in case of the former being acknowledged) (cf. Antaki, 1994). Either way, EMP2's turn can be seen as part of a (long, not shown) SNOC, and the lack of a character-bound display in response as noticeably absent (Schegloff, 1968).

Contrary to subject-side utterances, object-side accounts, descriptions, explanations or assessments aim at "producing versions of things and events" which serve to "build the factual status or objectivity of what they are saying" (Edwards, 2007, p. 31; Edwards & Potter, 2017). Neutrality can be claimed by using object-side assessments, accounts, etc. These are "produced as reflections of the things they are about" (Edwards, 2007, p. 31), and can be coded as indicators of orientation to speaker neutrality, and therefore to stake and interest.

Displaying, denying and negotiating bias

A strong suborientation to stake and interest is bias. One interactional strategy which aids the participants' appearing to be un-biased is doing "stake inoculation" (Potter, 1996). This is "a counter-dispositional practice in which the producer of a possibly dubious factual claim prefaces this with a self-characterization as pre-disposed to see things differently" (Edwards, 2007, p. 46). Edwards elaborates on stake inoculation:

> As we have noted, factual claims can be grounded by offering them as *counter-dispositional*: as reluctantly arrived at, or even precisely counter, not only to what others may think, but also to one's own presumptions and biases (Edwards, 2003: cf. Potter, 1996, on 'stake inoculation'). [This] is a way of denying that you believe what it suits you to believe, or what you believed before you looked – that is, of attending to a possible accusation of pre-judgment or prejudice.
>
> (Edwards, 2007, p. 36, emphasis in original)

As such, stake inoculation bears a resemblance to inoculation theory in the frameworks of communication studies and social psychology

(McGuire, 1961a, 1961b, 1964). It formulates resistance to persuasive influence as a messaging strategy, so that recipient attitudes can be inoculated against persuasive attacks in much the same way as a person's immune system can be inoculated against viral attacks (McGuire, 1964; Compton *et al.*, 2016). Examples of codable actions may be the provision of specific content in order to achieve "refutational preemption" (Pfau *et al.*, 1997, p. 188); that is, by raising and refuting potential counter-arguments to the position argued for.[5]

The following example of stake inoculation is from a video consultation between a general practitioner (GP) who is participating remotely from his consultation via video, a geriatric patient (PAT) at a live-in rehabilitation facility and her daughter (DAU). A health care worker (HCW) is also present, but only the GP and daughter are talking in this example. In the excerpt, the patient's daughter produces a subject-side explanation, which functions as a stake inoculation, to preempt a subsequent unfavorable assessment of her mother's health.

Example 6.4 I hate not being a sunshine story

```
1 DOC: sandy hvordan synes du weekenden er gået
       sandy how     think you weekend is gone
       sandy how do you think the weekend has gone
2      (1)
3 DAU: .hhh jamen eh:m (1.4) uh jeg hader og ikke og være
       .hhh but   eh:m (1.4) uh i   hate  and not and be
       .hhh now eh:m (1.4) uh I hate not being
4      en solstrålehistorie .hhh jamen [du  har  jo  haft lidt e:h
       a  sun shine story   .hhh but   [you have adv. had litte e:h
       a sunshine story .hhh but       [you have had a little e:h
                                       [((looks at mother, takes her hand))
5      du har haft lidt kvalme (.7) eh::m (.) eh stadigvæk
       you have had little nausea (.7) eh::m (.) eh still
```

The daughter responds to the GP's initial question about how the weekend has been with one second of silence (l. 2), which projects a dispreferred response (cf. Pomerantz, 1984a). After an inbreath, she starts with a preliminary ("now", l. 3) then pauses for another 1.4 seconds. Only then does she produce an answer, beginning with a subject-side assessment ("I hate", l. 3), followed by a description of what she hates not being, that is, "a sunshine story". This subject-side assessment serves to inoculate against her being someone overly disposed toward bringing bad news, or to exaggerating her mother's condition during the

5 Compton *et al.* (2016, p. 123) point out that: "As originally argued by McGuire (1964) and confirmed by a meta-analysis of inoculation theory studies (Banas and Rains, 2010), both refutational different (i.e., where the treatment refutes challenges that do not specifically appear in a future attack) and refutational same (i.e., where the treatment refutes specific challenges that are raised) treatments confer protection, supporting the premise that inoculation messages provide 'umbrella protection' against subsequent attacks".

weekend. In this sequential context, this utterance comes to function as a character-bound display of being someone not prone to exaggeration or complaint, but rather wishing to be a harbinger of good news. In this way she orients to her own (lack of) motives for producing a negative assessment of her mother's condition, and thereby also her lack of bias, regardless of the fact that she is the daughter of the patient. She then describes her mother's condition over the weekend with an object-side description ("you have had little nausea", l. 5) while looking at her mother and taking her hand. By choosing her mother, who the description is about, as the addressed recipient (cf. Goodwin, 1979; Goffman, 1981) of her utterance, the daughter gives her mother the opportunity to validate the description in front of the GP. The GP is thereby temporarily framed as a ratified but currently unaddressed recipient. By doing this, she displays an orientation to having the truthfulness of her own description (which is B-side knowledge) confirmed by the one with unlimited (i.e., A-side) knowledge of – and therefore epistemic authority over – the subject matter, namely the one whom the description concerns. The daughter's actions – subject-side assessment, self-description (not "a sunshine story"), an object-side description that is recipient-designed to be verified by the participant with the most knowledge on the subject – collaboratively constitute a cluster of codable features (and therefore also a CBD). These work together to indicate an orientation to being un-biased, honest and truthful. Together this adds up to a strong orientation to trustworthiness.

Negotiating benefactive status

Doing something for the reason of benefiting others and not serving self-interest is a key suborientation to stake and interest. Negotiations concerning who is the benefactor of an action may therefore be seen as part of an orientation to trustworthiness. Participants have been shown to locally negotiate the "benefactive status" of an action (Clayman & Heritage, 2014: 55; cf. Couper-Kuhlen, 2013), e.g. through proposals, offers and suggestions.

The best case examples of ongoing negotiations concerning an action's benefactive status are perhaps to be found in sales encounters. Good salesmanship classically involves selling products that benefit the customer or client. The sales arguments will therefore seek to promote those beneficial effects – but in the course of selling the product, the sellers also benefit their own economic situation, and of course that of the employing company (which is the reason for selling in the first place). Schenkein (1978) has shown how the benefactive stance of an insurance salesman is made relevant by the prospective client, due to the benefactive status being linked to his local identity as an 'insurance salesman' who has something at stake. The beginning of the sales encounter (involving the door-to-door insurance salesman) is a long stretch of (identity-related) talk about matters not insurance-related, until the householder says the following.

Example 6.5 I gather you also want to try to sell me some insurance (from Schenkein, 1978, p. 60)

PETE: I gather you also wanna try t'sell me
some insurance.
(2.0)
ALAN: Now– that doesn't sound like a bad
idea–no, ih– it *would* be nice. But
what I'd *like* to do,
(3.0)
ALAN: Uhh, do you *have* any insurance.

The prospective client forces the salesperson to get to 'the reason for the call' by verbalizing what he might relevantly have at stake. This is done by pointing to the fact that selling insurance is the reason for the call. In the leadup to this excerpt, Schenkein shows that the salesperson has done a lot of interactional work to construct his identity as more faceted than just a typical door-to-door salesperson, but that attempt is questioned as an untrustworthy attempt to hide his real agenda: selling insurance.

Negotiations of role compliance and living up to expectations

Orientation to stake and interest is sometimes made explicit in an interaction as something that may stretch beyond the local encounter. One example is a study of a project team whose members were asked by their CEO to design an organizational process for rebranding the organization. While meeting to plan a strategy seminar, they discussed whether or not to use yellow Post-it Notes in the seminar. What follows is this account, produced by one of the project group members.

Example 6.6 And I do know that they will laugh (from Nielsen, 2014, p. 118)

```
1 Kl:   og jeg ved godt de vil ↑grine,
        and I know well they will laugh
        and I do know that they will ↑laugh,
 2      når vi kommer med de der gule ↓lapper,
        when we come with those yellow patches
        when we appear with those yellow ↓postits there,
 3      (.)
```

```
 4        fordi
          because
 5 An:    mh he ↑HH, .HH
 6        >>ja, [jeg ka godt ↑si: dig jeg(strikker)]<<=
          year, I can well tell you I (knit)
          >>yeah, [I'll ↑tell you I (knit)]<<=
 7 Kl:    [det har vi lissom prøvet en gang]
          that have we sort of tried one time
          [that we sort of have tried once]=
 8 An:    ="nå::m så det' no'd med no'n gu:l la:pper"
          well so it's something with some yellow patches
          ="ri::ght then it's all about ye:lla po:stits"
 9        >og så'n no'd<
          and such something
          >and stuff like that<
10        >>si'r {Martin}<<
          >>says {Martin}<<
11        "↑NEJ, det ska' vær' ↑mere ↓kreativt"(H)
          NO, it must be more creative
          "↑NO, it must be ↑more cre↓ative"(H)
12        ((said with guttural Donald Duck voice))
```

The project group strives to identify key stakeholders in the designated design project, to share their own expectations of these key stakeholders' possible perceptions, to discuss the potential success criteria involved and to negotiate the values which are to govern the design team in the development process (Nielsen, 2014). When voicing reported and imaginary responses from others (e.g. "NO, it must be more creative" in l. 11–12 or "and I do know that they will laugh" in l. 1), interactants show an orientation to their own reputation being at stake as an outcome of this team meeting. Both the very local and the more global orientation to stake and interest shows a member's concern with both sociality and compliance with others' role expectations and with being trusted to deliver what is beneficial for the recipient, their colleagues and their superiors. What is at stake for them here is what portrays them as competent employees and strategy seminar planners. This orientation overlaps with an orientation to predictability (see Chapter 8). Every utterance regarding a future reaction from the CEO and their colleagues is orienting to the predictability and consistency of their behavior. In l. 1 Klara says that she "do[es] know that they will laugh" when the team at the seminar introduces the idea of using Post-it Notes, thus claiming high epistemic authority with regard to what will happen.

Conflicts, misconducts, blamings and complaints

When something is at stake, conflicts may occur. Separate lines of research focus on co-participants' interactional negotiations of transgressions and misconduct (Drew, 1998; Vöge, 2010), blamings and accusations (Drew, 1978; Pomerantz, 1978; Clift & Pino, 2020), complaints (Pomerantz, 1986; Holt & Drew, 1988; Drew, 1998; Edwards, 2005, 2007; Schegloff, 2005) and apologies (Heritage *et al.*, 2019). These studies touch on what the interactants may have at stake when doing these actions, such as how they build their own credibility, and thus also orient to their own trustworthiness, while complaining by "attending to [the complaint's] possible subjectivity" and managing its production "to best effect" (Edwards, 2007, p. 37). Codable strategies and moves in this suborientation include – but are far from limited to – participants' attending to their motives or grounds for doing the complaining as an integral part of the production of the complaint (Drew, 1998). Also, producing a complaint as having arisen from a legitimate complainable by using extreme-case formulations (Pomerantz, 1986); or self-categorizing as a member of the particular group one is complaining about, thereby orienting to and managing the implications of the complaint (Whitehead, 2013; cf. Rawls & David, 2005) are codable strategies.

An example of the latter can be found in a study by Whitehead (2013). In his example, a White caller to a radio show uses what Whitehead calls "self-deprecating self-categorization" (p. 316), before going on to complain about how differently the public responds to a White columnist's controversial statements, which were widely condemned as racist, and what the caller claims to be similar statements made by a prominent Black businessman.

Example 6.7 I'm sure from my accent the guys are gonna say (from Whitehead, 2013, p. 191)

Excerpt 1:

[102 - SAfm, 4-18-08]

```
1    C:   Uh: uh:: I- I just wanna put a bit o:f tongue in cheek
2         here be[cause I'm sure from my accent the guys are
3    H:          [Sure.
4    C:   gonna: gonna say "ja there's is the white (.) racist
5         bastard" you [know?
6    H:                [No, please [no.
7    C:                            [U::h bu- but (.) you know
8         especially coming from uh: Pofadder there by
9         (Karn[afel.)
10   H:        [Uhuh huh huh huh [huh huh
```

In this example, the caller simultaneously orients to his complaint not being perceived as biased by initially inoculating himself "against the possibility that recipients may take offense [at] his actions specifically on the basis of his racial category membership" (p. 316). This example shows how multiple codable actions and moves can work together when participants orient to stake and interest in order to display and/or negotiate their own trustworthiness in a sequential negotiation of character.

Another aspect of stake management in relation to complaints is working to undermine the factual grounds for others' complaints, for instance (Edwards, 2005, p. 9). One example of this is eloquently formulated by Derek Edwards, as follows.

> When speakers formulate the kinds of speech acts done in complaining, the word complain is not the only option. An ad hoc selection of related alternatives might include blame, accuse, criticize, slander, slag off, castigate, denigrate, censure and condemn. We have noted that some of these alternatives, such as accuse and criticize, while applicable to lots of actions that could also be called complaints, do not require the sense of transgression and grievance that complain possesses. But there is a further indefinitely extendable set of alternatives that not only include a sense of grievance, but also add an element of subjectivity and investment on the part of the complainer. These include moan, grumble, go on and on, gripe, carp, grouse, nag, bellyache and whinge.
> (Edwards, 2005, pp. 19–20)

Action ascription and description is therefore seen to be powerful in underlining or undermining the trustworthiness of the self or others, and the examples of codable actions that serve such purposes are bountiful.

Politeness and saving others' face

The study of 'facework' is a key suborientation to stake and interest. The face, understood as "the positive social value [of] a person" (Goffman, 1955, p. 213), of all participants is potentially at stake in any interaction. One line of research particularly relevant for the construction of trustworthiness therefore focuses upon the interactional work done specifically to 'save face' for oneself and other *in situ* (Goffman, 1955; Lerner, 1996; Pomerantz, 1984a). There are solid traditions within both pragmatics and symbolic interactionism for studying an interactant's concern or consideration for others in the interaction, and displaying such concern by attending to politeness and saving the interactants face (e.g. Brown & Levinson, 1978, 1987; Fraser, 1990; Goffman, 1955, 1967; Grice, 1975; Gumperz, 1982; Kasper, 1990; Leech, 1983; Ng & Bradac, 1993, to mention a few).

In this book, the interactors' concerns with face and politeness are considered relevant as a codable action when it has local implications for their orientation to trustworthiness. This is very often the case. Losing face is essentially about being revealed, put on the spot or otherwise called out with regard to one's properties such as motive, morale, consistency, composure, honesty, or abilities and knowledge. Since being considered trustworthy essentially depends upon these exact properties or abilities, facework often facilitates participants' orientation to any of them. Saving face is therefore a key element of being trustworthy, and interactants therefore have immense interest in attending to facework – both their own, and that of others. Conversely, making a person lose face can undermine the trustworthiness of that person in relation to that with which the loss of face is concerned. It is therefore unsurprising that research shows just how much interactional work goes into saving face.

It is worth noting that whether a given social negotiation of face can be seen as indicative of trustworthiness or not is dependent on the context. Foregrounding or orienting to the management of face can be seen as an orientation to some *aspect* of trustworthiness, particularly some aspect which is at stake locally – be it ability, truth, honesty or any other component of trustworthiness. In these cases, the actions that participants carry out as part of their ongoing facework can be seen and heard as one of several indicators of trustworthiness. This is the case in the following Example, with a native-speaking Danish policeman interviewing an applicant for citizenship.

Example 6.8 It might be a little silly in your case (from Fogtmann, 2007, p. 93)

```
1    Pol:  så stiller jeg dig lige et spørgsmål her det kan godt
           now I am going to ask you a question here it might be
2.         det er (.) det er lidt fjollet (.) øh i din forbindelse
           (.) it a little silly (.) ah in your case
3.         men har du nogen problemer med det danske sprog
           but do you experience any difficulties with the Danish language
4    Apl:  nej
           no
5    Pol:  nej (.) godt
           no (.) good
6    Apl:  det føler jeg i hvert fald ikke
           i do not think so anyway
7    Pol:  nej
           no
```

Here we see that the native-speaking Danish policeman is thematizing the irrelevance of questioning the applicant's language competence (probably because the preceding part of the interview was conducted in fluent Danish). One face saving effort here has to do with the applicant's ability and knowledge of the Danish language, which is a requirement for achieving Danish citizenship, and the fact that effort is oriented to saving the applicant's face. Another effort has to do with saving face for the policeman by preventing him from appearing clumsy, rigid or unable to assess the applicant's language skills – which have evidently been excellent throughout the interview. Both these efforts ultimately concern the interactants' abilities, and the positive assessment of these abilities which they both have at stake. They therefore represent an orientation to trustworthiness.

One subtle aspect of facework is how speakers in other-initiated repair orient themselves to a preference for the trouble sources with the least implications for the face for everyone involved. 'Not being able to hear', which puts (e.g.) background noise or one's own physical ability 'to hear' at stake, is preferred over 'not being able to understand', which potentially puts either one's own cognitive ability 'to understand', or even others' ability 'to express oneself clearly, precisely or correctly' at stake.[6] Rarely is the trouble source 'not being able to accept the talk' preferred, as this has the greatest implications for others' potential loss of face (Schegloff *et al.*, 1977; Svennevig, 2008). An example of just how face-threatening this can be is found in the following example, where a native-speaking Norwegian social worker questions the reliability of a client's claim.

Example 6.9 You can't have done nothing (from Svennevig, 2008, p. 340)

(3) Institutional interaction: C=Client (non-native speaker), S=Social worker (native)
S: Kan du fortelle litt om hva du (.) har gjort etter at du kom til Norge?
Can you tell me a bit about what you have done after you came to Norway?
C: Ingenting.
Nothing.
S: **Ingenting?**
Nothing?
C: Ja ha ha ha [ha ha]
Yeah
S: [ha ha] ha
.h Du kan vel ikke ha gjort ingenting?
You can't have done nothing can you? (you can well not have done nothing)
C: m:hm:,
S: **Du må vel ha gjort noe?**
You must have done something?
C: ha ha ha
S: Hæ?
Huh?
C: .hhh
S: Har du gått på no norsk-kurs?
Have you attended any Norwegian courses?
C: eh ja
uh yes

6 It is clear from this example that the different orientations inevitably branch into each other, as we have previously stated. Even though 'ability' and 'competence' are only indirectly made relevant here, what is foregrounded is the stake and interest in not having someone else lose face by appearing to be 'incompetent' and 'unable'.

The native-speaking Norwegian social worker questions the reliability of the client's claim to have done "nothing" since arriving in Norway, and thus questions the trustworthiness of the client by proxy. We see how confrontational it appears when repair has to do with lack of acceptance, when the answer is treated as 'hard to believe' in both l. 10 and 13 (Svennevig, 2008, p. 340) and proposed as being (factually) wrong and perhaps also (morally) inappropriate. Here the social worker's utterances in lines 5, 10 and 13 can be seen as quite direct prompts for some type of character-bound display. When the client fails to produce these, they are noticeably absent. We will not go further into a discussion of an interactant's orientation to aspects of trustworthiness when thematizing trouble sources, but this is potentially a considerable separate research object.

Summing up the orientation to stake and interest

In this chapter, we have reviewed studies of different aspects of interactants' orientation to stake and interest and argued their relevance for local interactional negotiation of trustworthiness. We have identified several codable actions, moves and interactional strategies that may display interactants' orientation to stake and interest. As is always the case, these actions, moves and interactional strategies do not necessarily accomplish trustworthiness, or the opposite, since they may be used interactionally to accomplish other social goals, as well. But they do represent possible indicators of local orientation to trustworthiness, depending on their context. As such, it will be relevant to focus on them in the data when exploring possible patterns of behavior.

In summary, we can see the following codable actions, moves and interactional strategies as potentially – but not exclusively – displaying interactants' orientation to stake and interest:

- 'Footing shift', to bring in others' concerns or voices while avoiding affiliation with the viewpoint that they report, thus displaying neutrality (Clayman, 1992).
- Extreme-case formulations to manage speaker investment while still maintaining neutrality (Edwards, 2000).
- Object-side or subject-side accounts, assessments, descriptions and explanations (Edwards & Potter, 1992; Edwards, 2007).
- Descriptions, explanations and assessments aiming at producing particular versions of things and events (Edwards, 2007; Edwards & Potter, 2017).
- Stake-inoculations to manage bias (Potter, 1996; Edwards, 2007), such as 'one could expect me to think/do/mean X, but I actually think/do/mean Y'.
- Offering factual claims as *counter-dispositional* – as reluctantly arrived at (Edwards, 2007).

- Offering factual claims as *counter-dispositional* to precisely counter not only what others may think, but also one's own presumptions and biases (Edwards, 2003).
- Voicing reported and imaginary responses from others as concerns at stake (Nielsen, 2014).
- Negotiation of or open displays of benefactive status (Clayman & Heritage, 2014), such as naming both the principal and secondary beneficiary of an offer or a request, or by listing both the pros and cons involved in accepting an offer (cf. Schenkein, 1978).
- Displays of compliance with the expectations of others by, e.g. quoting such formulations (Nielsen, 2014).
- Displays of keenness to deliver what is beneficial for a recipient by, e.g. in future encounters, making reference to potential dissatisfied responses from examples of such recipients (Nielsen, 2014).
- Attending to participants' motives or grounds for doing complaining as an integral part of the complaint's production (Drew, 1998).
- Producing a self-deprecating reference by, e.g. self-categorizing as a member of the group one is complaining about (Whitehead, 2013).
- Working to, e.g. undermine the factual grounds for others' claims or complaints (Edwards, 2005) by, e.g. substituting formulations of facts with diminished versions – i.e. from "many" to "a couple"; or by reformulating one part of a claim ("no-one got more than a few yards past me") with a question emphasizing, expanding or upgrading what the first speaker has downplayed ("So some people went past you?") (Atkinson & Drew, 1979, p. 157).
- Working with extreme-case formulations to inflate or deflate a description of what is at stake (cf. Pomerantz, 1986; Edwards, 2000).
- Miscrediting others' work on what is at stake for them by describing their talk as slandering, censuring, castigating, condemning, moaning, grumbling, going on and on, griping, carping, denigrating, grousing, nagging, bellyaching or whingeing (cf. Edwards, 2005), and therefore underlining or undermining the legitimacy of their stake and interest.
- Local facework to save both one's own face and that of others with regard to proprieties such as motive, morale, consistency, honesty, abilities or knowledge – i.e. glossing over others' mistakes; producing affiliative uptake on, or normalizing the formulation of, others' displays of lack of knowledge; acknowledging or encouraging cautiously produced suggestions; prefacing potentially difficult question with hedges that downgrade the expectations of recipients' knowledge; or choosing vernacular wording in a professional setting in which other participants may not know the right jargon.

We suggest that these social actions, moves and interactional strategies be coded in data so that analysts are able to identify *clusters* of indicators which may together serve to show whether and how interactants foreground an orientation to stake and interest in their interaction.

There is a range of studies within EM/CA regarding different expressions of other-concern, something that could potentially be seen as an interactional strategy aiming at considering others' stake or interests. These include empathy (e.g. Heritage, 2011; Versteeg & te Molder, 2016; Ford, 2017; Hepburn & Potter, 2007; Pudlinski, 2005) and sympathy (Bloch & Leydon, 2019; Goodwin, 2017; Butler, 2014; Laurier, 2013; Ogden, 2020; Pudlinski, 2005). However, we do not wish to confuse the matter by making all sorts of other-concerns relevant to the discussion either of stake and interest or trustworthiness. Even though empathy or sympathy (for example) could be seen as an interactional strategy aimed at considering others' stake or interests, and thus by proxy what might be at stake for them, this is not *per se* an orientation to trustworthiness.[7]

7 In Chapter 2, we have indeed used empathy as an example of an etic abstract phenomenon which has been studied thoroughly in EM/CA via inferences from observable actions and moves. Our interest in empathy in this book is solely to give an example of an abstract social phenomenon and not use it as an indicator or dimension of trustworthiness.

7 Orientation to knowledge and ability

Nobody can promise you the moon. Depending upon your perspective, it is not anybody's to give, it can't be done, they don't know how to do it, or they are just crazy in love. And you don't trust an honest fool who has a heart of gold with your savings, regardless of them being truthful to the best of their ability. You also don't trust your retirement funds with an honest and altruistic brain surgeon, because their expertise and knowledge are in another domain. If person A promises to do X, but is not entitled to deliver on that promise, person A is not trustworthy. For instance, a project manager cannot promise a team member a promotion

DOI: 10.4324/9781003280903-7

if promotions are not within the mandate of this manager. And if person B uses the wrong terminology about topic Y, person B is not trustworthy regarding this topic, due to lack of knowledge.

The third participant orientation in our study is to knowledge and ability. In terms of trustworthiness, this orientation is about being perceived as knowledgeable, qualified and competent[1], able to do the things at hand, and possessing the authority and ability to see it through. In this chapter, we distinguish between participants' orientation to knowledge, their orientation to those abilities dependent upon it, and purely having a mandate or authority to do something. However, these are often closely interconnected and found in the same stretches of interaction, as we will also demonstrate. As in the preceding two chapters, this one will explore different manifestations of participants' orientations to the dimension of trustworthiness in focus. The purpose of our analyses is to test both the theoretical conceptualization and the analytical program, and empirically to conceptualize trustworthiness as an interactional research object. All orientations may be present in all stretches of talk-in-interaction, but in each case, we will focus on the foregrounded orientations. Participants' abilities, mandates, capacities, knowledge, competences and areas of expertise are intertwined and negotiated as just that. But on the matter of pedagogy, we will focus first on orientation to knowledge, and then on orientation to ability and mandate.

Why knowledge and competence build trustworthiness

Knowledge is studied in a CA context as epistemics (Heritage, 2012a, 2012b; Heritage & Raymond, 2005; Raymond, 2018). Knowledge – or epistemic authority (Heritage & Raymond, 2005; Heritage, 2012a) – is the basis of this orientation, in the sense that interactants use displays and negotiations of knowledge to construct local identities as competent, skilled and well informed. This participant orientation to knowledge can be manifested interactionally in moves, strategies and actions displaying or challenging epistemic stance, status and authority.

1 We are aware that the term 'competence' has been widely used and debated (e.g. McClelland, 1973; Hayes, 1979; Dreyfus & Dreyfus, 1980; Sparrow, 1997; Rankin, 2002; Salaman, 2004). Our agenda is not to contribute to that debate, but strictly to explore it as a dimension of trustworthiness. For that purpose, we define competence here as the ability to do something successfully or efficiently as a result of skill, knowledge, qualification, capacity, role or mandate. Essential to the orientation in focus in this chapter is the notion that how person A may be showing knowledge of X and/or is confidently able to take relevant action with respect to X, contributing to person B's perception of A's trustworthiness with respect to X. In this chapter, we will explore trustworthiness related to capacity, role or mandate under the umbrella of ability; and trustworthiness related to skill, knowledge and qualification under the umbrella of knowledge.

Knowledge as a dimension of trustworthiness has to do with trusting somebody because of what that person knows, and consequently what skills and qualifications they have. Interactants "surrender their private judgment" (Starr, 1982, p. 10) and trust each other "on authority" (cf. Parsons, 1951; Heritage, 2005, p. 85). When this is the case, interactional contributions are treated as *pass-able* (cf. Nielson, forthcoming-a). Being in the know, K+, rather than unknowing, K– (Heritage, 2012a), is an attractive interactional position. Therefore, we often see interactional resources used to gain credibility with respect to knowledge.

Accepting knowledge

Treating each other as knowledgeable and competent most of the time is a fundamental part of the order of interaction. In Chapter 5, we showed how interactants exchange information in many different settings, without questioning them. They do that because they trust their co-participant to be knowledgeable of the matters in focus.

We will now show a typical example of interactants treating their co-participants as knowledgeable simply by accepting what they say. The following example is from a conference call between expert neurosurgeons in Denmark and Switzerland. The meeting was recorded in Denmark, so the only access to the neurosurgeon in Switzerland is via the screen. The Danish team shares their screen with the Swiss expert, showing him neuroimages, brain wave images and three videos of the patient's seizures. The screen provides visual access to the same material for all participants in the meeting, irrespective of their physical location.

Example 7.1 Conference call (clonic movement)

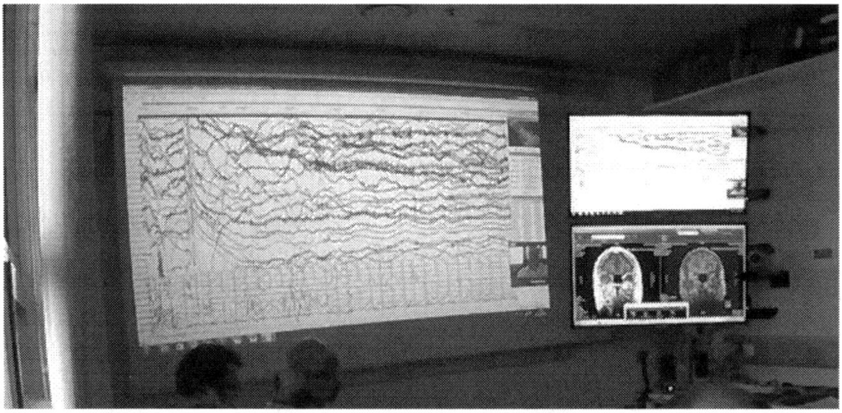

Fig. 7.1a. The Danish team share their screen with the Swiss expert, showing him brain waves during the patient's seizures.

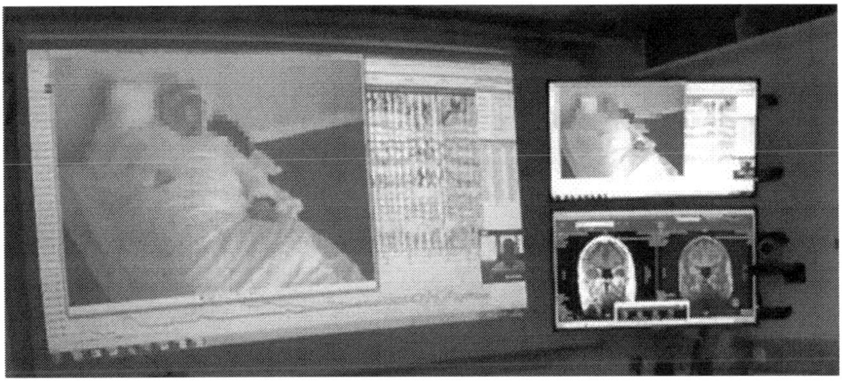

Fig. 7.1b. The Danish team share their screen with the Swiss expert, showing him videos of the patient during a seizure.

Fig. 7.1c. The Danish team gaze at the screen that they share with the French expert. A blue circle is drawn around Dr. C. This camera angle represents the French colleagues' perspective on the Danish group

At some point, the Swiss expert (DA) says the following:

```
DA:   [i ↑didn't see] a [clear pre↓dominence→
      o:f the clonic [mo:vement→]
      (.) on the: <left si:de>→
      o:f [the face↓]
      (0.5)
      which i:s→ of course→ [very important fea:[tu·re: o:f→]
      (0.5) [in this difficult] case [fo:r the] naturalization
```

Here, the Swiss doctor presents his observations, focusing on what he did not identify which could affect the diagnosis. He uses precise professional terms ("clonic movements", "naturalization"). Following is the Danish Dr. C's embodied response during the Swiss Dr. A's verbal statement:

A	[i ↑didn't see]	a	[clear pre↓domi	nence→
C	moves torso back from table, takes glasses of, moves torso back in seat, moves right hand up to cover mouth		tilts head to right	
A	o:f the clonic	[mo:vement→]	(.) on the: <left si:de>→	o:f
C		4 small headnods		
A	[the face↓]	(0.5)	which i:s→ of course→	
C	3 small headnods	3 small headnods		
A	[very important	fea:	[tu·re: o:f→]	(0.5)
C	2 small headnods		touches nose	
A	[in this difficult]	case	[fo:r the]	naturalization
C	touches other side of nose		right hand back to cover mouth	

Dr. C is an example of a recipient (one of many in the Danish hospital meeting room) of Dr. A's talk when he displays his expertise while assessing the patient. During that talk, we can see Dr. C's embodied (attentiveness and) acknowledgment of Dr. A's display of that expertise when he is talking on-screen. While the Swiss doctor is talking, we see Dr. C display intense concentration to co-assess the material. He repeatedly produces small nods of the head which visually confirm Dr. A's local identity as being competent, and his orientation to the importance of making accurate observations. The latter shows how participants in the wild often orient to several (of the theoretical) dimensions, here to knowledge and truth.

Confronting knowledge

Being confronted when stating, reporting or presenting things is the opposite of having co-participants surrendering to your judgment. An example of such post-action negotiation of epistemic authority is seen in Charles Goodwin's classic example (2003) of friends talking about cars. Here Mike states that a guy he knows from work has two Cords (very old expensive vintage cars), but Curt doubts that this is true:

Example 7.2 Confronting knowledge: Are you shitting me? (from Goodwin, 2003, pp. 153–154)

```
(4)
  1   Mike:   Lemme ask a guy at work.
  2           He's gotta bunch a' old clunkers.
                 (0.2)
  4   Mike:   Well I can't say that they're ol: clunkers=
→5            eez gotta Co:rd?
  6              (0.1)
→7   Mike:   Two Co:rds,
  8              (1.0)
  9   Mike:  [And
 10   Curt:  [Not original,
 11              (0.7)
 12   Mike:   Oh yes. Very original,
 13   Curt:   Oh:: reall[y?
 14   Mike:             [Yah. Ve(h)ry origi(h)nal.
 15   Curt:   °Awhh are you shittin m [e?
 16   Mike:                           [No I'm not.
```

Curt produces uptakes like "Not or*i*ginal" and "are *y*ou *sh*itting *me*?", openly showing his mistrust of Mike's story. This is because of the sheer unlikeliness that his colleague would be able to own not only one but two such cars. In the sequential negotiation of character (SNOC) found in l. 10–16, Curt orients to both Mike's knowledge about whether his colleague's cars are in fact "original" (l. 10), and also to whether Mike himself has the ability to tell the difference (l. 13).

Because others' acknowledgment of a person's knowledge is so attractive, but also has implications with respect to responsibility, for example (Stivers *et al.*, 2011, p. 9; cf. Raymond & Zimmerman, 2007), participants can be observed as being cautious in negotiating their respective trustworthiness based on knowledge. In what follows, we will explore three aspects of participants negotiating the quality of their knowledge: degrees, sources and primacy.

Negotiating and evaluating degrees of knowledge

Knowledge is not all-encompassing. It is compartmentalized and tied to certain domains. Moreover, you can have more or less knowledge regarding something, and be more or less certain of your knowledge of it.

Participants may display minimal knowledge or strong knowledge with regard to a domain, and thus assert their degree of epistemic authority using mitigating linguistic devices such as disclaimers, tag-questions and hedges (for example, Brown & Levinson, 1978, 1987; Andersen, 1986). They may also do this via different grammatical realizations of propositional content (Heritage, 2012a) or by design of polar questions (Heritage & Raymond, 2012). Participants will be fine-tuned in their local negotiations of the quality of their knowledge by calibrating their affinity with a given knowledge – for example, by doing word-search (Brouwer, 2003) or by try-marking their use of terms (Sacks & Schegloff, 1979).

The next example shows how participants may evaluate the quality of their knowledge using try-marking. This extract is from a video conference between a general practitioner (GP) in his doctor's consultation and a health care worker (HCW) in a meeting room at a rehabilitation center for geriatric patients. The GP is virtually "present" at the rehabilitation center via a BEAM telepresence robot, which is essentially a screen on a stick, mounted on a platform with wheels. He controls this from his consultation office located some 20 km away. The example begins with the HCW describing details regarding the circumstances of a wet patient.

Figure 7a The GP

Figure 7b The HCW

Example 7.3 Try-marking: So we talked a little about some swab

```
1* HCW: .hh og  det er kun  om  morgenen   det kommer
        .hh and it is  only on the morning it  comes
        .hh and it's only there in the morning

2*      og  hun kan være (.) drivhamrende våd af det
        and she can  be  (.)  soaking    wet of it
        and she can be soaking wet from it

3*      (1)

4* DOC:     [ok]

5* HCW: så [vi] snakkede lidt    om  noget po:de
        so [we]  talked  little about some  swa:b
        so we talked a little about some swa:b

6*        >prøv å  pode< for det eller et  eller andet
          >try 'n swab< for it    or  one  or   other
         >try 'n swab< for it or something
```

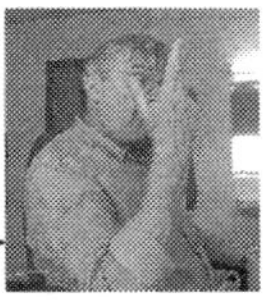

This is an inherently asymmetric interaction between two health care professionals with very different deontic (Stevanovic & Peräkylä, 2012) and epistemic statuses, rights and obligations (Heritage & Raymond, 2005; Lindström & Weatherall, 2015). The conference is initiated by the HCW, who needs advice regarding a patient who, every morning, is mysteriously soaking wet from an unknown liquid substance, even though she is equipped with a functioning catheter. The HCW has not seen the substance herself, but she has had it vividly described to her by colleagues, making the information she gives the GP a Type 2 knowable (Pomerantz,

1980) of a B-side event (see also Chapter 5, p. 60 on A/B-side access to events). As the GP is in his office, he has no visual or other access to neither the patient (who is not present), nor to the liquid substance, but only to the HCW via BEAM. This gives the HCW a local epistemic status as K+, even though her knowledge is not firsthand.

The recipient-designed sharing of details regarding the patient's clothes and linens in l. 1–2 shows an orientation to both knowledge and truth. The HCW's conspicuous use of vernacular terms ("soaking wet") might display an orientation to honesty, in that she chooses to provide the GP with details which she finds important, even though she does not know the professional terms for the phenomena. She therefore risks being seen as "less professional". Via embodied reactions, the GP displays alignment with the HCW's speculations regarding the patient's state, by raising his eyebrows when the latter describes a strange fact ("it's only in the morning it shows"). After one second of silence (at least partially due to the delay caused by the video mediation), he produces the response token "OK", thus leaving the floor open for the HCW. She goes on tentatively to suggest a possible course of action, presented as something already discussed with her co-workers – namely swabbing. The HCW thus claims both epistemic and deontic authority, albeit quite precariously. She uses deontic hedging both when introducing the suggestion ("talked a little about") and afterwards ("or something"). Furthermore, the syntactically incorrect use of "swab" in line 5 indicates that this is not a term that the HCW often uses. However, she self-corrects and suggests – quite hurriedly – that they "try 'n sw:ab" (l- 6), which can pass as a correct use of the term. The way the term sw:ab is initially produced (l. 5) with a prolonged vowel and an upwards intonation parallels try-marking (Sacks & Schegloff, 1979), albeit not to test if the GP knows the term, but to search for recognition and acceptance of her suggestion, and thereby also her knowledge in this turn at talk. We see lines 5–6 as a character-bound display whereby the HCW orients to her own knowledge, competence and honesty by using medical terms and delicately suggesting a relevant future course of action, despite her *per se* lesser deontic authority and her comparatively K− with regard to medical knowledge. We could argue that lines 1–2 are also a character-bound display oriented to appearing both truthful and knowledgeable about something that is locally relevant.

Already during the HCW's turn, her suggestion receives a clear multimodal uptake from the GP. As HCW mentions "swab", the GP raises his eyebrows, nods and subsequently raises his hand, pointing his index finger upwards. In this way, he displays recognition and acknowledgment of the HCW's knowledge, and her very cautiously suggested course of action. The GP's attending to her face, and thereby orienting to stake (see Chapter 6), becomes part not just of a co-construction of a locally relevant identity for the HCW as a trustworthy health professional, but also of a multimodal SNOC.

When participants negotiate and evaluate the quality and relevance of their knowledge by, for example, mitigating (e.g. Brown & Levinson, 1978, 1987; Andersen, 1986), try-marking their terms (Sacks & Schegloff, 1979) or adjusting their affinity with claimed or displayed knowledge, they locally orient to being perceived as trustworthy.

Negotiating the quality of sources of knowledge

One way of orienting to the quality of the knowledge one possesses is by deploying interactional strategies and moves that refer to the sources of that knowledge.

Examples of such interactional strategies and moves could be referring to sources of knowledge (Pomerantz, 1984b) as the following.

> If people ask for evidence, they are asking for grounds for believing that given assertions are true. One sort of evidence that people give is to tell the *sources* or *bases* of their believing given assertions. The source or basis of an assertion may not be relevant when an assertion's validity is assumed. When, however, its validity is called into question, the source or basis comes into play.
>
> (Pomerantz 1984b, p. 608)

> When people are concerned with being accountable for what they say, they may mitigate their accountability by presenting sources or bases for believing particular states of affairs, without accountably asserting the states of affairs that are suggested.
>
> (Pomerantz 1984b, p. 609)

> Attending to the sources or bases involves evaluating the sources as good or bad. That then bears on whether the version in question is believed or not. If a source is accepted as authoritative and reliable, a version may well be accepted as true. If an assertion from a credible source is presented as certainly true, it is more likely to be believed than if presented as a guess or an inference.
>
> (Pomerantz 1984b, p. 624)

The following is an example of giving the source and mitigating responsibility at the same time.

Example 7.4 I don't know. The desk called me (from Pomerantz, 1984b, p. 611)

	Desk:	What is the problem.
→	Caller:	I don't know. The desk called me and asked me, would you like to talk to the desk. They called and asked me to call an ambulance. We have one guest here that is ill.

Here, a caller to 911 is asked to state the reason for the call. By referring to not knowing the reason upfront, the caller pre-empts any further questions to that effect. The caller takes no responsibility for the legitimacy of the request, yet aligns with the report that they have a guest who is ill, making no attempt to downgrade the quality of "the desk" as a source. By referring to "the desk" as the source, the request for an ambulance is made institutional, and the professional inquiry "would you like to talk to the desk?" further establishes the request as coming from an institution. That carries the potential for seeking further information, should the 911 dispatcher want this.

When interactants are providing a basis to their claims, stating how they know and evaluate the quality of the sources involved (Pomerantz, 1984b; Potter, 1996; Sidnell, 2012), they strive to achieve trustworthiness based on their knowledge, on a very local turn-by-turn basis. Other examples of such interactional resources to that effect include referring to a third party (Clayman, 1992), animating (Clayman, 1992; Goffman, 1981) or ventriloquizing (Clifton, 2014; Cooren, 2010) a source of authority, or presenting things or documents (Benoit-Barné & Cooren, 2009) to mobilize authority[2] locally from policies or from superiors.

Negotiating primacy of knowledge: the right to know better

When there are conflicting sources in the interaction, referred to by different participants, the principle that "the Best Source's Version is more credible" (Pomerantz, 1984b, p. 614) may be applied. When working to decide that interactants may invoke the principle that "the most recent version is probably the right one" (Pomerantz, 1984b, p. 614). Or, when interactants negotiate the primacy of, and access to, their respective piece of knowledge (Heritage & Raymond, 2005; Raymond & Heritage, 2006; Stivers *et al.*, 2011), they may apply the principle that the identity category which is closest to the source of knowledge has primacy. This means that first-hand knowledge is better than second-hand access and second-hand knowledge (Raymond & Heritage, 2006). A person may have an epistemic advantage with respect to a certain field of knowledge due to his or her social category and social relations, and thus have A-access to person A–related events, rather than the B-access that person B has to A-events (Heritage, 2012a; Labov & Fanshel, 1977; Pomerantz, 1980). See also Chapter 5, p. 60 on A/B-side access to events.

In the following example, we see such a negotiation concerning primacy of knowledge. The extract is from a meeting in a communication department in a large corporation. In this example, the trainee, Louise

2 For rhetoricians, such strategies are known as 'appeal to authority', '*argumentum ab auctoritate*' or '*argumentum ad verecundiam*'.

(Lo), is reporting from a seminar that she and her senior colleague Jón attended the day before, at a posh conference hotel:

Example 7.5 We got it faster

1 Lo: ↑så va:r Jón og jeg på et u-ø:h:
↑then Jón and I attende:d a e:h
2 fant(h)a:stisk spæ:ndende:
fant(h)a:stically exi:ti:ng
3 seminar i går
seminar yesterday
4 (1.0)
5 **{name of expensive conference hotel}**
6 (.)
7 elendig frokost i øvrigt
lousy lunch by the way
8 (0.4)
9 ve du ikk gi mig ret i det?
don't you agree?
10 (.)
11 ?: **hhh**
12 (0.6)
13 **Ha:** det var jo ikk DERfor I gik te det
that was not WHY you attended it
14 vel?
was it?
15 (0.4)
16 Lo: næ
nah
17 (.)
18 det bare ikk
it's just not
19 altså je:g må indrøm: jeg- det var
really I: must admi:t I- it was
20 godt I to ikk brugt [tid på det
good the two of you didn't spend [time on it
21 Jó: [jo:rm altså
[yea:h but really
22 Lo: [det var altså ikk]
[it really wasn't]
23 Jó: [jeg ve da ikk-]
[I PT don't know-]
24 Lo: særlig godt
very good
25 **Ha:** →vi har læst det i aviserne i dag
we have read it in the newspapers today
26 Lo: **[*mm]**
27 **Ha:** →[så] vi fik det hurtigere
[so] we got it faster
28 (.)
29 Si: h e he ha
30 (.)

In l. 18, Louise assesses the seminar negatively (l. 18–21): It was a good thing that her department chair and one other colleague did not waste time on the seminar (l. 19–20), but apparently OK that Jón and she did. Her assessment constructs her superiors as being in a league above her. But the department manager responds by producing a "no news marker" in l. 25–27, claiming to have already read in the newspaper this morning what she is currently reporting from a seminar that she, due to her attendance, has A-access to (cf. Pomerantz, 1980). He, however, only has B-access from a third party report that he got before meeting her. This may not seem logical, but it serves to construct him as someone eager to position himself as better and earlier informed than her (Nielsen, 2010b, pp. 105–106).

Various social actions (reporting, informing, assessing, and so forth) are concerned with territories of knowledge (Heritage, 2012b; Heritage & Raymond, 2005). Participants are not just reporting, assessing, and so on (i.e. using their competence and knowledge); they are also stating (Asmuß & Oshima, 2012; Heinemann, 2006) or even defending their rights and responsibilities to do so (Heritage, 2012b; Heritage & Raymond, 2005; Raymond & Zimmerman, 2007). They are claiming a certain epistemic stance and authority, displaying their rights to know about or even to know better (Raymond & Heritage, 2006). Their co-participants may respond to their actions by accepting them, letting them pass, questioning them, modifying them, and so forth. Knowledge is thus not just a basis for informing, assessing, etc.; it is also "a moral domain" (Stivers *et al.*, 2011, p. 9) in which participants locally negotiate epistemic access, primacy and responsibilities.

Coming off as a knowledgeable insider

Low affinity can be conveyed by, for example, try-marking (also see Example 7.3). Conversely, strong affinity may be displayed by signposting names or objects (cf. "*Th*is guy had, a beautiful, thirty two Olds" (Goodwin, 2003, p. 153), just as different degrees of affinity may be embodied by glancing, pointing and touching (Glenn & LeBaron, 2011) at some object.

The negotiation of epistemic authority and stance differs, depending on the epistemic status of the participants. Professionals talking to other professionals receive different treatment from laypeople talking to professionals, partly because their actions imply a knowledge that is role-distributed. That role affords certain rights and responsibilities, partly because of the professionals' displayed knowledge of institutions and procedures (Whalen & Zimmerman, 1990). The use of specific terms and references is regularly employed to display what it means to be a cultural insider with a certain knowledge domain or territory (Heritage, 2012b). This is because making references does work other than merely referring. For instance, it illustrates membership of the domain from which it has been taken (Goodwin, 2003; Schegloff, 1972; cf. Kitzinger & Mandelbaum, 2013). Therefore, interactants may also demonstrate their knowledge and competence in a particular field by assessing and evaluating physical objects which are related to it (Goodwin, 2003). Likewise, the display of knowledge of a specialist field by using specialist vocabulary remains common (Kitzinger & Mandelbaum, 2013), or participants may make their institutional role relevant in order to gain advantage in discussions about who knows best how to improve a certain professional practice (Tranekjær *et al.*, in press).

The following example is from a management team meeting in a major bank branch in Sweden (Larsson & Nielsen, 2021, pp. 12–13). Participating in this sequence of the meeting are Peter (Pe), Charles (Ch) and Frederic (Fr). They are talking about a merger between their bank and Omega Bank, and are discussing some of this merger's consequences. At some point, Peter asks the following question.

Example 7.6 Substantial amounts coming to the branches

```
39 Pe:  du säger lägga >ut det på kontor<
        you say place >out it on branches<
        you say to delegate >it to the branches<

40      (.)

41      vad är det,
        what is it,
        what does that mean,

42      (1.1)

43      det är felräkningspengar,
        it is miscalculation money,

44      eller det är,
        or it is

45      (.)

46      stora °belopp som ska ut på° kontor=
        big °amounts that is coming out to° branches=
        °substantial amounts coming to° the branches=

47      =>jag vet inte vad dom< har tjänat Omega bank
        =>I don't know what they< have earned Omega bank
        =>I don't know how much profit< they've made Omega bank

48 Ch:  *nä* det vet inte,
        *no* don't know that,

49      (.)
```

```
50       ah:: vad tjänar dom,
         we::ll what do they earn,

51       >hundra miljoner< (.) tjänar dom?
         >hundred millions< (.) do they earn?
         >hundred millions< (.) could they?

52 Fr:   har jädra hög räntabilitet
         have damned high rentability
         got a damn high rentability

53 Pe:   jo
         yeah
```

By asking what "delegating it to the branches" means, Peter formally asks for information, but the content of the question shows that he knows a good deal already, because – in a category-bound display – he constructs a polarity between "miscalculation money" and "substantial amounts coming to the branches" as matters related to a bank merger. In this excerpt, Peter thus manages to gain relevant information and present himself as a knowledgeable insider at the same time.

There are different ways of using knowledge to construct a local identity as a trustworthy interactant, and different reasons for so doing. In the next section, we show how participants manage to allow interactional work like this to be interlaced with other power plays, in order to appear knowledgeable in a certain matter.

Flashing knowledge to bolster trustworthiness

Claiming epistemic primacy concerning something locally relevant is a member's concern, and a way of orienting to being trustworthy. One strategy is to flash your own knowledge by both referring to A-events and drawing in other knowing participants in order to create a consensus. An example of this can be seen in what follows. The data are from a multiparty conference call between two teams of Indian businesspeople, one being from a group of training institutes (TI) and the other from a large vehicle manufacturer (VM) that lacks trained workers.

Example 7.7 Oriya people are accustomed to better water price (from Clifton, 2012, pp. 120–121)

70 A so and I=I er so if they're working in Orissa no
71 problem or if some people are working in
72 Vizag or upto Hyderabad there's no issue

73		(.) but we're planning to send them to
74		Rajasthan=and you know Rajasthan we have
75		supplied how many people have we done?
76	C	fifty people °have gone°
77	A	fifty people have gone and all of them have
78		come back
79	C	er: they were there for at least six months and
80		[° er°]
81	A	[and] there were food and stay issues
82		you know but Rajasthan has a problem for
83		water (.3) and Orissa=Oriya people are
84		accustomed to better water price but Orissa
85		people have not been yet ↓
86	B	yeah

The VM manager, Baldev (B), initially had a preference for where the workers should come from, namely from the eastern region. Upon that request, manager Amrit (A) from TI explains why that is not the best solution, in light of workers going to Rajasthan to work. Amrit first produces an 'if-this but-that' construction, counterposing places where the Oriya people could work without problems, with where they are talking about sending them. In l. 74, he projects agreement ("you know") with B, before drawing on his own experience ("we have") about this and then drawing in his colleague Chadra (C) as a knowing participant to provide him with information about the number of people who have previously gone to Rajasthan. Provided with that number, Amrit again displays firsthand knowledge: that the workers have all gone back (l. 77–78) and that while they were there, "there were food and stay issues" (l. 81). Further, he can also provide a reason why (l. 82–85) – one which is also based on events to which he has primary access. Via A's ongoing displays of epistemic primacy, he works at achieving epistemic authority, and in this way he orients to being knowledgeable and trustworthy regarding this local issue concerning choice of workers.

Clifton, from whom this excerpt is taken, argues (2012) that Armrit's displays of "general truths of what 'anyone knows'" (p. 122), in combination with his extensive use of firsthand knowledge and other interactional moves aimed at achieving epistemic primacy, "is retrospectively oriented to by Baldev as a display of trustworthiness. This becomes apparent when Baldev later states "I think th=those very culture specific issues w=we could erm I would leave it to your judgment" (p. 114). Clifton further argues that his analysis is of " 'trust-in-action' as a situated members' achievement", but also that "there is nothing in the analysis that would allow a researcher to extrapolate an emic display of trust from the data" (p. 123) before Baldev's utterance previously cited. We dare to disagree, and argue with Sacks that both analysts and participants can see Amrit's strong orientations to displaying knowledge and ability, as in the two character-bound displays found in this excerpt (l. 70–74 and 80–85, respectively), as well as to truth, detail and transparency. Throughout more than 200 lines, we see a 'cluster of indicators' and thus a strong orientation to coming across as trustworthy.

When participants orient to knowledge, extensively 'flashing', by either claiming, showing, or demonstrating it (Schegloff, 1972) via A-event statements, signposting of names, objects or processes, and orient to both the source and quality of the knowledge they present, we see this as a strong orientation to one's own trustworthiness.

Testing others' knowledge

An orientation to knowledge can also be 'seen' when participants noticeably abstain from displaying it. It has been demonstrated how the use (or not) by professionals of terms from professional or specialist vocabularies, when addressing both peers and laypeople, can display a tacit assessment of others' (lack of) knowledge or competence. Professionals may design their talk to avoid using a word which might cause comprehension problems, and use vernacular explanations instead, or else explain the specialist term in vernacular language (Kitzinger & Mandelbaum, 2013). They might do this in order not to put the interlocutor "on the spot" by unveiling and displaying their lack of understanding or knowledge. Such strategies simultaneously show orientation to concern for others, and for saving their face, and thus to stake (see Chapter 6, p. 96). As we have seen, this is also a component in coming across as trustworthy. Likewise, asking questions to test whether a specialist term is known or understood is an orientation to knowledge. This may occur when professionals, who use specialist terms when speaking to laypeople, ask them if the term is known and understood. This is something we see in the following example, where the call-taker at a Birth Crisis help line is testing whether the specialist term 'doula' is known and understood by the caller:

Example 7.8 Do you know about doulas? (from Kitzinger & Mandelbaum, 2013, p. 181)

```
((Mother calling for help for her daughter who is pregnant again after a
traumatic first labor - the call-taker suggests first an independent midwife
and then a doula))
01  Clt:  If you want to get into a website .hhh www dot
02        independent midwi::[ves .hh] d-dot o:rg dot=
03  Viv:                     [y e a h]
04  Clt:  UK:.
05        (3.0)
06 Clt:→  .hhhh Now the other thing is uh d- do you know
07        about doula:s¿ hhh
```

```
08  Viv:  Pardon¿
09  Clt:  Do you know about doul:as.
10  Viv:  No.
11  Clt:  .hhh Well these are birth compa- paid birth compa:nions
12        who::: w- will be with the woman and be her >as it were<
13        advocate¿ .hh and tend to her personal nee:ds .hh and
14        they work along with the midwife but they are- it's
15        woman to woman stuff...
```

In this example, the call-taker is giving advice to the mother of the pregnant woman, first by referring to a website regarding independent midwives. After a silence, she goes on to suggest another thing, namely a doula (l. 6–7). The call-taker produces the first sound of the word, before cutting herself off and asking instead if the caller knows "about d*ou*la:s ¿" with a rising intonation that marks the term as possibly unknown to the caller. In so doing, she explicitly offers the caller an opportunity either to express recognition, or to reveal this possible lack of knowledge, thereby orienting to just that.

As with many of the actions and moves that display an orientation to one of the components of trustworthiness, try-marking as a way of testing others' knowledge does not necessarily – in and of itself – indicate that trustworthiness is at stake. We argue that it can function as one of many indicators, if a cluster of these can be identified in the sequential environment, and also that it may simultaneously be an orientation to stake and interest, since testing knowledge might also be sparing the layperson the potential loss of face involved in having to ask for clarification.

An example of the latter is presented in the following example – albeit in this case the professional, a GP, is not talking to a layperson but to a health care worker who has substantially less education than the doctor regarding the subject matter at hand. This excerpt is from the same meeting as Example 7.3. It begins 1 minute and 35 seconds after the previous excerpt, which concluded with the GP's agreement with the HCW's suggestion of swabbing the patient.

In l. 9–10, the GP asks the HCW if she knows what the specific swab kit needed looks like. The misplacement marker ("by the way") produced by GP after a micro-pause following the PCP in l. 9 can be understood as a belated realization of his own K– position regarding the extent of the HCW's knowledge of the practicalities of her future task. However, as the phrase is not prefacing the question, but is inserted with hearable pauses both before and after, in this instance it might also function as a hedge, downgrading the potential face-threat, which the question regarding the HCW's professional knowledge might pose. In this way GP displays orientation not just to knowledge, but also to stake. In l. 11, the HCW confirms with a type-conforming answer, before producing a request for affirmation regarding the kit with a very vernacular wording ("those sticks"). The HCW is clearly not claiming

Example 7.9 Do you know what it looks like?

```
09* DOC: altså       det sådan >ved du hvordan det ser  ud
         therefore it    so   >know you  how    it looks out
         so it's such >do you know what it looks like

10*      (.) for øvrigt  (.) det podesæt   °du skal bruge°
         (.) for moreover(.) that swab kit °you must use°
         (.) by the way (.) that swab kit °you need°

11*      (0.3) (0.7)

12* HCW: ja  er det er det de    der  pi↑nde
         yes it is  it is those there sti↑cks
         yes it is it is those sti↑cks

13*      (1.1)

14* DOC: .hh ja det såd'n (.) det et plastik
         .hh yes it such (.)  it  a plastic
         .hh yes it's such (.) it's a plastic

15* HCW: [°det°]
         [°it° ]

16* DOC: [øh. ] (.) [hylster]
         [eh. ] (.) [holster]

17* HCW:            [ja men ]
                    [yes but]

18* DOC: hvor der er både en pind og et glas
         where there is both a stick and a glass
         where there's both a stick and a tube

19* HCW: >ja  ja  jo<  mm: (.)det kender jeg godt (.)
         >yes yes yeah< mm: (.)it  know    i  well (.)
         >yes yes yeah> mm: (.) i know that. (.)
```

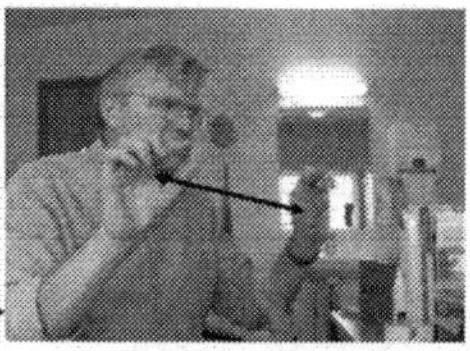

high epistemic authority, but she is simultaneously displaying whatever knowledge she has.

After a pause of 1.1 seconds, partially due to the delay of the video mediation (also see Seuren *et al*., 2021), the GP responds affirmatively and goes on to elaborate, describing the kit in detail. He uses more vernacular wording than what might be expected from a doctor (l. 13, 15, 17), while vividly gesturing in an attempt to animate what the kit looks like. In this way he is orienting to securing the HCW's knowledge, and doing so without putting the HCW on the spot. All the while, the HCW nods and verbally confirms that she understands and is familiar with the kit (l. 16, 18, 20), displaying understanding and recognition. She is therefore working at maintaining a certain epistemic stance. Only after the HCW verbally confirms that she knows the type of kit in l. 18 does the GP go on to use more professional wording (l. 19). This is now done with a SNOC, in which HCW's character-bound displays (l. 12 and 19) have left the GP trusting that the HCW understands his use of jargon, thus letting the HCW uphold her professional identity as a knowing and, therefore trustworthy, professional.

When interactants are testing others' knowledge, as seen in the examples here, it may, on the one hand, be about the speaker's own trustworthiness (when they orient to what is at stake for the other participant concerning, for example loss of face), or, on the other hand, the trustworthiness of the co-participant (who is being tested concerning one of the components of trustworthiness, knowledge). We may therefore see such negotiation as not just a case of unfolding steps of intersubjectivity, but as negotiations of character. The participants are also doing local identity work via their character-bound displays of knowledge and ability, as well as their negotiation of interest in what is at stake for the other. These displays may represent orientations to locally relevant components of trustworthiness.

Miscrediting others by spotlighting their lack of knowledge

Spotlighting others' lack of knowledge, especially regarding domains about which they might be expected to be knowledgeable about, is also an orientation to knowledge – and to the possible lack of trustworthiness of the participants. Using others' lack of knowledge or ability in a way that serves to miscredit them can be done through the use of interactional strategies such as other-initiated other-repair (Schegloff *et al.*, 1977). This is usually strongly dispreferred, not least due to its face-threatening character. It may also be a strategy to make another person appear less than trustworthy, which the following two examples demonstrate.

Example 7.10 Other-correcting: Motor (from Jefferson, 1987, p. 87)

```
[9] Engine
[from Jefferson, 1987 p. 87]
01  Ken:  And they told me how I could stick a th-uh::
02        Thunderbird motor? (0.5) in my Jeep?  And
03      →I bought a fifty five [Thunderbird motor.
04  Rog:→                      [Not motor, engine.
05        You speak of [electric motor and a gasoline engine.
06  Ken:               [Okay
```

Here, Roger unabashedly corrects Ken regarding the correct jargon – both in the overlapping speak in l. 4, and in the almost lecture-style elaboration of what Ken got wrong in l. 5. This leaves Ken appearing to be clearly less trustworthy when it comes to knowledge of car repair.

Example 7.11 Other-correcting: toxemia (from Kitzinger & Mandelbaum, 2013, p. 189)

```
01  Kat:→... <I suffered (0.2) toxemia pre-eclampsia (.)
02         you name it.  I suffered it.
03         (.)
04  Clt:→Toxemia IS pre-eclampsia by [the  way]
05  Kat:                             [Oh sorry] yes.
06         [(                )]
07  Clt:   [It's alright I just]= SAY that because if you're
08         dealing with paralegal (.) things and everything
09         it's: important to know.
10  Kat:   mm[m]
```

In this example, which is from a Birth Crisis help line, the other-initiated other-repair is concerned with a particularly delicate matter – that is, the caller's own health problems during her pregnancy. The caller claims to have suffered from both toxemia and pre-eclampsia, two terms for the same condition. She is corrected (l. 4) by the call-taker, who informs her that the two are the same thing. The caller apologizes for the overlap with a misplacement marker produced right after the correction, indicating the delicacy of the correction. Also, the call-taker goes on to produce a reason for her correction (l. 7–9): namely, that it is important for the caller to be able to be specific and to be able to provide the correct knowledge in another situation where her trustworthiness is paramount; that is, when "dealing with paralegal things". The call-taker's local project here is not to make the caller appear untrustworthy, but potentially to bolster her in displaying trustworthiness in another important situation.

Other examples of interactional moves designed to make it transparent that others are not trustworthy because of lack of knowledge would include asking questions to which the recipient is unlikely to know the answer, designing talk concerning the vocabulary in order to make it obvious how others are not trustworthy because of their lack of knowledge, or accusing others of doing just that.

Using lack of knowledge as a resource for escaping responsibility

The primacy of knowledge can also be seen in the way that " 'not knowing' and 'not remembering' serve as accounts because of the norm that speakers should base their reports on knowledge" (Pomerantz, 1984b, p. 610; see also Goodwin, 1987). The following example, as J is asking V about when J's son phoned V, is an example of this.

Example 7.12 I don't know what time it was (from Pomerantz, 1984b, p. 610)

In 'giving the time', a speaker is accountable for the time being right. This presumes that speakers would know (or think they know) the right time if they 'give the time'. The presumption that a speaker properly has knowledge of the state of affairs being asserted, may be used when persons decline to give information. The following excerpt illustrates this. *J* is asking *V* to tell her what time *J*'s son phoned *V*.

J: Well what time was it, I left you at about twenty to five.
(0.4)
→ *V*: I don't know what time it was Jenny, I can't remember really,

One of *J*'s immediate concerns, expressed in the question, *What time was it*, is to have *V* give the time that her son phoned. While *V* understands *J*'s concern she does not cooperate with it. If she were cooperating and were unsure of the exact time, she might have indicated an approximate time. Or she might have taken what *J* said, *I left you about twenty to five* as a starting point and worked on arriving at an estimated time. In fact, she gives nothing helpful toward that concern. She first says that she does not know and then adds that she does not remember. 'Not knowing' and 'not remembering' serve as accounts because of the norm that speakers should base their reports on knowledge.

The rationale is that (cf. Pomerantz, 1984b, p. 610) reporting should be based on knowing, and such usage makes the speaker accountable for being right. Therefore, accounting for not responding with reference to "not knowing" or "not remembering" frees the participant from responding with a report (of e.g. a specific time), and also from the implications of the content of the report (i.e. here, the use that J will make of the information). In the preceding example, speaker J assumes that speaker V has that knowledge, treating V as a trustworthy source of information – a source that J has A-knowledge about, being a fellow A-knowledge owner. Nonetheless, speaker V steps back from that endorsement, probably because of the implications of being treated as a trustworthy source of that information toward a third party.

Why ability, capacity, mandate and entitlement build trustworthiness

Ability is a component of trustworthiness which is related directly to a speaker's capacity, role or mandate. Speaker A is only to be trusted doing action X if it is doable or within reach for A. These aspects cannot be reality-checked within the interaction. This is because the interactants often do not have access to the relevant 'data'. Interactant B cannot leave the scene to check if interactant A has either the ability or the deontic status to do something, or to make it happen. But when interactants orient to the 'skills or ability to do' in the interaction then they orient to a dimension of trustworthiness. Doing X presupposes the ability and/or entitlement to do X. By undertaking actions such as reporting, stating, informing and assessing, participants do not just report, inform, assess, and so forth (i.e. use their competence and knowledge); they also state (Asmuß & Oshima, 2012; Heinemann, 2006), or even defend, their rights and responsibilities to do so (Heritage, 2012b; Heritage & Raymond, 2005). Equally, their co-participants may respond to their actions by accepting them, letting them pass, questioning them, modifying them, and so forth, i.e. acknowledge these rights (cf. M.F. Nielsen, forthcoming-a).

Having the right – or mandate – to decide, propose or announce a future action is studied in CA as "deontic authority". According to Stevanovic and Peräkylä, "epistemic authority is about knowing how the world "is", whereas "deontic authority is about getting the world to match the words; . . . about determining how the world 'ought to be'" (Stevanovic & Peräkylä, 2012, p. 298; cf. Lindström & Weatherall, 2015).

This section is not about ability and entitlement. It is about participants orienting to someone's trustworthiness due to their ability, capacity, mandate or entitlement – by means of interactional strategies and moves displaying, demonstrating or questioning the abilities, rights, mandates and capabilities necessary to perform a certain action, or to deliver on one. In the following subsections, we will explore these components of trustworthiness.

Accepting others' ability

As in the other sections on different orientations, we consider the default setting to be interactants living their lives, including the moments where they make promises and execute decisions for a range of different purposes and are not treating such actions as anything out of the ordinary.

In the next example from the Danish headquarters of an international company, we see two colleagues, Zaki (ZAK) and Kurt (KUR), next to the coffee machine in a company café area. They are talking about pricing services in IT projects, while a third colleague, Fabio (FAB), is sitting in the café area with his laptop.

Example 7.13 Extremely complicated (from Nielsen & Toft, in review-a)

```
1   ZAK   *▲■men(it▲ ▲projekter)■ kan jo faktisk være ekstremt
           but it projects can actually be extremely
          *gazing toward KUR-->
    kur    ▲gazes toward cup of coffee▲ ▲gazes toward ZAK-->
```

```
                ■picks up cup of coffee from coffee machine■
2          komplicerede fordi alt +det her med tid og mandskab▲
           complicated because all this with time and crew
                                   +gestures with left hand-->
    kur                                                   -->▲
3          ▲[hvad er der]+
           what is there
                     -->+
    kur       ▲gazes toward kitchen counter-->
4   KUR    [det er alt  ] ■fra at skifte▲ ▲et system
           it is everything from replacing a system
                                     -->▲ ▲gazes toward ZAK-->
                        ■puts cup of coffee on kitchen counter
5          [%og så# op til▲% ▲det helt]
           and then up to the really
            %gestures with both hands%
                        -->▲  ▲gazes toward cup of coffee-->
    Fig          #fig.25
6   ZAK    [ja lige præcis men også]
           yes exactely but also
7   KUR    store■ og▲ ▲så ■hvordan prissætter+*# du +det■
           big and    so how do you put a price on that
               ■picks up cup of coffee on kitchen counter
                -->▲ ▲gazes toward ZAK-->
                        ■gestures with left hand------■
    zak                                       +turns head toward FAB
                                               *gazes toward FAB
                                                   +nods
    fig                                         #fig.26
8          ■og+*▲ [så vid**ere   ]
           and so on
           ■turns body toward FAB
               ▲gazes toward FAB-->
    zak      +turns head toward KUR
              *gazes toward KUR* *gazes toward FAB-->>
```

In the data extract, we see Zaki and Kurt discuss the complexity of pricing services, e.g. their IT projects (l. 1–7). Zaki makes a statement (l. 1–3) which Kurt not only treats as acceptable by progressing the talk, but also contributes with an example (l. 4–5). Zaki acknowledges this and strongly agrees with it (l. 6), before continuing with the topic (l. 7f). Kurt treats Zaki as a trustworthy source of information by accepting and continuing the talk, never problematizing the statement or Zaki's ability or right to make it. We will return to this conversation in more detail. But, for now, we will focus on the exchange in l. 1–6.

Confronting others' ability

In a business project, it is pivotal for the effectiveness of collaboration that one professional can trust the assessments made by another professional, including the basis on which such assessments (or statements, or predictions or other social actions) are made. We see participants verbalize exactly the latter when, for example, they problematize methods of reasoning or the reliability of data. One participant may very well let things pass in a way that others will not. In what follows, we see the continuation of the exchange between Zaki, Kurt and Fabio, with Kurt trailing off from his report on the complexities of pricing IT services.

Example 7.14 How do you get that kind of knowledge? (from Nielsen & Toft, in review-a)

```
 8   KUR   ■og+*▲ [så vid**ere     ]
           and so on
           ■turns body toward FAB
               ▲gazes toward FAB-->
     zak     +turns head toward KUR
              *gazes toward KUR* *gazes toward FAB-->>
 9   FAB           [hvordan# fanden]
                    how the hell
     fig                   #fig.27
10   FAB   undskyld jeg■ afbryder men hvordan fanden
           sorry I am interrupting but how the hell
     kur               ■leans agains counter facing FAB
```

```
11   FAB   øh har +du hvordan får du sat dig ind i det der+
           ehm have you how do you get that kind of knowlegde
     zak         +steps toward high table where FAB is sitting+

12         +(0.9)
     zak   +puts hand on table
13   FAB   [altså]
           i mean
14   ZAK   [men  ] det øh (0.4) øhm alstå▲▲#der er jeg jo nødt til
           but    that ehm      well there I do need to
     kur                                  -->▲ ▲gazing toward ZAK-->>
     fig                                       #fig.28
15         at snakke med folk
           talk with people
```

While Zaki and Kurt discuss the complexity of the IT projects (l. 1–7) and how to price services, Fabio is positioned at a standing table directly in front of the coffee machine. He is visibly orienting to their discussion. In l. 9, Fabio initiates a question, while also apologizing for interrupting their conversation (l. 10). He addresses (l. 11) the complexity of IT projects and questions Zaki's ability to get the kind of knowledge that he has just implied he is in possession of. During the following conversation (not shown, due to its length), it appears that

Fabio's job description is to define the pricing of services, and he was not aware that Zaki also worked on it as a part of his job. A participant with more knowledge of "extremely complicated" matters (l. 1–2 in Example 7.13) may therefore not treat another speaker as a trustworthy source, even after that person has built a rapport with a third party by talking about it and having their identity as knowledgeable confirmed.

Doubting trustworthiness by confronting ability

Participants may express doubts with respect to, for example, a mutual project by pointing to their lack of trust in its foundation. In the following example, we will see an even more confrontational example of that from a business meeting between four managers. Here one manager (EMP1) represents collaborating partner A, and three managers (EMP2, EMP3 and EMP4) represent the collaborating partner B.

Example 7.15 If this is how the cooperation is at the kick off

```
133 EMP3 so a lot of time is spent in trying to align
         ourselves
134*     (.)
135      to the common goal
136      instead of actually spending a constructive time
137*     sitting down and working out a plan
138      on how to achieve it
139      I mean
140*     we have not even reached the knowledge transfer level
141      (.)
142      if this is how the cooperation is at the kick off➔
143*     then I'm extreme(h)ly(h) uh reluc(h)tant to say that
144*     the knowledge transfer will actually work ↑right
145* EMP2 [yea]
```

In this example, we see EMP3 from partner B argue that partner B has spent "a lot of time" "trying to align" themselves (l. 133–134) to "the common goal" – that is, they have made an effort to deliver on their deliverables, despite the obstacles presented by partner A not making it possible for them to spend "constructive time sitting down and working out a plan on how to achieve it". However, partner A in the collaboration does not work toward "the common goal", which leaves "the knowledge transfer" as a goal that partner A cannot be trusted to cooperate in making "actually work". EMP3 is implicitly challenging the ability (or agenda, cf. Chapter 6) of partner A to perform professionally, in order to make the knowledge transfer from partner A to partner B work. In so doing, she is questioning the trustworthiness of partner A.

Example 7.16 Part of your specialties

```
21* GP:  yes  det må  du  meget gerne få  fat  i
         yes that may you very  adv   get hold in
         yes it would be very good if you could get hold of that

22*      og  så lave en podning på det .hh
         and so make a  swab    on it  .hh
         and then do a swab on it .hh

23* HCW: for at pode hende
         for to swab her
         to swab her

24* GP:  [ja ] (.) o:g  ø:hmm (1.3)
         [yes] (.) a:nd e:hmm (1.3)
         [yes] (.) a:nd e:hmm (1.3)

25  HCW: [ja ]
         [yes]

26* GP:  den øh >ja  det kan  du        lige så godt gøre<
         it  eh >yes it  can you(sng) just so well do<
         it eh >yes you just might as well do that<

27*      (.) det synes jeg det kø det hører  med  til jeres    specialer
         (.) it  think  i  it  ce it  belong with for your (pl) specialities
         (.) i think it is ca is part of your specialities

28* HCW: #ja=
         #yes=

29* GP: =altså  jeres kompetencer
         =that is your  competenceses

30*      at  det kan  i        godt vælge  (.) °syns  jeg°
         that it can you (pl) well choose (.) °think i°
         that you can chose that (.) in my opinion

31*      (1.8)

32* HCW: jaeh↓
         yeah↓
```

Negotiating and assessing ability and capacity

Confronting and doubting the ability of others may be harsh. More subtle methods are also used, and with more amicable results. Assessing the trustworthiness of others and displaying one's own trustworthiness can be achieved via negotiating ability and capacity. In the above example, which is from the same meeting as Example 7.3 and Example 7.9, the GP is undertaking an assessment of the HCW's ability and deontic authority, while also performing character-bound displays of his own. Just before this excerpt begins, the GP and the HCW have established that the HCW does in fact know what a swab kit is.

In l. 21 and 22, the GP urges the HCW to "get hold of" the kit and "do a swab", which can be seen as an uptake on the HCW's verbal and embodied identity, including work done during and after the GP's explanation as seen in Example 7.9. When the HCW confirms, by reformulating "to swab her" in l. 23, the GP initially agrees and then looks away, pausing for just more than a second, while keeping his gaze to the side before he continues with what may be termed 'contemplating out loud'. Here, he shares his thoughts about whether he finds it within the professionally permissible actions of the HCW and her colleagues (l. 26), and within their field of competence (l. 27 and 29) to perform the swab. As analysts, we cannot know whether he is trying to remember what type of examinations HCWs are legally permitted to do, or whether he is simply making a personal evaluation. But in l. 30, the GP expands the deontic authority of the HCW and her colleagues by stating that not only does he believe ("in my opinion") that they have the ability to swab, but also that they have the deontic authority to decide whether or not to do so. In this way, GP orients to the competence, ability, and mandate of both himself and the HCWs. The GP asserts his epistemic status by being the one considering and ultimately deciding that it is permissible for HCWs to make the decision to swab. Then he leaves them with the responsibility for future action, thereby deeming them trustworthy with regard to this, and himself as trustworthy with regard to evaluating and delegating such tasks. We see the collective stretch of talk in Example 7.3, Example 7.9 and Example 7.16 as containing at least one cluster of indicators of the negotiation of trustworthiness.

Using lack of mandate as a resource for rejection

Lack of ability has been shown to be an interactional resource in enacting rejections. Compare how pointing to one's own inability as grounds for not complying with requests is preferred over rejecting help for others (Drew, 1984; Heritage, 1988). The latter is a matter of motive and therefore an orientation to stake and interest (see Chapter 6). Claiming inability is not, *per se*, related to trustworthiness. But it is evidence that the ability to perform some action is a necessary precondition for the person executing it to do so (see also Austin, 1962, on felicity conditions). Therefore, others trusting the person performing the action relies on the conditions for doing just that.

In Chapter 5, on orientation to truth and honesty, we saw how telling all or more than necessary could indicate an orientation to trustworthiness – that is, in order to create transparency. Conversely, by doing more than requested, a participant may disclose reasons to do less than is asked for in the local sequential environment, and thus still orient to being trustworthy. This could be achieved by means of accounting for the inability to appear open and honest (cf. Chapter 5), and without hidden agendas (cf. Chapter 6). Essentially, it is about being open and transparent about not being open and transparent. The following example is from a department meeting in a communications department of a large corporation. The head of the department (H) is making an announcement about a video clip that is "possibly" going to be edited into the company movie – one that the department has been working on.

When one of the editors, Robert (R), asks a very specific question (l. 8), the department chair is orienting to some facts that he is not mandated to share:

Example 7.17 I have some inside knowledge that I can't tell you

1 H: jeg forstod på Thornø i morges
I understood from Thornø this morning
2 (.)
3 at hanøh (.) muligvis godt kunne (.) forestille sig
that heeh (.) possibly well might (.) imagine
4 at vi lige klippede en ekstra eller to ting ind i den
that er just cut an extra or two things into it
5 (.)
6 R: ja
yeah
7 H: øhøh før den kunne bruges som koncernfilm
eheh before it could be used as corporate film
8 R: så tager vi [navn på datterselskab] væk
so take we [name of subsidiary company] away
so then we remove [name of subsidiary company]
9 H: øhøh
eheh
10 (.)
11 nu (.) øh ligger jeg med noget inside viden
now (.) eh lie I with some inside knowledge
now (.) eh I have some inside knowledge
12 (.)
13 som jeg ikke (.) desværre ikke kan fortælle jer nu
that I not (.) unfortunately not can tell you now
that I can't (.) unfortunately can't tell you at this point
14 (.)
15 Jo: ja
yeah
16 H: så jeg (.) er i den situation
so I (.) am in that position
17 (.)
18 atøh (.) jeg ved (.) noget
thateh (.) I know (.) something
19 (.)
20 K: som sk- -
that wi- -
21 H: som vil ske
that will happen
22 (.)
23 som vil få indflydelse på den video
that will have influence on that video
24 (.)

The department chair makes it accountable (l. 9–13 and 16–23) that he is not able to respond to the question raised in l. 8, but that he acknowledges that by not doing that, he is not telling the whole truth concerning what he knows about it. He also acknowledges that it would have been relevant and necessary for him to do so. Reasons for not being able to relate this information could include the idea that business matters such as selling off a company would entail informing the stock exchange before everybody else. But that is also a fact which he cannot share without implying that the company mentioned in l. 8 is about to be sold. By accounting for not adhering to the (tacit) norm of answering by telling what he knows about the matter, since he does state that there is something to tell (l. 1–4), he makes it locally relevant and orients to exactly that.

In this example, the department head accounts for his reluctance to answer by reference to a lack of mandate, not a lack of knowledge or the irrelevance of the question. In doing so, he produces a self-initiated category-bound display as he orients to coming across as trustworthy while still (perhaps also due to being able to) keeping facts confidential. So the displayed lack of mandate also becomes a display of ability to navigate and follow protocol, and of respect for what he has the mandate to do or not. This shows how participants can be very skilled in their mutual negotiation of ability and knowledge.

Concluding discussion of orientation to knowledge and ability

Knowledge and ability as a dimension of trustworthiness has to do with trusting somebody because of that person's skills, knowledge and qualifications, as well as their mandate. It is important to bear in mind that the social negotiation of knowledge and ability as indicative of trustworthiness is dependent upon context. There is, for example, a big difference between a private conversation between friends using moves such as mocking, specialist terms or flashing knowledge, and the same interactional moves being used in inherently asymmetrical institutional settings. In the latter, the interlocutors' epistemic and deontic statuses are often institutionally defined. A layperson using vernacular language when enquiring about something, or explaining something to a specialist, may likely not display orientation to a component of trustworthiness, and probably not to the recipients' possible lack of knowledge. Their choice of wording may merely be the result of lacking knowledge about medical jargon, for instance. On the contrary, when a specialist is doing the same, they more likely orient to the recipients' presumed lack of knowledge of jargon, and thereby displays orientation to, for example, not appearing unapproachable, not putting the layperson (or anyone with K–, cf.

Heritage, 2012a) on the spot. They thereby avoid risking face-loss for the other (as seen in Example 7.9), and therefore orients to appearing trustworthy.

Interactional strategies, moves and actions indicative of this orientation to knowledge and ability include the following.

- Orientation to epistemic authority (Heritage & Raymond, 2005; Heritage, 2012a) when confronting and doubting knowledge via codable actions such as stating, reporting or presenting information, thereby negotiating trustworthiness; and by accepting others' statements, letting them pass or conversely by questioning them or modifying them (M.F. Nielsen, forthcoming-a).
- Orientation to degrees of knowledge, from minimal to strong, by means of codable linguistic mitigating devices such as disclaimers, tag-questions and hedges (e.g. Brown & Levinson, 1978, 1987; Andersen, 1986), via different grammatical realizations of propositional content (Heritage, 2012a) or design of polar questions (Heritage & Raymond, 2012).
- Orientation to the quality of own knowledge and that of others by codable actions such as try-marking (Sacks & Schegloff, 1979) or adjusting one's affinity with claimed or displayed knowledge of, for example, facts.
- Orientation to the quality of knowledge sources via actions and moves such as asking for evidence or presenting sources as certainly true (Pomerantz, 1984b), or strategies such as presenting a source but simultaneously mitigating responsibility.
- Orientation to the primacy of knowledge via codable actions and moves such as giving the most recent version of events by claiming or displaying A-side knowledge (Heritage, 2012a; Labov & Fanshel, 1977; Pomerantz, 1980), by producing a "no news marker" in the face of others' displayed or claimed knowledge, by reporting and informing, by assessing others' knowledge or by drawing in knowledgeable participants.
- Orienting to doing being a knowledgeable insider, displaying strong affinity to one's own knowledge via codable actions and strategies such as using jargon or specialist vocabulary, making relevant one's own institutional role and assessing and evaluating objects or information or by signposting names or objects (Goodwin, 2003).
- Orientation to testing others' knowledge by means of codable actions such as asking questions, try-marking or using or abstaining from using specialist vocabulary, explaining and pursuing confirmation of understanding and knowledge.
- Orientation to spotlighting others' lack of knowledge, thereby miscrediting their trustworthiness via codable actions such as other-initiated other-corrections, asking questions designed to reveal lack

of knowledge, using jargon, or by directly accusing others of not being knowledgeable.
- Orientation to confronting a presumed lack of others' ability via codable actions and strategies such as problematizing methods of reasoning or the reliability of data, and by questioning the ability to cooperate.

As is the case with regards to all the components of trustworthiness, the examples of codable actions, moves and strategies that we have identified and listed do not necessarily accomplish trustworthiness or the opposite *per se*. Although we see them as possible indicators of local orientation to trustworthiness when the local sequential environment makes it relevant to do so, they remain context-sensitive.

This chapter has explored different manifestations of participants' orientations to knowledge and ability, competence and mandate, all as foregrounded in stretches of talk. We have treated these two vast research areas together, recognizing that the research fields of epistemics and deontics are usually the appropriate homes of such discussion. This decision is debatable. We have, however, chosen to point to the components of trustworthiness which encompass different aspects of competence, and which epistemics and deontics embrace.

'Being in charge' is an aspect of ability which is detached from being knowledgeable. Solely having the mandate or the deontic authority (Stevanovic & Peräkylä, 2012; Lindström & Weatherall, 2015) to make decisions or to call the shots is possible without being knowledgeable. So that, in and of itself, does not make a person trustworthy. On the contrary, being skilled and capable requires knowledge about what a participant is skilled in or capable of. This illustrates the intertwined character of the four orientations that we have thematized earlier in this book, to which we will return in the concluding discussion.

8 Orientation to consistency and predictability

If people are to consider you trustworthy, it cannot just be on a lucky day. They need to see a pattern of behavior and appearance that suggests you are to be trusted. The best thing is to be consistently trustworthy in all aspects all the time – that is, by building a track record and earning goodwill. The next best thing is to be trustworthy in some respects, so that it becomes predictable when you are being honest, competent and altruistic, and when you are not. That way, if people know they cannot trust you in a certain respect, they should at least be able to predict your behavior because they trust their experience of you. If you are a loose cannon, people will be cautious.

Since everything happens on the 'surface', as we discussed in Chapter 2, we do not really *know* if we can trust a person. We can only judge from their actions and appearance, and these can be faked, as has also been evident from the last three chapters. Scammers and con artists may have similar member's competences to honest people, drawing on the same common-sense knowledge about societal 'normalcy' and plausible stories and behavior. They may also be capable of producing locally relevant character-bound displays, potentially creating inferences of trustworthiness (Garfinkel, 1967, pp. 76–103; Sacks, 1995, Part 1, pp. 113–117, 255; cf. Komter, 2003). However, as Abraham Lincoln has been famously quoted as saying, "You can fool all the people some

DOI: 10.4324/9781003280903-8

of the time, and some of the people all the time, but you cannot fool all the people all the time". Even the most skilled swindlers, excelling in their ability to exploit how to appear trustworthy, may eventually fail to be consistent. There is probably always some corner of their life where the truth will come out. Therefore, consistency is important for being trustworthy.

In this chapter, we explore how trustworthiness is related to predictability, orderliness and consistency. Predictability is a local as well as a global matter, and a general as well as a personal concern for participants. In the interaction, we see participants orient to it all, and we argue that it is both a local concern and a meta-orientation. We will show how predictability may be seen in at least three different ways: as social-systemic predictability of the interactional order, as based on experience and as a matter of local interactional projectivity. As is the case in the three previous chapters, more than one orientation may be present in any stretch of talk-in-interaction, but in each excerpt, we focus on the orientation(s) foregrounded by the participants *in situ*.

Doing being normal provides social-systemic predictability

For decades, predictability, consistency and normalcy have consistently (*sic!*) been in focus in EM/CA. Consistency and predictability are related to normalcy, because only by knowing what 'normal' looks like can one act accordingly, thereby displaying an orientation to doing what ordinary people predictably and consistently do in a given situation. What constitutes normalcy, norms and members' orientation and adherence to those, was a keen interest for Garfinkel. In his 1963 "trust" paper, he pointed to the tacit norms and rules that people take for granted through their reactions to the systematic disruption of games and ordinary social routines. In his later work further exploring those routines, Garfinkel pointed to members of society orienting to specific, "concrete" norms of conduct:

> A society's members encounter and know the moral order as perceivably normal courses of action – familiar scenes of everyday affairs, the world of daily life known in common with others and with others taken for granted.
>
> (Garfinkel, 1964, p. 225)

Garfinkel pointed to norms being tacitly but constantly oriented to by people: When explaining a "normal action", such as returning a greeting with "hello", people merely cite the norm, whereas "to explain breaches of the norm, we cite accounts which are overwhelmingly treated as excuses or justifications for the breach: 'I didn't hear him,' 'I had a terrible hangover, . . . ' " (Heritage, 1984, p. 116; Garfinkel, 1964). In other words, the more basic the questions that appear 'out of the ordinary', the more pressure is applied to test for normalcy. This was made very visible in Garfinkel's breaching experiments, when he asked his students to seek clarification of people's commonplace remarks without them knowing why. An example is set out next.

Example 8.1 What's the matter with you? (Garfinkel, 1967, p. 43)

"On Friday night my husband and I were watching television. My husband remarked that he was tired. I asked, 'How are you tired? Physically, mentally or just bored?'"

(S) I don't know, I guess physically, mainly.

(E) You mean that your muscles ache or your bones?

(S) I guess so. Don't be so technical.

(After more watching)

(S) All these old movies have the same kind of old iron bedsteads in them.

(E) What do you mean? Do you mean all old movies, or some of them, or just the ones you have seen?

(S) What's the matter with you. You know what I mean.

(E) I wish you'd be more specific.

(S) You know what I mean! Drop dead!

The core of the breaching experiment that the wife exposed her husband to here was not to do the expected: namely, to produce an acknowledgment or co-assessment or sympathetic remark of sorts, but instead to inquire about the type of tiredness or the kind of movies, and to insist on asking follow-up questions until he specifically objected to it ("Don't be so technical", "You know what I mean! Drop dead!"). Asking for clarification was treated as 'not normal' in that situation, and an offensive action.

Via these breaches, Garfinkel was able to point to the taken-for-granted background assumptions, tacit behavioral norms and "perceived normal" courses of conduct through which ordinary members of society constitute ordinary social scenes (cf. Heritage, 1984). Members' competences include understanding these norms and orienting to them, and members gain these competences by living in, and experiencing, the world (Garfinkel, 1963). The point we are trying to make here is that people have experience with how things normally work, and therefore very specific knowledge of what to expect and how 'normal' people behave. This equips them to reproduce that normalcy. Also, people orient very strongly to coming across as, or acting as, 'normal' in their social setting.[1]

Sacks also took an interest in what constitutes "normal" or "ordinary" behavior when people were 'doing being ordinary'. He declared: "You cannot have a nervous breakdown because you happened to see an automobile accident. You cannot make much more of it than what anybody would make of it" (Sacks, 1984, p. 427). Also, you cannot call people in the middle of the night without having a reason for calling, and without stating that reason at the beginning of the call (*ibid.*, p. 427). Behaving out of the ordinary would be accountable and treated by co-participants as such.

Building on Sacks, Gail Jefferson also studied how 'normal' is achieved. When people encounter or witness extraordinary events and are later giving reports of these, they often use a "normalizing device". That is, first giving an explanation of the incident as something ordinary or 'normal', before presenting the extraordinary event they realized had actually happened later. This, Jefferson – inspired by Sacks (1984) – has coined the "At first I thought X, Then I realized Y" format (2004a, p. 145). It can be seen in example 8.2 on p. 139, taken from the hearings conducted after John F. Kennedy was shot. Reportedly, the first thought that came to mind for this witness was not that the president was under attack, but that something 'ordinary', like a motorcycle backfiring, was happening.

Using these normalizing devices, such as the "At first I thought X, Then I realized Y" format, orient to being perceived as not prone to exaggeration, not being overly dramatic, etc. As such, participants are oriented to being normal, that is, consistently and predictably recounting things as they usually 'are'.

Later, Edwards deals with the issue of normalizing and normalcy and points to "doing being ordinary" as being "not prone to tell tall stories, nor to experience and report extraordinary events, nor [to] over-interpret mundane events as extraordinary" (Edwards 2007, p. 33). He also points

1 What constitutes such normalcy is entirely dependent upon the specific social system, but that is an (important) discussion which is beyond the scope of this chapter.

Example 8.2 I heard what I thought was the backfire of a motorcycle (Jefferson, 2004a, p. 153)

(44) [Warren Report, Written Statement, William R. Greer, SS, p. 320]
((Greer was driving the Presidential limousine))

I was looking at the overpass that we were about to pass under in case
→ someone was on top of it, when I heard what I thought was the backfire of a motorcycle behind the President's automobile. After the second shot, I glanced over my right shoulder and saw Governor Connally start to fall.
→ I knew then that something was wrong and I immediately pushed the accelerator to the floor...

to Wooffitt (1991), who found systematic use of another device related to the one Jefferson pointed out: "I was just doing mundane X, when extraordinary Y happened" (p. 34). This can be found in reports of supernatural experiences. Edwards points out that what these devices do is to "manage subjectivity in the course of relating a potentially dubious factual account" (Edwards 2007, p. 34), making it salient that what happened was actually happening in the world and "not in the speaker's head or imagination" (p. 34).

Heritage and Clayman show how callers to emergency dispatchers are not only providing descriptions of a problem for which they are seeking help, but also working at being perceived as "genuine", "trustworthy", and "believable" by the call-taker (2010, pp. 72, 76). In addition to using normalizing devices (Jefferson, 2004a), as mentioned earlier, they orient to their normal, everyday reason for being at the location where something extraordinary takes place, and to their doing normal activities when they encounter the unusual problem that they have called to report (Heritage & Clayman, 2010, cf. Bergmann, 1993). This is evident in Example 8.3.

Example 8.3 I was just walking up University Avenue (from Heritage & Clayman 2010, p. 76)

(11) [MCE 17: 11–12: 20]

```
1 911:       Midcity p'lice an' fire,
2            (0.5)
3 Clr:       Ye:s, I'd like to report an a:cciden'
4            (0.8)
5         →  igh- augh- I was just walking up University Avenue
6         →  an' jus' seen two cars colli:de...
```

Here the caller orients to doing the ordinary activity of "just walking up University Avenue" (l. 5) when he sees the collision he has just called to report. We see l. 5 as an example of a character-bound display of normalcy.

Overall, Heritage and Clayman (2010) draw attention to callers explaining and accounting for why they were at a scene, their claiming of proper motivation for calling, their orienting to appearing as someone doing routine and normal activities – and therefore being not just normal but believable, trustworthy; that is, as someone doing predictable activities rather than being dramatic or prone to jump to conclusions.

One kind of predictability is thus the socially constructed normalcy which is related to predictable behavior within a respective social system whereby members orient to tacit norms of sociality when they are living out their everyday lives, and when doing so, come off as normal or ordinary. This represents a social-systemic predictability of the interactional order.

Predictability and experience

Another kind of predictability is related to the co-participants' experience with a specific person. This represents a 'global predictability'. In other branches of trust research, this is studied as 'particularized trust', which is defined as being based on experiences with concrete persons in their mutual social relations. That means having knowledge about that person's behavior, ethics, morals, etc., to a point where the 'guess' that someone is trustworthy or not can be qualified (Sztompka, 1999). Such perceptions are based on an individual assessment of the other's motives and competences (Misztal, 1995; Uslaner, 2002; Hardin, 2004; Grimen, 2009). This point is so fundamental to certain strands of trust research that the very definition of trust relies on the perceived consistency and predictability of the trustee's behavior (see Hardin, 2001, 2002; Reiersen, 2017; Lewicki & Brinsfield, 2015; Cook & Santana, 2017). We will not be discussing this line of research or this aspect of trustworthiness further here. We do, however, suggest that this kind of very specific member's competence (i.e. in knowing a particular person in their usual social habitat, and using such knowledge to determine the concrete others' predictability and consistency) constitutes a very specific knowledge of what interactional order to expect adherence to. We also find that its study might benefit from taking further into account Garfinkel's breaching experiments, as well as EM/CA work on sequentiality and references to persons.

For analysts to detect the behavioral patterns which form such a 'meta' orientation would require a longitudinal study beyond the scope of this book. Even so, interactants sometimes explicitly voice matters of consistency and predictability as a concern in their local interaction, making it a locally relevant orientation. In social interaction, we see this orientation to consistency and predictability across encounters and domains. It is oriented to in references to predictable behavior or reactions like "he/she is gonna say", "my mom's gonna be angry" or "don't worry; he always does that". Other examples of global predictability are references to persons as always (or never) showing up on time, always (or never) hiding facts, etc.

In what follows, we look at an extract from a meeting in the communications department of a large global corporation. Two of the employees (M2 and M3) discuss with the department chair (M1) and his secretary (W1) the cross-cultural understanding of the color of a recently produced company calendar which will be used worldwide.

Example 8.4 If they can trip over something

1	M2	så sagde jeg (.) nå (.) hvad med den blå farve (.) det er jo en sorgens farve (.) så sagde hun ah (0.8) nobody cares (0.5) **then I said (.) well (.) what about the blue color (.) it is y'know a color of grief (.) then she said ah (0.8) nobody cares (0.5)**
2	M	når når [M2] lige føjer den er jeg (.) fordi [navn på vice CEO] som jo altid skal blande sig (.) havde jo (.) øh sagt (.) da han havde fået kalenderen i hånden (0.6) det er jo en helt skrup forkert blå farve (.) den betyder sorg i Kina (.) eh eh (.) og I kender (.) divisionshaverne i **when [M2] right now adds this I am (.) because [name of deputy CEO] who y'know always must interfere (.) had y'know (.) eh said (.) when he had got the calendar in his hand (0.6) that is an entirely grossly wrong blue color (.) it means grief in China (.) eh eh (.) and you know (.) the executive officers in**
3	M2	nå for Satan **oh my lord**
4	M1	det her hus her (.) hvis de kan falde over noget (.) der i den grad joøh med stor glæde (.) så (.) hugger de til (.) **this house here (.) if they can trip over something (.) that indeed y'know eh with great pleasure (.) then they go for the throat**
5	M3	med stor glæde **with great pleasure**
6	W1	når det hele er udsendt HEH he **when it is all sent out HEH he**

In this extract, we see the participants agreeing on, and sharing their frustrations about, how one of the executive officers tends to interfere ("who y'know always must interfere", l. 2), and how all the executive officers take pleasure in finding flaws and pointing them out (l. 4–5), preferably in retrospect (l. 6). The group continues talking about how they manage these top managers with a "stiff upper lip" (quote not shown in the preceding extract), since their judgment is not to be respected. The communications department treats this behavior by executive officers as habitual and predictable, apparently not building their credibility as executive decision-makers. We can see this extract as an interactional negotiation of (others') predictability, but the identities as predictable are ascribed by the participants to the non-present executive officers, based on their former actions. The reported utterances of the executive officers are interpreted and discussed in retrospect by the now locally present participants, who thereby orient to the predictability of the former.

Being perceived as trustworthy across sequences, encounters, situations and social contexts would entail trustworthiness to be a primary identity for the participant. Therefore, consistency is a meta-orientation which is drawn upon in matters of reputation and goodwill, in comparison with the 'global predictability' mentioned previously.

Predictability and interactional projectivity

A third locus for observing predictability is situational normalcy. Examples of local (situated) predictability are people saying "sorry" when bumping into one another. The orderliness of predictable moves has been examined by Liberman in his study of pedestrians and drivers at a busy street crossing, for example, (2013). The earliest CA work on turn-taking, possible completion points, overlap, preference organization, second pair part restrictions and turn projectability (Pomerantz, 1984a; Sacks *et al.*, 1974; Schegloff & Sacks, 1973) represents a strong research interest in uncovering this kind of very fundamental predictability – the kind which constitutes and enables the interaction order.

An aspect of this is the ability to predict not just when, but how, a turn will end. Collaborative or anticipatory completions are examples of this (Lerner, 1996; Bolden *et al.*, 2019). One taken from mundane interaction between friends can be seen in Example 8.5.

Example 8.5 Wait another three weeks (from Bolden et al., 2019)

```
Ger:    .hh Bec'z, (.) we don't wanna see one another, (.) .k.hh
        onna weekend where we jist have (.) yihknow two da:ys if
        e[ ven tha] :t.
Shi:      [ Right, ]
        (.)
Shi:    .t I[ don't blame you.]
Ger:        [ tuh relate tuh o] ne another. .hh Yihknow we'd like-
        (.) a little bit longer then tha:t.
        (0.2)
Shi:    Right,=
Ger:   I mean I don't (.) that much. But he does.
       (0.4)
Shi:   Ri[ ght.
Ger:     [ En it doesn't matter et this point I've waited this long
       I[ c'n (wait).
Shi:    [c'n wait another three wee:ks.
Ger:   Ye:ah,
Shi:   .hh W'l that's good.
       (0.2)
```

Here, Geri and Shirley are talking about how Geri and her boyfriend might not be seeing each other for some time. In l. 16, Shirley produces an anticipatory completion of Geri's sentence. Bolden *et al.* argue that Shirley uses this anticipatory completion to "demonstrate her support and affiliation with the stance Geri is formulating" (2019, p. 145). The way she does this requires more than turn projectability. Being able to finish each other's utterances may also rely on a member's competence and personal experience with that person, and the topics and interests that he or she consistently has, or that are well known within the social system to which the interactants belong. All of this is an orientation to predictability. Also, the competence involved in being able to perform such anticipatory completions is the kind of very specific member's knowledge of a particular person in their usual social habitat, which we discussed in the preceding paragraph, or of the specific social system(s) they belong to. Being consistent may, therefore, contribute to smooth social encounters – but however intriguing this is, it is a topic beyond the scope of this chapter. This kind of predictability (that is, interactional projectivity) does not have to do with trustworthiness *per se*. However, as we discussed in Chapter 3 and Chapter 5, breaches to such norms of the interaction order by means of, for example, producing misaligned, misplaced, unfitted or delayed utterances, when compared to what would be the local sequential norm, might be perceived as fishy or untrustworthy behavior.

Predictability and role compliance

Normalcy, projectability, predictability and consistency all bleed into role expectations (also see Chapter 6, p. 93 on "Negotiations of role compliance and living up to expectations") which members of society have toward one another: Teachers, lawyers, 911 dispatchers, doctors and so on are all expected to act in a certain way. This can be seen as being oriented to when they do something perceived as being outside their role.

One example whereby role expectations, normalcy, and consistency are oriented to strongly is in 911 calls. Here, the call-takers have the role of gate-keepers (Heritage & Clayman, 2010). They make sure that the call is about a genuine problem by holding callers accountable for presenting a problem-based justification for their request for assistance, and by seeking assurance that they are not mistaken about what has happened, that they are not giving malicious reports and they are not suffering from irrational paranoia. A basic example of this can be seen in Example 8.6.

In l. 6, the caller presents the problem as "an emergency", before requesting assistance from the police (PD). The PD orients to this as insufficient – as can be seen in l. 10, where PD asks for clarification, especially in l. 12, where the caller is ordered to "find out". When the caller cannot provide a description of the problem, the PD takes on the

Example 8.6 We have to know what we are sending on (from Zimmerman, 1992, pp. 436–437, as cited in Heritage & Clayman, 2010, p. 69)

```
(2) [Zimmerman, 1992: 436–7]
 1  PD:    Police Department.
 2         ( )
 3  Clr:   Yes This is the Ambassador Hotel Em- Ambassador Hotel?
 4         ((echo: Hotel))
 5  Clr:   Do you hear me?
 6         (.)
 7  PD:    Yeah _I hear you.
 8  Clr:   Uh they have an emergency=They want thuh police to thuh
 9         kitchen right away.
10  PD:    What kind of an emergency?
11  Clr:   I don't know honey They hung up I don't know [what's happening
12  PD:                                                 [Well find out,
13         (.)
14  PD:    We don't send out without=
15  Clr:   =I beg your pardon?
16         (0.5)
17  PD:    We have to know what we're sending on.
```

gatekeeper role, informing her/him that "We don't send out without=" (l. 14), before continuing in l. 15 with an explanation of what knowledge must be provided for them to send out police assistance. The caller's assessment of what constitutes an emergency is not treated as trustworthy, and therefore, the caller is not treated as trustworthy. The reason is that the caller is not behaving like a caller to an emergency service is expected (or instructed) to by dispatchers. A remedy is suggested ("find out", l. 12), which is connected with two of the other components of trustworthiness – knowledge and ability – as well as with truth and honesty.

Claims of deviant behavior and inconsistency as defense material

Consistency – or rather, the lack of it – is also a resort. Participants may resort to claims of their own inconsistency when they are defending themselves against negative implications, or resisting accusations. Arminen (2005) has pointed toward participants' orientation to consistency and coherence in psychotherapy sessions (p. 155) or job interviews (p. 159), when they make claims and link this to personal integrity.

The flip side of this is using inconsistent actions as a defense strategy against accusations of malefic or illegitimate behavior. We can see examples of this in interaction when someone is reportedly acting "out of character", or is noticed or commented upon with such expressions as "you don't usually do X", or that someone is "not the person I know".

In the following example, we can see an example of this from a police interrogation about theft and possible violent behavior.

Example 8.7 I'm not that type of person (from Edwards, 2006a, p. 476)

S: I didn' push the woman or nothin, (0.5) I really
did not do that.= I'm not that type of person
y'know what I me:an. .h Fair enough I stole the
→ ciggies, (0.9) I wouldn' hurt an old lady.

Here, the suspect (S) uses the self-characterization "I'm not that type of person" – that is, someone who would "hurt an old lady". He orients to being a person who lives up to the norms regarding how one treats older women, and the social expectations of a man who might steal cigarettes but who would never push an old woman. We see that move as a character-bound display.

Edwards (2006a) has pointed out that suspects in police interrogations use the modal verb "would" to claim their disposition to act in ways inconsistent with whatever offense they are accused of committing. One example, taken from the same police interrogation as Example 8.7, can be found in what follows.

Example 8.8 I wouldn't do that (from Edwards, 2006a, p. 479)

(1) PW:1:15
P: But she said (0.2) that she was pushed backwards
by yourself.= Now I've been to see this lady
yesterday. .hhh And at the (.) bottom: r:ight hand
side of her back (0.4) she's got a (.) brui:se
about the size about a fifty pence piece.=
S: =Well then somebody else has done that mate.
→ I wouldn'I ↑wouldn't do that. No I'll admit to
stealin the ciggies, right .hh but they were on the
counter, .h I did not jump over no counter for them.

We see the move in l. 7 ("I wouldn'I ↑wouldn't do that") as a character-bound display (CBD), and the entire example as a sequential negotiation of character (SNOC).

Studies of courtroom interaction have identified a range of interactional strategies used in interrogations and cross-examinations to (mis) credit witnesses, plaintiffs or defendants in courtrooms – such as pointing to their prior experiences and actions (Atkinson & Drew, 1979, also see Drew, 1985), either to magnify or mitigate the problematic character of their reported actions. Consistency and inconsistency are therefore important in courtroom interaction, especially when establishing trustworthiness and guilt. It is aggravating if a person has undertaken some deed several times, or repeatedly over decades. Equally, it is a mitigating circumstance if something only happened once, or accidentally. Moreover, in courtroom interaction, the extreme-case version of resorting to inconsistency claims as a defense is the temporary insanity plea, which must be the ultimate claim to inconsistency in order to build trustworthiness.

Predictability of untrustworthiness as last resort

The last suborientation is to be predictable if nothing else. Sometimes, people are found to be neither truthful nor honest, neither capable nor knowledgeable, but rather dishonest, self-serving and/or incompetent – and they are found to be consistently so. One can say that they are predictably untrustworthy. Such predictability can be the last resort, because if trustworthiness is not expected of someone, at least one knows what else to expect and how to behave accordingly. This is exactly the type of people management that the meeting participants are discussing in Example 8.4 where the two employees orient to the executive officers being predictably nosy and consistently meddling in the business of others ("always must interfere"). Also, they are seen as going "for the throat" at any opportunity. Such behavior does not build their credibility as executive decision-makers.

Summing up the orientation to consistency and predictability as a member's concern

This chapter has explored how interactants orient to consistency and predictability when they negotiate trustworthiness mutually, in interaction. The essence of orientation to consistency is that trustworthiness is linked to predictability, and predictability is linked to what members in a given social context construct as the normal thing to do in that context or the experience of what a particular person usually does. Interactional strategies indicative of this orientation to normalcy and predictability includes different normalizing devices, and other codable moves such as the following.

- Orienting to normalcy by accounts of one's actions as being not out of the ordinary by using normalizing devices (Jefferson, 2004a; Sacks, 1984; Edwards & Fasulo, 2006) and by treating breaches of norms as just that, explaining them through accounts involving excuses and justifications (Garfinkel, 1964; Heritage, 1984).

- Orienting to predictability and living up to expectations by self and other characterizations as "(not) that kind of person" (Edwards, 2006a, p. 476, 479) and the use of never/always in, for example, compliments and accusations.
- Orienting to consistency and predictability by referring to (future, potential) predictable behavior, or reactions such as "he/she is gonna say", "my mom's gonna be angry" or "don't worry; he always does that".
- Orienting to predictability and role expectations by adhering to, or making locally relevant, protocol, rules and 'how things are normally done'.
- Orienting to something being deviant or 'out of character' by using "would" to claim a certain disposition.

Being perceived as trustworthy across sequences, encounters, situations and social contexts would entail trustworthiness being a primary and consistent identity for the participant. This orientation is, therefore, both a local members' concern and a meta-orientation.

9 Concluding discussion

We have not studied trustworthiness. Figuratively speaking, our study of trustworthiness resembles René Magritte's famous painting, *Ceci n'est pas une pipe*. Just as his painting was a picture of a pipe, not the real pipe, we have not studied trustworthiness *per se*, as it is a mental concept.

DOI: 10.4324/9781003280903-9

In the first section of the book, we introduced the research in rhetoric, together with different strands of research in trustworthiness which serve as a backdrop for our study, revealing our pathway to this book and why we find the examination of interactional orientation to trustworthiness such a worthwhile endeavor. We have then approached trustworthiness as a social phenomenon within an EM/CA framework. We have done so by ethnomethodologically re-specifying trustworthiness. We have further conceptualized and studied it using premises, methods and analytical techniques found in EM/CA.

Our research endeavor has thus been to reconceptualize an abstract social concept and study it as an empirical interactional research object. We have defined trustworthiness as an interactional phenomenon in the following way:

> A perceptual outcome (i.e. a social construct) achieved in dynamic interactional negotiation of identity, realized by person A's observable interactional actions, moves, and strategies that manifest orientations to one or more components of trustworthiness (those being truth and honesty, stake and interest, ability and knowledge, and/or consistency and predictability) in interaction with person B; which may be identifiable and codable, which may appear in clusters of displays, or be noticeably absent or misplaced, and which may therefore foreground one or more components.

We have been particularly inspired by the hundreds of CA analyses carried out over the past sixty years which have paved the way for our own exploration of abstract identity projects as a valid EM/CA research object. We have supported our analyses of orientations to trustworthiness with research conducted within the EM/CA framework. Many of our examples have come from exemplary CA research on the equivalents of character and character traits. We have reviewed these as examples of EM/CA studies of local micro-level manifestations of participants' displays of traits and features, which each of the four orientations encompass. None of these studies were conducted with trustworthiness in mind. Even so, they are all concerned with one or more of the actions, moves or strategies that we have now identified in our research as potential indicators of orientations to trustworthiness. In this way, we have acknowledged a large number of EM/CA studies which have independently explored niches and corners of our orientations, seeing them as inspiration for our own study.

Our theoretical and empirical contribution

What we have presented in this book is not traditional CA. We have stepped away from the tempting blackboxing (cf. Latour, 1999) of the concept of "members' competence". We have approached an etic and abstract social phenomenon and reconceptualized it in an EM/CA context. We have therefore taken seriously that, if there is such a thing in the social world as 'being trustworthy', then we not only regard it as any participant's concern to achieve and identify it – we also find it to be a phenomenon worthy of scholarly treatment.

We have pointed out how interactants continuously make social judgments of each other based on observations of their mutual behavior, and that trustworthiness is an example of an abstract term inferred from such judgments. Thus, it is below the line of observable behavior. We have therefore taken time to explore the link between above-the-line, observable, physical and embodied actions *in situ*, and below-the-line assessments of our own or others' trustworthiness. We have argued that being perceived as trustworthy is an identity project for participants in interaction, and that this endeavor is observable as displayed to co-participants, as well as to analysts. Also, assessing the trustworthiness of others is a participant's concern, oriented to in interaction, and thus observable both to co-participants and to analysts.

Four orientations

Building on rhetoric, trust research in the social sciences, psychology and EM/CA, as well as the study of some aspects of trustworthiness in discursive psychology and our findings from analysis of our own data, we have identified four orientations to trustworthiness: truth and honesty, stake and interest, knowledge and ability, and consistency and predictability. We have explored these orientations as empirically observable phenomena via analyses of data excerpts that show interactants foregrounding very different aspects of trustworthiness. What is foregrounded depends upon their relation, situation, and additional interactional projects. We have then used this analytic work to further inform our theoretical conceptualization via an abductive process.

Character-bound displays and clusters of indicators

Our theoretical conceptualization of trustworthiness as an interactional phenomenon has been provided using an analytical EM/CA framework. We have explored how an etic construct such as trustworthiness may be identified and analyzed through clusters of indicators by breaking it down to four participant orientations, all of which manifest themselves on the 'observable surface' of human interaction. Via our empirical conceptualization, we have defined trustworthiness as a social and dynamic phenomenon in which interactants may foreground and negotiate (clusters of) indicators of trustworthiness. One term we have proposed for interactional strategies, moves and actions that may be seen or heard as orienting to the participants' own character traits related to trustworthiness is 'character-bound displays' (CBDs). We took inspiration from Sacks' notion of category-bound activities (Sacks, 1992) when proposing our notion of the character-bound display of one's own trustworthiness, and we explored the sequentially negotiated orientation to character, both one's own and that of others, by means of actions, moves and interactional strategies. These CBDs include participants' displays of orientation to one or more components of trustworthiness relevant for a particular encounter which might activate a perception of a certain character; that is, they can be seen as or heard that way (cf. Sacks, 1972a) by the other participant(s). These character-bound displays can either be unprompted/self-initiated or initiated by others in the interaction. This work on displays is fundamental and may be expanded to the study of the 'doing of' the interactional accomplishments of other social identity aspects.

Sequential negotiation of character and socially distributed clusters

We have pointed out how social character is socially negotiated over stretches of talk in sequences of embodied talk-in-interaction. We have proposed the term 'sequential negotiation of character', this time abbreviated SNOC, for this phenomenon. We believe that this idea may also be extended to the study of other phenomena than the ones covered in this book.

When working with clusters of indicators manifested over multiple turns at talk in sequential negotiations of character, we have speculated if they could be seen as 'socially distributed clusters of indicators'. We find this to be a phenomenon just as compelling as socially distributed cognition (cf. Due, 2016). However, both phenomena might be mere aspects of intersubjectivity, or simply 'interactional negotiation'. This could form a topic for examination in an independent paper.

Indicators of orientations to trustworthiness

Our study has distilled the social construct of the character trait 'trustworthiness' into four components to which participants orient, each carved into a range of subcategories that are respectively manifested in several indicators in the shape of social actions, moves and interactional strategies, as illustrated in Figure 9.1.

Material listed in the figure is far from an exhaustive list, as such lists are impossible. It is meant merely to be an illustration of what is possible. In our case, they are useful in the sense of being pedagogical, but will always be a work in progress. Interactants can demonstrably implement and combine codable strategies, moves and actions through an almost endless range of linguistic formats. Exemplifying everything is

Character trait	Components	Practices (selected examples)	Indicators (selected examples), not constitutive or stand-alone, but potentially codable actions, moves, and interactional strategies
Trustworthiness	Truth & honesty	• Negotiating the quality of facts and information • Creating openness and transparency by giving access to information • Pursuing response in cases of reluctance and minimalism	• Correcting factual information • Describing procedure in detail • Asking follow-up questions to evasive answers
	Stake & interest	• Negotiating stance and subjectivity • Doing neutrality • Displaying, denying, and negotiating bias • Negotiating benefactive status	• Making footings shift to bring in other voices • Offering factual claims as reluctantly arrived at • Working to undermine factual ground for others' claims • Questioning the neutrality of others • Voicing the potential expectations of others
	Knowledge & ability	• Confronting presented facts • Negotiating degrees of knowledge • Assessing the quality of sources of knowledge • Testing others' knowledge • Miscrediting others by spotlighting their lack of knowledge	• Using mitigation devices • Referring to A/B-side knowledge • Try-marking references • Referring to lack of knowledge in order to evade responsibility • Using lack of mandate as a resource for rejection
	Consistency & predictability	• Doing "being normal" • Voicing predictability • Formulating role expectations • Adhering to or voicing procedure • Conforming to interactional projectivity	• Using normalizing devices • Including "never"/"always" in, e.g., compliments and accusations • Making references to locally relevant protocol, rules, and "how things are normally done" • Formulating predictable behavior by referencing future third-party reactions • Claiming an action to be "out of character"

Figure 9.1 Our proposed components of trustworthiness, which in combination constitute our theoretical and empirical conceptualization, and some of the identified indicators of each component (with inspiration from Clayman and Heritage's study from 2002 on adversarialness with respect to character trait, dimensions, and indicators).

self-evidently impossible here; neither is it what we have set out to do. What we have pointed to as codable phenomena here are not specific micro-level actions, formats or tokens, but the range of actions, strategies and moves participants use locally to orient to one or more dimensions of their own and others' trustworthiness. As stated in Chapter 2 and Chapter 3, none of these isolated actions, strategies or moves are indicative of trustworthiness *per se*; rather, it is their local turn-by-turn sequential unfolding in a context whereby the orientation to trustworthiness becomes apparent – especially when these actions, strategies, and moves appear as clusters of indicators.

Our contribution to prior research

Following this discussion of our research contribution, we would also like to discuss how we see our work contributing to the theoretical backdrop outlined and reviewed in Chapter 3.

Our contribution to rhetoric research includes showing that a research interest in trustworthiness may be extended to social interaction, and that applying an EM/CA approach to this study may produce new and multifaceted findings. We do find that our study has propelled century-long research interest in ethos into new and greener pastures, and we anticipate a new subfield of rhetoric research growing from this.

Our main contribution to trust research in the social sciences is to expand and reconceptualize the research object and analytical material for studying trust and trustworthiness, and to develop a theoretical model which can inspire and affect much current research. Strands of research concerned with trust as action and behavior, or trust as mental or social process, might especially find our theoretical (as well as our empirical) conceptualizations to be worthy of further exploration. Datatypes more frequently used in these views include elicited data, such as experimental data, contextual inquiry, think-aloud protocols and – particularly – self-reported data (Nielsen & Nielsen, in review). Applying discourse or narrative analysis to self-reported data, such as interviews, might contribute to insights into participants' self-construction, and their own perception and conception of self with regard to the elements of our theoretical and empirical conceptualization, thus offering a different perspective (cf. Nielsen & Nielsen, in review).

Our contribution to psychology is to show how the study of perceived character in a diverse range of social settings may benefit from an open mind with respect to research methodology and the *loci* of concepts such as character traits or dispositions, which are traditionally studied as internal to the individual (also see Nielsen & Nielsen, in review). We find our exploration of the social machinery for the perceptions and strategies that interactants have to work with bringing new insights to the table.

We acknowledge that our work questions a good number of assumptions behind much research into trust-related matters, both in psychology and in the social sciences. We propose that our methodology provides some of the answers posed by this questioning. For the same reasons, we do not expect our work to be universally welcomed – but if we do manage to trigger a sincere research debate within the various trust research communities, we feel that we will have accomplished an important mission.

Our contribution to discursive psychology (DP) is to show what may further come out of applying a mixture of text and interaction analytical tools to the study of human sociality, and also what is traditionally perceived as psychological phenomena. We have found that our object of analysis is very much within the realms of DP, and we believe that our colleagues from that field will take our ball and run with it. We cannot wait to applaud the goals they will score in doing that!

Our contribution to EM/CA is to widen the scope for which social phenomena the methodology may be applied to, to make a first step in the direction of a systematic study of character in social interaction and to develop an analytical apparatus of concepts and categories for that purpose. We believe that our work is a necessary and solid stepping stone toward further exploration and study of trust and trustworthiness in this field, because we have applied our apparatus to a broad range of different social settings.

We also see our work, especially our identification and analysis of codable – and thus, in principle, countable – indicators of components of trustworthiness and our work on clusters, as the first step toward an operationalization of trust, trustworthiness or both in future quantitative EM/CA studies. Quite possibly, it may also pave the way for quantitative CA studies of other abstract and complex social phenomena in interaction (A.M.R. Nielsen, in review). See also Chapter 2 for an overview of EM/CA and DP studies of complex social phenomena studied via inference from action.

While these may sound like big claims, we strongly believe that the legitimacy and efficacy of our research and our research object is clearly demonstrable from this book. The prospects of our decade-long research reside in the nitty gritty details of social negotiation of social identity, and not in the least trust and trustworthiness.

Discussion of our theoretical and empirical conceptualization

Our book offers both theoretical and empirical conceptualizations of trustworthiness, and neither is flawless. In what follows, we will raise and address a couple of significant issues that the theoretical conceptualization makes relevant.

Some orientations are more basic than others

As mentioned in Chapter 5, we find truth and honesty to be the basic and fundamental components of trustworthiness, and therefore, the most basic orientation to it, as well. If a person is not perceived by others to be honest and truthful, that person's trustworthiness is endangered with regard to everything else. In that context, any orientation to stake and interest, ability and knowledge, or consistency and predictability is essentially in vain, because they could just be part of the lie (see also Kjøller, 1991a). It is unsurprising, therefore, that we see orientations to truth and honesty branching out into all the other orientations. Participants' efforts to disclose their stake and interest in a matter, to claim or display the ability to do something, their knowledge about it, and their claim to normalcy and consistency – all these are often oriented simultaneously to truth and honesty.

In contrast to the other components, we argue that orientation to consistency and predictability can be identified as both a local concern and a meta-orientation to patterns oriented to in participants' references to predictable behavior, or in their reactions across encounters and domains that lie outside the current *in situ* interaction. This orientation also stands out because participants sometimes orient simply to someone being consistently and predictably 'not trustworthy' regarding all other components – that is, being neither truthful nor honest, nor open or transparent, nor knowledgeable or capable.

Overlapping orientations

The fact that one component is more fundamental than the others is visible in the overlaps in orientation to the components that we have identified. Orientation to stake and interest, or truth and ability, are rarely seen as standing alone, and a cluster of indicators will often consist of displays of (or other types of) orientations to two or more components, one being to truth and honesty. As evident from our review of CA literature and our analyses in Chapters 5–8, people in real-life conversations often orient to – and thus make relevant – two or even three or more components of trustworthiness in a given stretch of talk. One orientation may be foregrounded, while others may be backgrounded or used to facilitate the orientation, which is thereby made most locally relevant by the participant(s). For instance, facts – and thereby implicitly an orientation to knowledge and truth – may be part of a trade negotiation in which stake and interest are questioned and, therefore, mostly oriented to by participants.

However, we do argue that when we as analysts can see, identify and show in the data the participants' orientation to one or more components, it is meaningful to do so. Also, we believe that the benefit of our approach lies in the fact that we take seriously the interactants' emic endeavor: their being able both to construct themselves as trustworthy and to detect whether they can trust others by exploring the foundations for making such character assessments *in situ*. However, a relevant discussion to be had is whether it is valid to explore trustworthiness in any given analysis by pointing to only one or two orientations, those being the most pertinent and relevant ones for the interactant(s) in a given situation, even if they serve only pedagogical purposes. This distinction is theoretical and etic. It is a member's concern to assess trustworthiness, and as analysts, we share the resources to assess it. People's orientations to these can self-evidently be intertwined in many ways (e.g. disclosing one's lack of knowledge can display an orientation to honesty, knowledge and stake management), and the orientations will therefore be seen branching out into each other.

Discussion of the empirical approach

As with overlapping or interlacing orientations, there is no one-to-one relation between a codable phenomenon and an inferred orientation. We see a couple of challenges for carrying out this empirical work in practice.

When is a display a display?

By no means do we argue that all orientation to something is a matter of displaying something. Indeed, we are not sure that we can even grasp all the implications of such a sentence. In this book, we have chosen not to probe deeply into a discussion of what constitutes orientation as a member's phenomenon, when it is evidently an analyst's concept. We have used Nielsen and Toft's definition:

> We define "participant orientation" as an action, an etic category to describe participants' situated embodied (i.e., verbal, visual, facial, gestural, postural) moves that may display (to the analyst as well as to co-participants) their attention to some social, physical or procedural target in a scene in order to monitor, display availability to, and/or participate in it; in order to make topics, issues, incidents, objects or norms locally relevant to co-participants; or in order to pinpoint their orientation or shift of orientation. The orientation may be full or divided, foregrounded or backgrounded, single or multiple, upgraded with layered modalities in use or not, with change-of-orientation markers deployed or not, interactionally coordinated or not.
>
> (in review-b, p. 8–9)

While we have been watching more hours of video data than we can number, and have analyzed thousands of multimodal actions, we have paid close attention to what constitutes a display. In Chapter 3, with inspiration from Sacks (1972a), we define the concept of 'character-bound displays' (CBDs) as "interactional strategies, actions, and moves that might activate a perception of a certain character; that is, they can be seen as or heard that way by the interlocutor". As analysts, we argue that, using the very members' competences that Sacks pointed to, we are able to recognize specific (clusters of) displays oriented to making one's own character trait relevant. However, we still find it fruitful to discuss when a display *is* a display, and when someone orienting to another person doing or being something may also be considered a component of trustworthiness.

First, when someone says, "She always shows up on time" or "She never delivers properly", they certainly orient to the consistency, predictability and orderliness (or otherwise) of another person. But it is a statement ascribing an identity to somebody else which has to do with trustworthiness as character. It may very well contribute to the third-party perceptions of the person. However, we argue that no utterance can be a 'character-bound display' on behalf of another person who might not even be present. Also, it is not data that are comparable to, for example, observing a person joining a meeting ten minutes later than everybody else – while a co-participant demonstrably visibly looks at her watch, and the latecomer then promptly begins to produce excuses and accounts, as in the example discussed in Chapter 3. Here, Psathas's notion of *action-generated categories* (1999, p. 155) could prove a fruitful inspiration for future work on character, where exploring what actions function as displays of character in different contexts and settings might prove a useful addition to this line of research.

What is worth considering – and further examining – is whether, if a participant's assessment of a co-participant's consistency and predictability is negative, this assessment is then a character-bound display of their own consistency and predictability by comparison, or by calling out the lack of someone else's. Or is it merely part of a SNOC? It is certainly a foregrounded concern. Such matters, partly of philosophical and theoretical interest, need looking into further. We suggest taking Watson's notion of category-tied predicates (1978, 1983; also see Psathas, 1999) as a point of departure. These predicates are 'characteristics' of a category, and they are used by members to ascribe a specific category explicitly to a person, to oneself or to another, as they are commonsensically bound to these (e.g. "this mother [category] cares [predicate] tremendously for her baby" [Stokoe, 2012, p. 281]). Moreover, it might be fruitful to investigate and discuss the feasibility of a concept that might consequently be coined as 'character-tied predicates' as indicative of one or more of the four orientations.

Baseline required – and debatable

To see and recognize that something is being oriented to, one must know what it looks like when this is not the case. Therefore, a baseline for 'non-orientation' is required. This baseline, or the 'normality of mutual trust' from which our analyses of the participants' foregrounding of orientations to components of trustworthiness differ or stand out, is quite complicated to identify. We have made our best effort. We therefore begin each of our chapters on a particular orientation with an example of a trivial instance whereby we do not see any component of trustworthiness being made relevant by the participants. It is pertinent to discuss whether these baseline examples are just that – if trust and trustworthiness are so intertwined in every part of a social interaction that it is not feasible to identify when it is *not* oriented to, or if some settings are so low-risk for the participants that there is no need to orient to trustworthiness (cf. Watson, 2009), or indeed, if this aspect is actually the manifestation of ontological trust that Garfinkel set out to explore. Even so, we argue that when no orientation is foregrounded or made relevant by participants in the interaction, it is the baseline of 'normalcy', also when that normalcy is not being oriented to as such.

Note that when we use the word 'normalcy' here, we refer to trusting others as the default situation. We are not questioning their honesty, motives or expertise. The fact that we as authors are born and raised in a country that frequently rates as a 'high-trust society' (using a methodology that we are critical of, by the way) could also be a reason why we tend to think that social encounters with seemingly high levels of mutual trust are 'normal', and could therefore constitute a baseline. Examples of that high-level trust are people setting up tables outside their houses alongside public roads with fresh strawberries and change in little jars, expecting people to pay for them on trust; or young parents going to cafés with their newborn baby sound asleep in a huge pram parked right outside the café window, never expecting anybody to walk away with it.

If we are correct that this kind of upbringing might affect our sense of normalcy with respect to trust, our study might conceivably be differently designed and conducted. This could lead to different results, had we not had an upbringing equipping us with membership of trustful relationships and communities. We might have been able to 'see' other features of the interaction – and not see others – if we had lived other lives in other contexts ourselves. This is always true, however, and is a highly philosophical discussion which we are not really suited to participate in. Its implications are beyond our imagination. Moreover, making matters even worse, being able to recognize a baseline is a member's competence – so we as authors may only have the competence to see deviations from normalcies in social systems that we ourselves are familiar with. With this sentence, we are potentially pulling the rug from under half of our book, but this is the place to be honest about that.

Choice of data

We have mainly looked at what might be termed 'ordinary settings' rather than 'high-risk' ones. As mentioned previously, where we have looked at breaches of trust, we have – in the spirit of Sacks and following Watson – sought out "naturally occurring, naturally situated breaches rather than contrived ones" (Watson, 2009, p. 494). This means treating 'trust is the rule' as our baseline in the proposed data chapters.

Moreover, most of the data used in this book are from institutional settings. This makes the analyses it contains more comparable than would be the case if we also included (for example) parent–child interactions. But our data do not include all kinds of social settings, and that fact could have an impact on our results. However, we have no reason to believe that matters of truth and honesty, stake and interest, ability and knowledge, and consistency and predictability, do not apply to social encounters between friends and family, and children and adults. Still, showing that in the data would be needed in order to make that claim authoritatively.

By choosing data from 'ordinary' mostly low-risk settings, we may have made our project more difficult for ourselves. It is much harder to recognize trust if, in fact, it is the rule, than the opposite. This is a deliberate choice. We do believe that focusing on data where (mutual) inherent mistrust is the agenda would skew our results. Compare how some approaches to psychoanalysis have been criticized for being developed by studying mentally ill patients, and how some models of social assessment which have been developed by studying the motivation of alcoholics and other substance abusers (Miller *et al.*, 2008) have subsequently been used to conduct interviews screening for unemployment benefits, even though they are arguably not suited for this purpose (Miller & Rollnick, 2009; Hogden *et al.*, 2012). Of course, studying trust negotiations between participants in all walks of life – and in all kinds of settings – is necessary for developing a solid empirical base. But the foundation for that work, we believe, is to study the negotiation of trust in ordinary settings.

Breaches of norms, trustworthiness and perspicuous settings

We believe that it is worth raising the question as to whether CBDs, SNOCs or any other indicators of (e.g.) trustworthiness are actually more often found in contexts of breaches of norms and expectations. Garfinkel studied trust in the context of breaches (1963), and his 'trust conditions' were a result of his observations of such breaches. Watson points to "perspicuous instances" where orientation to others' trustworthiness can be clearly identified (2009, p. 490). He suggests that these perspicuous settings might render both trust and trustworthiness "particularly accessible and 'grasp-able' to the researcher" (p. 492).

In the tradition of Garfinkel's interventions, we see a supplementary approach being the option of looking at breaches of trust, since any orientation to the locally relevant components of trustworthiness would be foregrounded in such a situation. We agree with Rose that the study of breaches of trust should, indeed, be only supplementary at best. This is because:

> Doubt interrupts and is rare. Trust commonly prevails. . . . Trust as a rule is the rule, doubt the exception. As a rule people have to do

> with things through the exercise of trust pared by doubt occasionally, hardly ever by the exercise of doubt relieved occasionally by trust.
> (Rose, 1992, p. 170, as quoted in Watson, 2009, p. 494)

However, we do not know if instances of 'breaches of norms' are particularly perspicuous, and it is beyond the scope of this book to conclude this. What we do see, after all, is that in some situations, local identity projects (and thus the SNOC that indicates the orientation to trustworthiness) is foregrounded, whereas in other situations, it is backgrounded. Perhaps this is because it is presumed, or simply not deemed locally relevant.

Coding what is missing

Some discussion is needed regarding the codability (or not) of the absence of moves, strategies and actions oriented to some aspect of trustworthiness, or abstention from performing an action; that is, not volunteering information or detail, not telling the whole truth, not disclosing one's own stake and interest in a matter, etc. Sometimes we can recognize that something is noticeably absent (cf. Schegloff, 1972, p. 76; see also Pomerantz, 1984a). For example, we have identified what can be recognized as quite direct prompts for some type of character-bound display in our data. Equally, when the co-participant fails to produce these displays, they are noticeably absent. If a slot is created for a CBD, then the absence of it (a non-CBD, so to speak) is potentially a CBD in itself. At other times, however, determining whether something is noticeably absent is not even an option. This issue of determining whether something *could* have occurred (and is therefore potentially 'missing') in a given sequential context is not new. Schegloff dedicated large parts of his seminal paper on quantification in CA to this very challenge. He termed slots where a certain phenomenon could (or should) potentially be found, and thus, where they could be coded as missing, as "environments of possible relevant occurrence" (Schegloff, 1993, p. 102). It is beyond the scope of this book to delve further into this ongoing and complex discussion here (but see Heritage, 1995; De Ruiter, 2013; Stivers 2015; A.M.R. Nielsen, in review). However, this underlines the point that what *can* be studied here is not trustworthiness – or the lack of it – as a concept, but rather the participants' orientation to it. And that is exactly our research object.

Coding an action depends on the local and global context

The interactional construction and negotiation of trustworthiness is both context- and role-specific. For example, if two friends are talking casually over coffee, and one uses a specialist term in their conversation, other factors are at play than would be the case if a patient and a doctor were talking during a consultation, and the patient used a specialist term. (For examples and a discussion of the use of specialist terms in asymmetrical, institutional encounters, see Chapter 7, p. 117.) The participants' epistemic and deontic stances vary, making different displays relevant as orientations to trustworthiness, depending on the contexts and what the participants have at stake. The same moves, strategies and actions may therefore do very different work locally, and must be coded as displays of completely different orientations, dependent upon the local context. What should be a topic of an ongoing discussion is the question of how to ensure that any codable action, move or interactional strategy (or the lack of one, where it should relevantly occur) may indeed be indicative of an *in situ* orientation to trustworthiness – always taking into account not just the sequential context but also the larger context.

Defining clusters of indicators

We have argued that trustworthiness is an inferred social judgment based on members' observations of what we term 'clusters of indicators', and we have explored what may constitute such clusters. An obvious implication of our study would be to explore if and how the interactional moves, strategies and actions oriented to one or more component of trustworthiness may appear in clusters, so that impression management (cf. Goffman, 1959) is to be viewed as using particular micro-strategies that form a pattern. In the example with the Greek driver's license (see Chapter 5, p. 71), it was not the fact that the citizen repeatedly redesigned her utterances, or the detailed information she provided, that rendered her appearance suspicious *per se*. Rather, it was the combination of a pre-launched, lengthy account, marked by numerous redesigns incorporating shifts in tempo; her volunteering of unnecessarily detailed information; her resort to ambiguity even when it was possible to say something very precise ("50 km"), as well as the fact that the two citizens conferred with each other at low volume and used code-switching (to Greek) – that is, privately, to avoid being heard or understood by the (Danish-speaking) professional. Such a combination may ultimately be an example of a cluster of indicators which add up to potentially being seen and heard as not being trustworthy. It is, however, debatable as to whether it is fair and feasible to see and hear a strong focus in the interaction toward one orientation as an overly foregrounded orientation, and thus an indication of a lack of trustworthiness. More research is needed on this. If, for instance, a person is just very nervous about the severe potential implications of an encounter with a professional, then that person may strive so hard to appear trustworthy that merely trying too hard could turn it into a doomed interactional project. Compare this with the 'Othello error' (Ekman, 1992) shown in studies that non-criminals may produce the same lie implicating actions, moves and strategies as criminals – not because they lie, but because they fear not being believed by the police (Bond & Fahey, 1987; Ofshe & Leo, 1997a; Memon *et al.*, 2003, pp. 16, 29).

Participant versus analyst resources for determining components of trustworthiness

When exploring trustworthiness, we have found that it is crucial to distinguish between resources available to participants within the interaction and those available to analysts of the interaction. Even when drawing on one's own member's competence as an analyst, the two roles require different data and competence. They also use different languages about their observations in, or of, a social interaction. To illustrate this, we have set out in Figure 9.2 a sketch of the data, competencies and language available to participants and analysts, respectively. We have used the orientation to consistency as an example because it is also a meta-orientation, and because the possible/potential resources available to an interlocutor and an analyst, respectively, are likely to vary more than is the case with the other components, which are solely micro-orientations and thus local concerns. (See Chapter 8).

	Participants in a social encounter	**Analysts of social encounters**
Potentially available data for reviewing consistency	Prior experience with persons, situations and courses of action; acquired scripts related to genres and situations	Collections of examples of the same phenomena, e.g., uses of extreme case formulations (Pomerantz, 1986) containing "always" or "never". Longitudinal studies (Pekarek Doehler *et al.*, 2018; Wagner *et al.*, 2018)
Competence and strategies used to assess consistency	Member's competence, personal experience	Literature reviews, comparative studies, collection studies, member's competence
Linguistic forms and interactional strategies for referring to consistency or inconsistency	Expressions like: Normally, usually, always, habit, "normally I would but" vs. never, rarely, accidentally, "out of character", "I was not myself". "This is not you", "You know I am not like that", "I thought you would X, but then you Y"	Presenting default cases and using informal quantification: "overwhelmingly", "frequently" "typically" vs. "outlier", "infrequent", "atypical", "unusual", "out of the ordinary", "exception"

Figure 9.2 Examples of different data, competence and expressions used from the perspective of participants and analysts, respectively, when observing and referring to consistency.

We see a lot of potential in taking different perspectives as a point of departure, and in applying different research methodologies to a study of a given component of a character trait. However, in the next section, we will touch upon a couple of concerns related to the issue of methodology.

Time will test our project of revisiting trustworthiness

Since our approach to the study of trustworthiness – and thus, by proxy, also the trust someone is worthy of or not – is novel, it is obvious to ask if it is bold and ambitious and points forward; or whether, over time, it will come to seem tangential. Only time will tell. However, we can set out a couple of indicators that our work is pointing forwards, and may well inspire future work.

Our trustworthiness as scholars, or the credibility of our study

Even though trustworthiness is generally perceived as an attractive social identity, it is not necessarily considered advantageous in any and all situations. This is because trustworthiness implicates responsibility. We have therefore sought to show how core dimensions – such as lack of knowledge, ability or consistency – can be used to evade responsibility and reduce trouble.

We are happy to take on responsibility – and in our work, we do hope to come off as trustworthy ourselves. We feel strongly about the mission of basic university research – the search for truth and understanding. This book reflects our genuine aspiration to explore the concept of trustworthiness and, through that, to learn more about human sociality. We have worked hard to understand the many aspects of our work, as well as the work of others. Also, we have spent many hours reading, reflecting, analyzing, discussing, outlining, rethinking, rewriting and starting over again. This has been a journey which has enabled us to become better equipped to undertake this kind of work than we were at the outset. We have made an effort to credit all of our many excellent colleagues who have inspired this work, and we hope that we have been open about the shortcomings of our work. When we have, for example, quoted the works of others (findings, arguments, data excerpts), we have always made the declaration of those origins very visible. We have done this out of respect for their work, and in order to be able to present our arguments and findings in a pedagogic manner. We do not have anything particular at stake with respect to building research empires, or schools for specific approaches. That said, our reputation is at stake, of course. We have a strong interest in disseminating knowledge and letting wider audiences benefit from education. We hope that we have made sure to do this consistently throughout the book. We know that writing a paragraph like this, though often with slightly different wording, is also a rather predictable thing to do in the final pages of a book communicating the results of thousands of hours of work. We like that trait of the research community. We try to learn from each other, and we try to be open about how to go about this. We consider it a responsibility, and one that we are proud to share in.

Methodological prospects of our study

The study presented in this book is part of a larger research project on trust-in-action. Another study we have conducted within the scope of this project concerns the empirical study of trust as a relational and a social phenomenon from a multimethodological perspective (Nielsen & Nielsen, in review). In what follows in this section, we will elaborate upon and discuss how the present study in this book supports – and is contextualized by – our other study on trust methodology.

The trust methodology study is a review of trust conceptualizations and an ethnomethodologically founded method critique applied to commonly used trust research methods. In two maxims of empirical research inspired by EM we argue that: a) you cannot directly study social constructs and concepts found below the line of what is sensorially discernible by participants or analysts alike, since these etic constructs must be inferred from what is sensorially discernible (along the lines of the argumentation of Chapter 2 in this book); and b) that people's plans, perceptions and propensities – as well as any other social construct not sensorially discernible in social action – must be analytically distinguished from people's actual actions. The trust methodology study reviews ten different views of trust as identified in the trust research literature over the last decades. The review spans across the social sciences, psychology and political science, and we propose a taxonomy corresponding to trust conceptualizations. Subsequently, we explore how different types of data, sorted by what kind of access to peoples' actual real-life actions they afford, are currently used to study different aspects of trust and trusting in various strands of trust research. This critical review leads us to discuss the challenges concerning what it is possible to conclude about different aspects of trust based on different types of empirical data, and what it is not possible to conclude. We confront the lines of trust research broadly across the social sciences and psychology, which today base conclusions on research methodology which we would argue does not permit reaching the kind of conclusions made.

The trust methodology study also aims to contribute to the development of the empirical explication and examination of trust, trusting and trustworthiness (all three), by drawing together different methodologies and disciplines. It particularly recommends the application of more natural data (Labov, 1972), such as observation methods and video ethnography, to trust research. This is just as we have set out to do in our study of trustworthiness in this present book, exploring trustworthiness 'in the wild' instead of trustworthy behavior in research labs or in survey-induced retrospective recollections of trustworthy or trusting actions. We contend that this present book on trustworthiness backs up our claim that there is great potential in exploring and putting together methods which are rarely combined in current trust research, in order to improve the quality of the study not just of trust and trustworthiness, but of a range of complex, abstract social phenomena (cf. A.M.R. Nielsen, in review). We sincerely believe that, over time, the use of natural data will outlive elicited data in the study of trust and trustworthiness. The work of this book therefore also points toward more methodologically solid grounds for making assertions of trustworthiness.

Cross-disciplinary verifications of our study

As we noted in Chapter 2, we expect our components and subcategories to be further developed over time by our colleagues, as well as by ourselves. We consider our approach to the study of trustworthiness to be novel and ambitious, but we also hope that our findings will be supported by means of a range of other research methodologies and theoretical approaches.

The studies reviewed in Chapter 2 of this book are descriptive, and so are our analyses in Chapters 5–8 as they uncover the order that the interactants orient to. Some of the studies we refer to are based on massive amounts of data from real-life interactions. Their findings have implications for the study of building, maintaining or rebuilding trustworthiness. When, for instance, it is documented that interactants prefer self-correction over other-correction (cf. Schegloff *et al.*, 1977), we have found it encouraging that this seems to be consistent with the very different studies which use methodologies designed to test perception. For example, a study of corporate responses to accusations (from external actors) of unethical behavior (Bradford & Garrett, 1995) tested (in a mail survey to alumni and parents of current students) five different categories of potential communicative responses (no response, denial, excuse, justification and concession) which were meant to defend their corporate image to third parties. Bradford and Garrett found that their respondants, from a third-party perspective, found concession to be the most effective and robust communicative option. This corresponds with both the observations of Schegloff *et al.* (1977) regarding preference for self-initiated self-correction, and also our own finding in the opposite direction – namely, that other-initiated other-corrections can be used to orient to, or spotlight, others' lack of knowledge, thus miscrediting their trustworthiness (see Chapter 8, pp. 121).

Another example that gives us confidence (here, with respect to our own study) is a large meta-study which, independently of our line of research, reached similar conclusions to ours. The first three orientations we pointed to in this book (truth and honesty, stake and interest, and knowledge and ability) are basically backed up by a large meta-study of neutralization techniques, defined as "techniques that help to argue away, fully or partly, someone's responsibility for the deviant behavior ('I am not to be blamed') so that there is no or less guilt" (Kaptein & van Helvoort, 2019, p. 1262). Neutralization theory is a subfield of criminology and deviant sociology which investigates how criminals – including white-collar criminals – attempt to justify and rationalize their crimes, norm violations and deviant behavior. Kaptein and van Helvoort "examined the academic and professional literature in the following disciplines: deviance, criminology, (social) psychology, (business) ethics, and management" for quotes citing neutralizations and using keywords like excuses, justifications and rationalizations, as well as terms like distortions, illogical arguments and fallacies. They also "explored the electronic databases Blackwell Synergy, EBSCO, Google, Google Scholar, ISI Web of Knowledge, JSTOR, ProQuest, ResearchGate, and SSRN". They "conducted a manual search of all articles published in the top-tier journals in the abovementioned disciplines", and they "identified and examined other relevant publications cited within the retrieved publications" (Kaptein & van Helvoort, 2019, p. 1263). After identifying 1,251 different kinds of neutralizations, they sorted them by means of a theoretical model involving four different categories that they had developed. In that process, they identified sixty further subcategories. To test the discriminant validity of the model, they "randomly selected 30 examples of neutralizations and asked 9 academics and practitioners to allocate them to one of the 60 subtechniques that were briefly described to them. In 85% and 93% of the cases, the participants attributed the example to the same subtechnique and technique, respectively", as Kaptein & van Helvoort proposed. "For two of the examples more than one third of the panel members attributed it to another subtechnique" (Kaptein & van Helvoort, 2019, p. 1264). This led them to adjust the relevant technique and its corresponding description.

We have chosen to devote a considerable amount of space to the methodology adopted by this study, because Kaptein and van Helvoort's theoretical model and its 'empirical manifestation', together with verification from the nine participants, supports the relevance of elements within our own theoretical model. Their review study points to four categories of neutralization: a) distorting the facts (by nuancing, denying and inventing facts); b) negating the norm (reducing norms to facts, appealing to another norm and relativizing the norm violation); c) blaming the circumstances (limited options, limited role and limited choice); and d) hiding behind oneself (claiming to have imperfect knowledge, capabilities or intentions).

As we interpret it (and we do hope that we are not stretching this), Kaptein and van Helvoort's model could: (a) relate to 'truth and honesty';

(b) relate to 'stake and interest'; (c) relate to 'knowledge and ability'; and (d) relate to 'knowledge and ability', as well as to 'stake and interest'. But it seems that all categories and subcategories in Kaptein and van Helvoort's meta-study relate in some aspect to truth and honesty, stake and interest, or knowledge and ability. Furthermore, they have identified a category (d, hiding behind oneself) which consists of working strategically within the interaction using our three first orientations. It is beyond the scope of our present study to go further into this discussion. In our book, we have indeed explored trustworthiness as a construct in which neutralization techniques play a significant role in (re)establishing trustworthiness. However, we have not explored neutralization techniques *per se*.

So even though EM/CA is skeptical about the feasibility and usability of elicited data (A.M.R. Nielsen, in review), and even if our cross-disciplinary research methodology and focus on naturally occurring data collected among (mostly) non-criminals in everyday (and especially) institutional interaction is very different from every study reviewed in Kaptein and van Helvoort's study, we have nevertheless found that our findings are supported to an extent by this particular work – and thus by much other work from criminology and deviant sociology. Their review study represents an acid test of sorts, since their object of study (crime, norm violation and deviant behavior) would be deviant or extreme cases in our research field, which is devoted to the study of the social construction of normality and the continuous negotiation of the interactional order (Garfinkel, 1963; Goffman, 1971; Misztal, 2001). Although we have some objections and reservations regarding some methodological choices in Kaptein and van Helvoort's study,[1] their key findings are still

1 We are aware that both the data and the methodology of Kaptein and van Helvoort's study differ significantly from our own, but we have still found that – due to the particular methodology of their review study – their key findings, as mentioned here, can defensibly be used to verify our own theoretical conceptualization, as well as its empirical manifestations. However, there are aspects of their study that we find lacking in transparency and documentation of empirical data compared to what are the norms in EM/CA studies. For example, we find problematic the lack of transparency with regard to the precise profession of, and distribution between, the nine participants in the panel asked to allocate the thirty examples. Also, there is a troubling lack of information regarding which examples they were presented with, in what form they were presented (that be either as quotes like "I didn't do it for myself" or as conceptual examples from the model, such as "The hiding behind imperfect, etc., self-restraints"), and whether they came from elicited or naturally occurring data. Again, there is the question of the ecological validity of the 'empirical data' (here understood as the very allocation of techniques to subcategories). The validity of such experimental elicitation can potentially be limited by the presence of motivational confounds (A.M.R. Nielsen, in review) and the fact that nothing real is at stake for the participants (Garfinkel, 1963), except their own self-perception (cf. Nielsen & Nielsen, in review). That is why these methods are scarcely used in EM/CA studies. However, regardless of both their profession and the type of examples that they were presented with, the participants do likely have the same lived experience and

one of many reasons why we are confident that our model will stand the test of time, even if we hope to see it developed much further.

Practical application?

It could seem like an open-and-shut case to discuss whether it would be possible to take our work further and outline its practical implications. Can our work be turned into a recipe for how to appear trustworthy and how not to? Such endeavors have been suggested (e.g. Kjøller, 1991a). The whole point of the three appeal forms that Aristotle suggested (logos, ethos, pathos) was originally very practical, i.e. to persuade an audience by coming across as credible and trustworthy, and thus as authoritative and convincing. Our results may indeed resonate with examples of common defense strategies in the settings of crime and courtroom: "Even if I wanted to do it, I would not be capable of doing it because of X" (borrowing from 'ability' to reduce problematic 'stake and interest'); "I admit that I have again and again wanted him dead, but I did not kill him" (borrowing from 'truth and honesty' to reduce problematic 'stake and interest'); and "I know that I have no alibi, but why should I do it? I have no motive!" (borrowing from 'stake and interest' to reduce problematic 'ability'). The practical application is indeed a thriving focus in rhetoric studies when discussing how to create a trustworthy persona, work with stake inoculation and use of strong character traits to compensate for weaker ones. Also, the interest in practical application of research outcomes has increased in CA, especially in the last decade and a half (Antaki, 2011). As trust and trustworthiness are further explored as interactional concepts, results from these future studies – so we imagine – might very well inform professional practice further.

Future research awaits

The study presented in this book – and the larger research project on trust-in-action of which it is a part – represents just one necessary step in our ambition to respecify a range of abstract social phenomena as empirical research objects.

members' competences for commonsensically assessing and evaluating the example techniques. So do both the people who produce and use them in their everyday life, and the authors of the review article – or, for that matter, us as analysts. Furthermore, even though the allocation might be somewhat biased by the participants' unconscious taking into account of their self-perception and desired identity (cf. A.M.R. Nielsen, in review), this particular task of sorting instances of something into categories – rather than directly relating them to their own past or future choices or to their own moral, ethics or identity – lowers the risk of these type of validity issues detrimentally affecting the results.

Our contribution stresses the importance of cross-disciplinary research. We think that all schools of research – formal trust research in both psychology and the social sciences, discursive psychology, rhetoric and conversation analysis and ethnomethodology – benefit by each being provided with pieces to the greater puzzle of conceptualizing social phenomena like trustworthiness. We also think that recent developments in research methodology across a range of scientific fields provide material toward the greater endeavor of operationalizing such social phenomena for quantitative analysis.

In this present study, we can see how each research discipline is being brought together, and also brought to its boundaries by that proximity. Indeed, as we have pointed out previously, classic trust research has been invited to explore the *in situ* communicative behavior (in naturally occurring social interaction) that forms the basis for trustors' decision-making about whether to trust the trustee. Also, the study of rhetoric has been invited to include social interaction as data and to use video ethnography to explore it, and ethnomethodology has been invited to embrace abstract social phenomena that are not directly observable in data, and to identify patterns of behavior as indicators of that phenomenon.

We hope to see future studies explore trust and trustworthiness and:

- to see our categories and subcategories explored further in large, collection-based, inductive EM/CA studies, some of which might test whether and how trustworthiness can be examined further in a quantitative study;
- to see if orientations differ in strength depending upon the social context (e.g. if truth is a strong orientation for at least one of the participants in professional settings, whereas precision and quality in decision-making processes might be institutional priorities);
- to see in which sequential environments the same codable action, move or interactional strategy might appear as a potential indicator of different components of trust or trustworthiness;
- to see clusters of character-bound displays, or other indicators, studied in different settings with different issues at stake;
- to see sequential negotiation of (different kinds of) character analyzed in a range of settings;
- to see the orientation to consistency and predictability further explored with respect to the three other orientations (i.e. truth and honesty, knowledge and ability, and stake and interest), hopefully from both a participant's and an analyst's perspective;
- to see the relation between character-bound displays and sequential negotiations of character investigated, in order to explore how the former plays a part in the construction of the latter;
- to see studies exploring in detail how character-bound displays are negotiated;

- to see if instances of 'breaches of norms' are particularly often seen in perspicuous settings – that is, whether sequential negotiation of character indicating orientation to trustworthiness is especially foregrounded;
- to see studies of breaches and deviant behavior turned into lists of codable indicators consisting of participant actions, moves and interactional strategies, in order to examine and possibly conceptualize *lack of* trustworthiness; and
- to see how all this will support or falsify our own study.

We are also eager to see the concept of trustworthiness connected to the study of what we term *trust-in-interaction*. We would love to participate in some of these research endeavors. Others we will enjoy discussing with our excellent colleagues around the world. Revisiting trustworthiness is just one building block in the larger endeavor of studying the interactional achievement of trust in social interactions.

References for the monograph

Revisiting Trustworthiness in Social Interaction

Alexander, M., & Stokoe, E. (2020). Characterological formulations of persons in neighbourhood complaint sequences. *Qualitative Research in Psychology, 17*(3), 413–429.

Andersen, J. E. (1986). Adverbier – sprogvidenskabens stedbørn. In Selskab for Nordisk Filologi (Eds.), *Årsberetning 1985–86.* (pp. 45–53). Selskab for Nordisk Filologi, Københavns Universitet. ["Adverbs – the stepchild of linguistics"].

Anne, R., Levine, T., Ching, P., & Yoshimoto, J. (1993). The influence of perceived source reward value on attributions of deception. *Communication Research Reports, 10*, 15–27.

Antaki, C. (1994). *Explaining and arguing: The social organization of accounts.* SAGE.

Antaki, C. (2003). The uses of absurdity. In H. van der Berg, M. Wetherell, & H. Houtkoop-Stenstra (Eds.), *Analyzing race talk: Multidisciplinary approaches to the interview* (pp. 85–102). Cambridge University Press.

Antaki, C. (2011). *Applied conversation analysis, intervention and change in institutional talk.* Palgrave Macmillan.

Antaki, C., & Rapley, M. (1996). Questions and answers to psychological assessment schedules: Hidden troubles in 'quality of life' interviews. *Journal of Intellectual Disability Research, 40*(5), 421–437.

Antaki, C., & Widdicombe, S. (1998). Identity as an achievement and as a tool. In *Identities in talk* (pp. 1–14). SAGE.

Aristotle. (350 BCE/1983). Ancient Greek: Ῥητορική, romanized: Rhētorikḗ, latin: Ars Rhetorica, English: Rhetoric, Danish: *Retorik.* Translated 1983 to Danish by Thure Hastrup. Museum Tusculanum.

Arminen, I. (2005). *Institutional interaction: Studies of talk at work. Directions in ethnomethodology and conversation analysis.* Ashgate Publishing Company.

Asmuß, B., & Oshima, S. (2012). Negotiation of entitlement in proposal sequences. *Discourse Studies, 14*(1), 67–86.

Atkinson, J. M. (1982). Understanding formality: The categorization and production of 'formal' interaction. *The British Journal of Sociology, 33*(1), 86–117.

Atkinson, J. M., & Drew, P. (1979). *Order in court.* Palgrave Macmillan.

Austin, J. L. (1962). *How to do things with words.* Oxford University Press.

Banas, J., & Rains, S. (2010). A meta-analysis of research on inoculation theory. *Communication Monograph, 77*(3), 281–331.

Barnes, R., & Moss, D. (2007). Communicating a feeling: The social organization of 'private thoughts'. *Discourse Studies, 9*(2), 123–148.

Barr, A. (2003). Trust and expected trustworthiness: Experimental evidence from Zimbabwean villages. *The Economic Journal, 113*(489), 614–630.

Ben-Ner, A., & Halldorsson, F. (2010). Trusting and trustworthiness: What are they, how to measure them, and what affects them. *Journal of Economic Psychology, 31*(1), 64–79.

Benoit-Barné, C., & Cooren, F. (2009). The accomplishment of authority through presentification: How authority is distributed among and negotiated by organizational members. *Management Communication Quarterly, 23*(1), 5–31.

Benwell, B., & Stokoe, E. (2011) *Discourse and Identity.* Cambridge Core.

Berg, J., Dickhaut, J., & McCabe, K. (1995). Trust, reciprocity, and social history. *Games and Economic Behavior, 10*(1), 122–142.

Bergmann, J. (1992). Veiled morality: Notes on discretion in psychiatry. In P. Drew & J. Heritage (Eds.), *Talk at work: Interaction in institutional settings* (pp. 137–162). Cambridge University Press.

Bergmann, J. (1993). *Discreet indiscretions: The social organization of gossip.* Aldine de Gruyter.

Bilmes, J. (2012). Truth and proof in a lawyer's story. *Journal of Pragmatics, 44*, 1626–1638.

Black, E. (1965). *Rhetorical criticism: A study in method.* University of Wisconsin Press.

Bloch, S., & Leydon, G. (2019). Conversation analysis and telephone helplines for health and illness: A narrative review. *Research on Language and Social Interaction, 52*(3), 193–211.

Bolden, G. B., Hepburn, A., & Potter, J. (2019). Subversive completions: Turn-taking resources for commandeering the recipient's action in progress. *Research on Language and Social Interaction, 52*(2), 144–158.

Bond, C. F., & Fahey, W. E. (1987). False suspicion and the misperception of deceit. *British Journal of Social Psychology, 26*, 41–46.

Bradford, J. L., & Garrett, D. E. (1995). The effectiveness of corporate communicative response to accusations of unethical behavior. *Journal of Business Ethics, 14*(11), 875–892.

Brouwer, C. E. (2003). Word searches in NNS – NS interaction: Opportunities for language learning? *Modern Language Journal, 87*(4), 534–545.

Brown, P., & Levinson, S. C. (1978). Universals in language usage: Politeness phenomena. In E. N. Goody (Ed.), *Questions and politeness* (pp. 56–289). Cambridge University Press.

Brown, P., & Levinson, S. C. (1987). *Politeness: Some universals in language usage.* Cambridge University Press.

Burbules, N. C. (2001). Paradoxes of the web: The ethical dimensions of credibility. *Library Trends, 49*(3), 441. Retrieved December 3, 2021, from www.ideals.illinois.edu/bitstream/handle/2142/8352/librarytrendsv49i3f_opt.pdf?sequence=1&isAllowed=y

Burke, K. J. (1966). *Language as symbolic action: Essays on life, literature and method.* University of California Press.

Burke, S., & Demasi, M. A. (2019). Applying discursive psychology to 'fact' construction in political discourse. *Social and Personality Psychology Compass, 13*(5), e12449.

Burks, S. V., Carpenter, J. P., & Verhoogen, E. (2003). Playing both roles in the trust game. *Journal of Economic Behavior & Organization, 51*(2), 195–216.

Butler, C. (2014, July). Whining and crying: Children's affective displays in family interaction. Paper presented at ICCA 2014, Los Angeles, CA.

Butler, J. K. (1991). Toward understanding and measuring conditions of trust: Evolution of a conditions of trust inventory. *Journal of Management, 17*(3), 643–663.

Candlin, C. N., & Crichton, J. (Eds.). (2013). *Discourses of trust*. Palgrave Macmillan UK.

Cheney, G. (1991). *Rhetoric in an organizational society. Managing multiple identities*. University of South Carolina Press.

Christie, R., & Geis, F. L. (1970). *Studies in Machiavellianism*. Academic Press.

Clayman, S. (1988). Displaying neutrality in television news interviews. *Social Problems, 35*, 474–492.

Clayman, S. (1992). Footing in the achievement of neutrality: The case of news interview discourse. In P. Drew & J. Heritage (Eds.), *Talk at work* (pp. 163–198). Cambridge University Press.

Clayman, S. (2002a). *The news interview journalists and public figures on the air*. University Press.

Clayman, S. (2002b). Tribune of the people: Maintaining the legitimacy of aggressive journalism. *Media, Culture & Society, 24*(2), 197–216.

Clayman, S. E., Elliott, M., Heritage, J., & McDonald, L. (2006). Historical trends in questioning presidents, 1953–2000. *Presidential Studies Quarterly, 36*(4), 561–583.

Clayman, S. E., & Heritage, J. (2002). Questioning presidents: Journalistic deference and adversarialness in the press conferences of U.S. Presidents Eisenhower and Reagan. *Journal of Communication, 52*(4), 749–775.

Clayman, S. E., & Heritage, J. (2014). Benefactors and beneficiaries: Benefactive status and stance in the management of offers and requests. In P. Drew & E. Couper-Kuhlen (Eds.), *Requesting in social interaction* (pp. 55–86). John Benjamins.

Clayman, S. E., Heritage, J., Elliott, M. N., & McDonald, L. L. (2007). When does the watchdog bark? Conditions of aggressive questioning in presidential news conferences. *American Sociological Review, 72*(1), 23–41.

Clayman, S. E., & Loeb, L. (2018). Polar questions, response preference, and the tasks of political positioning in journalism. *Research on Language and Social Interaction, 51*(2), 127–144.

Clift, R., & Pino, M. (2020). Turning the tables: Objecting to conduct in conflict talk. *Research on Language and Social Interaction, 53*(4), 463–480.

Clifton, J. (2012). 'Doing' trust in workplace interaction. In S. Măda & R. Săftoiu (Eds.), *Dialogue studies* (Vol. 17, pp. 107–132). John Benjamins Publishing Company.

Clifton, J. (2014). Small stories, positioning, and the discursive construction of leader identity in business meetings. *Leadership, 10*(1), 99–117.

Coleman, J. S. (1990). *Foundations of social theory*. Harvard University Press.

Compton, J., Jackson, B., & Dimmock, J. A. (2016). Persuading others to avoid persuasion: Inoculation theory and resistant health attitudes. *Frontiers in psychology, 7*, 122.

Cook, K. S., & Santana, J. J. (2017). *Trust and rational choice* (E. M. Uslaner, Ed.; Vol. 1). Oxford University Press.

Cooren, F. (2010). Ventriloquie, performativité et communication. Ou comment fait-on parler les choses [Ventriloquism, performativity, and communication. Or how to make things speak]. *Réseaux, 5*(163), 33–54.

Cordeiro, L., Soares, C. B., & Rittenmeyer, L. (2017). Unscrambling method and methodology in action research traditions: Theoretical conceptualization of praxis and emancipation. *Qualitative Research, 17*(4), 395–407.

Coulter, J. (1990). *Mind in action*. Polity Press.

Couper-Kuhlen, E. (2012a). Exploring affiliation in the reception of conversational complaint stories. In A. Peräkylä & M. -L. Sorjonen (Eds.), *Emotion in interaction* (pp. 113–146). Oxford University Press.

Couper-Kuhlen, E. (2012b). On affectivity and preference in responses to rejection. *Text & Talk, 32*(4), 453–475.

Couper-Kuhlen, E. (2015). What does grammar tell us about action? *Pragmatics. Quarterly Publication of the International Pragmatics Association (IPrA), 24*(3), 623–647.

Davidson, J. (1984). Subsequent versions of invitations, offers, requests, and proposals dealing with potential or actual rejection. In J. M. Atkinson & J. Heritage (Eds.), *Structures of social action: Studies in conversation analysis* (pp. 102–128). Cambridge University Press.DeBruine, L. M. (2002). Facial resemblance enhances trust. *Proceedings of the Royal Society B: Biological Sciences, 269*, 1307–1312.

DeBruine, L. M. (2005). Trustworthy but not lust-worthy: Context-specific effects of facial resem-blance. *Proceedings of the Royal Society B: Biological Sciences, 272*, 919–922.

Delgado, M. R., Frank, R. H., & Phelps, E. A. (2005). Perceptions of moral character modulate the neural systems of reward during the trust game. *Nature Neuroscience, 8*(11), 1611–1618.

DePaulo, B. M., Lindsay, J. L., Malone, B. E., Muhlenbruck, L., Charlton, K., & Cooper, H. (2003). Cues to deception. *Psychological Bulletin, 129*, 74–118.

Deppermann, A. (2013). Multimodal interaction from a conversation analytic perspective. *Journal of Pragmatics, 46*(1), 1–7.

De Ruiter, J. (2013). Methodological paradigms in interaction research. In I. Wachsmuth, J. De Ruiter, P. Jaecks, & S. Kopp (Eds.), *Advances in interaction studies* (Vol. 6, pp. 11–32). John Benjamins Publishing Company.

Dietz, G., & Den Hartog, D. N. (2006). Measuring trust inside organisations. *Personnel Review, 35*(5), 557–588.

Doehler, S. P., Wagner, J., & González-Martínez, E. (2018). *Longitudinal studies on the organization of social interaction*. Palgrave Macmillan Limited.

Drew, P. (1978). Accusations: The occasioned use of members' knowledge of 'religious geography' in describing events. *Sociology, 12*(1), Special Issue: Language and Practical Reasoning, 1–22.

Drew, P. (1984). Speakers' reporting in invitation sequences. In J. Maxwell & J. Heritage (Eds.), *Structures of social action: Studies in conversation* (pp. 129–151). Cambridge University Press.

Drew, P. (1985). Analyzing the use of language in courtroom interaction. In T. A. van Dijk (Ed.), *Handbook of discourse analysis: Vol. 3, discourse and dialogue* (pp. 133–147). Academic Press.

Drew, P. (1997). 'Open' class repair initiators in response to sequential sources of troubles in conversation. *Journal of Pragmatics, 28*(1), 69–101.

Drew, P. (1998). Complaints about transgressions and misconduct. *Research on Language and Social Interaction, 31*(3/4), 295–325.

Drew, P. (2003). Precision and exaggeration in interaction. *American Sociological Review, 68*(6), 917–938.

Drew, P., & Heritage, J. (1992). *Talk at work, interaction in institutional settings.* Cambridge University Press.

Drew, P., & Heritage, J. (2006). *Conversation analysis* (Vol. 1–4). SAGE.

Dreyfus, S. E., & Dreyfus, H. L. (1980). A five-stage model of the mental activities involved in directed skill acquisition [Manuscript, University of Berkeley].

Due, B. L. (2016). Co-constructed imagination space: A multimodal analysis of the interactional accomplishment of imagination during idea-development meetings. *CoDesign, 14*(3).

Due, B. L., & Lange, S. B. (2015). Videobased reflection on team interaction (The ViRTI-method). *Working Papers on Interaction and Communication, 1*(3), 1–38.

Edwards, D. (1994). Script formulations: An analysis of event descriptions in conversation. *Journal of Language and Social Psychology, 13*(3), 211–247.

Edwards, D. (1995). Two to tango: Script formulations, dispositions, and rhetorical symmetry in relationship troubles talk. *Research on Language and Social Interaction, 28*(4), 319–350.

Edwards, D. (2000). Extreme case formulations: Softeners, investment, and doing nonliteral. *Research on Language and Social Interaction, 33*(4), 347–373.

Edwards, D. (2003). Analyzing racial discourse: The discursive psychology of mind-world relationships. In H. van der Berg, M. Wetherell, & H. Houtkoop-Stenstra (Eds.), *Analyzing race talk: Multidisciplinary approaches to the interview* (pp. 31–48). Cambridge University Press.

Edwards, D. (2005). Moaning, whinging and laughing: The subjective side of complaints. *Discourse Studies, 7*(1), 5–29.

Edwards, D. (2006a). Facts, norms and dispositions: Practical uses of the modal would in police interrogations. *Discourse Studies, 8*(4), 475–501.

Edwards, D. (2006b). Discourse, cognition and social practices: The rich surface of language and social interaction. *Discourse Studies, 8*, 41–9.

Edwards, D. (2007). Managing subjectivity in talk. In A. Hepburn & S. Wiggins (Eds.), *Discursive research in practice: New approaches to psychology and interaction* (pp. 31–49). Cambridge University Press.

Edwards, D., & Fasulo, A. (2006). "To be honest": Sequential uses of honesty phrases in talk-in-interaction. *Research on Language and Social Interaction, 39*(4), 343–376.

Edwards, D., & Potter, J. (1992). *Discursive psychology.* SAGE.

Edwards, D., & Potter, J. (2017). Some uses of subject-side assessments. *Discourse Studies, 19*(5), 497–514.

Edwards, D., & Stokoe, E. (2011). "You don't have to answer": Lawyers' contributions in police interrogations of suspects. *Research on Language and Social Interaction, 44*(1), 21–43.

Ekman, P. (1992). *Telling lies: Clues to deceit in the marketplace, politics and marriage*. W. W. Norton.

Ekman, P. (2009). Lie catching and microexpressions. In *The philosophy of deception*. Oxford University Press.

Enfield, N. J. (2012). Reference in conversation. In J. Sidnell & T. Stivers (Eds.), *The handbook of conversation analysis*. Wiley-Blackwell.

Enfield, N. J., & Kockelman, P. (2017). *Distributed agency*. Oxford University Press, Oxford University Press USA – OSO.

Engell, A. D., Haxby, J. V., & Todorov, A. (2007). Implicit trustworthiness decisions: Automatic coding of face properties in the human amygdala. *Journal of Cognitive Neuroscience, 19*(9), 1508–1519.

Erikson, E. H. (1993). *Childhood and society* (2nd rev ed.). Wiley. (Original work published 1950)

Evans, A. M., & Krueger, J. I. (2009). The psychology (and economics) of trust. *Social and Personality Psychology Compass, 3*(6), 1003–1017.

Everett, J. A. C., Pizarro, D. A., & Crockett, M. J. (2016). Inference of trustworthiness from intuitive moral judgments. *Journal of Experimental Psychology: General, 145*(6), 772–787.

Fan, X., Miller, B. C., Park, K.-E., Winward, B. W., Christensen, M., Grotevant, H. D., & Tai, R. H. (2006). An exploratory study about inaccuracy and invalidity in adolescent self-report surveys. *Field Methods, 18*(3), 223–244.

Fogtmann, C. (2007). *Samtaler med politiet: Interaktionsanalytiske studier af sprogtestning i danske naturalisationssamtaler* [PhD Dissertation]. Department of Scandinavian Studies and Linguistics, University of Copenhagen.

Ford, J. (2017). *Empathy in doctor-patient palliative care consultations: A conversation-analytic approach* [Doctoral Thesis]. University of Loughborough.

Fraser, B. (1990). Perspectives on politeness. *Journal of Pragmatics, 14*, 219–236.

Freeman, R. E. (1984). *Strategic management: A stakeholder approach*. Pitman.

Freeman, R. E., & Reed, D. L. (1983). Stockholders and stakeholders: A new perspective on corporate governance. *California Management Review, 25*(3), 88–106.

Gambetta, D. (1988). Can we trust trust?. In D. Gambetta (Ed.), *Trust: Making and breaking cooperative relations* (pp. 213–237). Blackwell.

Garfinkel, H. (1963). A conception of, and experiments with, trust as a condition of stable concerted actions. In O. J. Harvey (Ed.), *Motivation and social interaction: Cognitive approaches* (pp. 187–265). Ronald Press.

Garfinkel, H. (1964). Studies of the routine grounds of everyday activities. *Social Problems, 11*(3), 225–250.

Garfinkel, H. (1967). *Studies in ethnomethodology*. Prentice-Hall.

Garfinkel, H. (1991). Respecification: Evidence for locally produced, naturally accountable phenomena of order, logic, reason, meaning, method, etc. in and as of the essential haecceity of immortal ordinary society (I) – An announcement of studies. In G. Button (Ed.), *Ethnomethodology and the human sciences* (pp. 10–19). Cambridge University Press.

Garfinkel, H. (1996). Ethnomethodology's program. *Social Psychology Quarterly, 59*(1), 5.

Garfinkel, H., & Sacks, H. (1970). On formal structures of practical action. In I. J. C. McKinney & E. A. Tiryakian (Eds.), *Theoretical sociology: Perspectives and developments* (pp. 337–366). Appleton-Century-Crofts.

Geis, F. L., Christie, R., Schachter, S., & Festinger, L. (2013). *Studies in machiavellianism*. Academic Press.

Gibson, J. J. (1979). *The ecological approach to visual perception*. Psychology Press (s. 63–68).

Gillespie, N. (2015). Survey measures of trust in organizational contexts: An overview. In F. Lyon, G. Möllering, & M. Saunders (Eds.), *Handbook of research methods on trust*. Edward Elgar Publishing.

Glenn, P., & LeBaron, C. (2011). Epistemic authority in employment interviews: Glancing, pointing, touching. *Discourse & Communication, 5*(1), 3–22.

Goffman, E. (1955). On face-work: An analysis of ritual elements in social interaction. *Psychiatry, XVIII*, 213–231.

Goffman, E. (1959). *The presentation of self in everyday life*. Doubleday.

Goffman, E. (1961). *Encounters: Two studies in the sociology of interaction*. Bobbs-Merril.

Goffman, E. (1967). *Interaction ritual: Essays on face-to-face behavior*. Doubleday Anchor.

Goffman, E. (1971). *Relations in public: Microstudies of the public order*. Basic Books.

Goffman, E. (1981). *Forms of talk*. University of Pennsylvania Press.

Goldman-Eisler, F. (1968). *Psycholinguistics: Experiments in spontaneous speech*. Doubleday.

González-Martínez, E. (2001). Comment agir en confiance avec un partenaire dont on se mefie? *Réseaux, 108*(4).

González-Martínez, E., & Mlynář, J. (2019). Practical trust. *Social Science Information, 58*(4), 608–630.

Goodwin, C. (1979). The interactive construction of a sentence in natural conversation. In G. Psathas (Ed.), *Everyday language: Studies in ethnomethodology* (pp. 97–121). Irvington Publishers.

Goodwin, C. (1981). *Conversational organisation: Interaction between speakers and hearers*. Academic Press.

Goodwin, C. (1987). Forgetfulness as an interactive resource. *Social Psychology Quarterly, 50*(2), 115–130.

Goodwin, C. (2000). Action and embodiment within-situated human interaction. *Journal of Pragmatics, 32*(10), 1489–1522.

Goodwin, C. (2003). Recognizing assessable names. In P. Glenn, C. LeBaron, & J. Mandelbaum (Eds.), *Studies in language and social interaction: In honor of Robert Hopper* (pp. 151–161). Lawrence Erlbaum.

Goodwin, M. H. (2017). *Haptic sociality*. Oxford University Press.

Grice, H. P. (1975). Logic and conversation. In P. Cole & J. Morgan (Eds.), *Syntax and semantics, volume 3: Speech acts* (pp. 41–58). Academic Press.

Griesel, D., & Yuille, J. C. (2007). Credibility assessment in eyewitness memory. In *The handbook of eyewitness psychology, Vol I: Memory for events* (pp. 339–370). Lawrence Erlbaum Associates Publishers.

Grimen, H. (2009). *Hva er tillit*. Universitetsforlaget.

Gumperz, J. J. (1982). *Discourse strategies*. Cambridge University Press.

Gunnthorsdottir, A., McCabe, K., & Smith, V. (2002). Using the Machiavellianism instrument to predict trustworthiness in a bargaining game. *Journal of Economic Psychology, 23*(1), 49–66.

Hansen, F., & Kock, C. (2003). Evaluation of public spokespersons. *Nordicom Review, 24*(1), 27–31.

Harder, P., & Kock, C. (1976). *The theory of presupposition failure*. Akademisk Forlag.

Hardin, R. (2001). Conceptions and explanations of trust. In K. S. Cook (Ed.), *Trust in society* (pp. 3–39). Russell Sage Foundation.

Hardin, R. (2002). *Trust and trustworthiness*. Russell Sage Foundation.

Hardin, R. (Ed.). (2004). *Distrust*. Russell Sage Foundation. Retrieved April 13, 2021, from www.jstor.org/stable/10.7758/9781610442695

Hayes, J. (1979). A new look at managerial competence: The AMA model for worthy performance. *Management Review, 68*(11), 2–3.

Heinemann, T. (2006). Will you or can't you? Displaying entitlement in interrogative requests. *Journal of Pragmatics, 38*, 1081–1104.

Hendry, J. (2002). The principal's other problems: Honest incompetence and the specification of objectives. *The Academy of Management Review, 27*(1), 98–113.

Hepburn, A. (2002). *An introduction to critical social psychology*. SAGE.

Hepburn, A., & Potter, J. (2007). Crying receipts: Time, empathy, and institutional practice. *Research on Language and Social Interaction, 40*(1), 89–116.

Hepburn, A., & Wiggins, S. (Eds.). (2007). *Discursive research in practice: New approaches to psychology and interaction*. Cambridge University Press.

Heritage, J. (1984). *Garfinkel and ethnomethodology*. Polity Press.

Heritage, J. (1988). Explanations as accounts: A conversation analytic perspective. In C. Antaki (Ed.), *Understanding everyday explanation: A casebook of methods* (pp. 127–144). SAGE.

Heritage, J. (1995). Conversation analysis: Methodological aspects. In U. M. Quasthoff (Ed.), *Aspects of oral communication*. De Gruyter.

Heritage, J. (2002a). Designing questions and setting agendas in the news interview. In J. Mandelbaum, P. Glenn, & C. LeBaron (Eds.), *Studies in language and social interaction*. Routlegde.

Heritage, J. (2002b). The limits of questioning: Negative interrogatives and hostile question content. *Journal of Pragmatics, 34*(10), 1427–1446.

Heritage, J. (2005). Revisiting authority in physician-patient interaction. In J. F. Duchan & D. Kovarsky (Eds.), *Diagnosis as cultural practice* (pp. 83–102). Mouton de Gruyter.

Heritage, J. (2007). Intersubjectivity and progressivity in person (and place) reference. In T. Stivers & N. J. Enfield (Eds.), *Person reference in interaction: Linguistic, cultural and social perspectives* (pp. 255–280). Cambridge University Press.

Heritage, J. (2011). Territories of knowledge, territories of experience: Empathic moments in interaction. In: T. Stivers, L. Mondada, & J. Steensig (Eds.), *The morality of knowledge in conversation* (pp. 159–183). Cambridge University Press.

Heritage, J. (2012a). Epistemics in action: Action formation and territories of knowledge. *Research on Language & Social Interaction, 45*(1), 1–29.

Heritage, J. (2012b). Epistemics in conversation. In J. Sidnell & T. Stivers (Eds.), *The handbook of conversation analysis* (pp. 370–394). John Wiley & Sons.

Heritage, J. (2013). Action formation and its epistemic (and other) backgrounds. *Discourse Studies, 15*(5).

Heritage, J., & Clayman, S. (2010). Gatekeeping and entitlement to emergency service. In *Talk in action* (pp. 69–86). John Wiley & Sons.

Heritage, J., & Greatbatch, D. (1991). On the institutional character of institutional talk: The case of news interviews. In D. Boden & D. H. Zimmerman (Eds.), *Talk and social structure* (pp. 93–137). University of California Press.

Heritage, J., Raymond, C. W., & Drew, P. (2019). Constructing apologies: Reflexive relationships between apologies and offenses. *Journal of Pragmatics, 142*, 185–200.

Heritage, J., & Raymond, G. (2005). The terms of agreement: Indexing epistemic authority and subordination in talk-in-interaction. *Social Psychology Quarterly, 68*(1), 15–38.

Heritage, J., & Raymond, G. (2012). Navigating epistemic landscapes: Acquiescence, agency and resistance in responses to polar questions. In J. P. De Ruiter (Ed.), *Questions: Formal, functional and interactional perspectives* (pp. 179–192). Cambridge University Press.

Heritage, J., & Roth, A. L. (1995). Grammar and institution: Questions and questioning in the broadcast news interview. *Research on Language & Social Interaction, 28*(1), 1–60.

Heritage, J., & Sefi, S. (1992). Dilemmas of advice: Aspects of the delivery and reception of advice in interactions between health visitors and first time mothers. In P. Drew & J. Heritage (Eds.), *Talk at work* (pp. 359–417). Cambridge University Press.

Heritage, J., & Stivers, T. (1999). Online commentary in acute medical visits: A method of shaping patient expectations. *Social Science & Medicine, 49*(11), 1501–1517.

Hoff-Clausen, E. (2004). *Set gennom nettet*. Samfundslitteratur.

Hoff-Clausen, E. (2008). *Online ethos*. Samfundslitteratur

Hogden, A., Short, A. E., & Dugdale, P. (2012). Health coaching and motivational interviewing: Evaluating the chronic disease self-management toolbox as a resource for person-centered healthcare. *The International Journal of Person Centered Medicine, 2*(3), 520–530.

Holt, E., & Drew, P. (1988). Complainable matters: The use of idiomatic expressions in making complaints. *Social Problems, 35*(4), 398–417.

Houtkoop-Steenstra, H., & Antaki, C. (1997). Creating happy people by asking yes-no questions. *Research on Language & Social Interaction, 30*(4), 285–313.

Huisman, M. (2001). Decision-making in meetings as talk-in-interaction. *International Studies of Management & Organization, 31*(3), 69–90.

Husserl, E. (1970). *The crisis of European sciences and transcendental phenomenology: An introduction to the phenomenological philosophy* (trans. David Carr). Northwestern University Press. (Originally published in 1938).

Isocrates (390 BC/1986). *Fire taler*. Museum Tusculanum. The four speeches "Mot sofistene", "Helena", "Busiris" and "Antidosis" were translated to Danish 1986 by Thure Hastrup, using the Danish spelling Isokrates.

Iversen, C. (2014). 'I don't know if I should believe him': Knowledge and believability in interviews with children. *British Journal of Social Psychology, 53*(2), 367–386.

James, H. S., Jr. (2014). You can have your trust and calculativeness, too: Uncertainty, trustworthiness and the Williamson thesis. *Journal of Trust Research, 4*(1), 57–65.

Jefferson, G. (1973). A case of precision timing in ordinary conversation: Overlapped tag-positioned address terms in closing sequences. *Semiotica, 9*, 47–96.

Jefferson, G. (1974). Error correction as an interactional resource. *Language in Society, 2*, 181–199.

Jefferson, G. (1987). On exposed and embedded correction in conversation. In G. Button, & J. R. E. Lee (Eds.), *Talk and social organization* (pp. 86–100). Multilingual Matters.

Jefferson, G. (2004a). "At first I thought": A normalizing device for extraordinary events. In G. H. Lerner (Ed.), *Conversation analysis: Studies from the first* (pp. 131–167). John Benjamins.

Jefferson, G. (2004b). Glossary of transcript symbols with an introduction. In G. H. Lerner (Ed.), *Conversation analysis: Studies from the first generation* (pp. 13–31). John Benjamins Publishing Co.

Jones, K. (2012). Trustworthiness. *Ethics, 123*(1), 61–85.

Kaptein, M., & van Helvoort, M. (2019). A model of neutralization techniques. *Deviant Behavior, 40*(10), 1260–1285.

Kasper, G. (1990). Linguistic politeness: Current research issues. *Journal of Pragmatics, 14*, 193–218.

Kitzinger, C., & Mandelbaum, J. (2013). Word selection and social identities in talk-in-interaction. *Communication Monographs, 80*(2), 176–198.

Kiyonari, T., Yamagishi, T., Cook, K. S., & Cheshire, C. (2006). Does trust beget trustworthiness? Trust and trustworthiness in two games and two cultures: A research note. *Social Psychology Quarterly, 69*(3), 270–283.

Kjøller, K. (1991a). *Manipulation – en håndbog*. Borgen.

Kjøller, K. (1991b). *Politisk argumentation. En teori om offentlig politisk argumentation i et velfærds-demokrati*. Borgen.

Kjøller, K. (2007). *Manipulation – En håndbog. NU med indoktrinering, vold og hjernevask* (2nd ed.). Borgen.

Knudsen, M. (2001). Krop og suverænitet – om to måder at skabe tillid på. In A. Bordum & S. B. Wenneberg (Eds.), *Det handler om tillid* (pp. 15–24). Samfundslitteratur.

Komter, M. (2003). The interactional dynamics of eliciting a confession in a Dutch police interrogation. *Research on Language and Social Interaction, 36*(4), 433–470.

König, L., & Jucks, R. (2019). Hot topics in science communication: Aggressive language decreases trustworthiness and credibility in scientific debates. *Public Understanding of Science, 28*(4), 401–416.

Krueger, J. I., Massey, A. L., & DiDonato, T. E. (2008). A matter of trust: From social preferences to the strategic adherence to social norms. *Negotiation and Conflict Management Research, 1*, 31–52.

Krumhuber, E., Manstead, A. S. R., Cosker, D., Marshall, D., Rosin, P. L., & Kappas, A. (2007). Facial dynamics as indicators of trustworthiness and cooperative behavior. *Emotion, 7*, 730–735.

Labov, W. (1972). *Sociolinguistic patterns*. University of Pennsylvania.

Labov, W., & Fanshel, D. (1977). *Therapeutic discourse: Psychotherapy as conversation*. Academic Press.

Larsson, M., & Nielsen, M. F. (2021). The risky path to a followership identity: From abstract concept to situated reality. *Journal of Business Communication, 58*(1), 3–30.

Lasswell, H. (1948). The structure and function of communication in society. In L. Bryson (Ed.), *The communication of ideas*. The Institute for Religious and Social Studies.
Latour, B. (1999). *Pandora's hope: Essays on the reality of science studies*. Harvard University Press.
Laurier, E. (2013). *Youtube: Using third party video as research data* [Unpublished Reseach paper]. *School of GeoSciences*, University of Edinburgh.
Leech, G. (1983). *Principles of pragmatics*. Longman.
LeFevre, K. B. (1987). *Invention as a social act*. Southern Illinois University Press.
Lerner, G. H. (1987/2004). *Collaborative turn sequences* [Unpublished doctoral dissertation]. University of California. Published 2004 in: G. H. Lerner (Ed.), *Conversation analysis: Studies from the first generation* (pp. 225–256). John Benjamins.
Lerner, G. H. (1996). Finding "face" in the preference structures of talk-in-interaction. *Social Psychology Quarterly, 59*(3), 303–321.
Lerner, G. H., Raymond, G., & Heritage, J. (2017). Schegloff and the founding of a discovering discipline. In G. Raymond, G. H. Lerner, & J. Heritage (Eds.), *Enabling human conduct: Studies of talk-in-interaction in honor of Emanuel A. Schegloff* (pp. 1–12). John Benjamins Publishing Company.
Levinson, S. C. (1983). *Pragmatics*. Cambridge University Press.
Levinson, S. C. (2012). Action formation and ascription. In *The handbook of conversation analysis* (pp. 101–130). John Wiley & Sons.
Lewicki, R. J., & Brinsfield, C. (2015). Trust research: Measuring trust beliefs and behaviours. In F. Lyon, G. Möllering, & M. Saunders (Eds.), *Handbook of research methods on trust*. Edward Elgar Publishing.
Lewis, J. D., & Weigert, A. (1985). Trust as social reality. *Social Forces, 63*(4), 967–985.
Liberman, K. (2013). *The local orderliness of crossing Kinkaid. Chapter one in: More studies in ethnomethodology*. State University of New York Press.
Lindström, A., & Weatherall, A. (2015). Orientations to epistemics and deontics in treatment discussions. *Journal of Pragmatics, 78*, 39–53.
Local, J., & Walker, G. (2008). Stance and affect in conversation: On the interplay of sequential and phonetic resources. *Text & Talk, 28*(6), 723–747.
Lui, L., & Standing, L. (1989). Communicator credibility: Trustworthiness defeats expertness. *Social Behavior & Personality: An International Journal, 17*(2), 219–221.
Lynch, M. (1994). *Scientific practice and ordinary action: Ethnomethodology and social studies of science*. Cambridge University Press.
Lyon, F., Möllering, G., & Saunders, M. (2015). *Handbook of research methods on trust*. Edward Elgar Publishing.
Macaulay, M. (1996). Asking to ask: The strategic function of indirect requests for information in news interviews. *Pragmatics, 6*, 491–509.
MacMartin, C. (1999). *Discursive constructions of child sexual abuse: Conduct, credibility and culpability in trial judgments* [PhD thesis]. University of Guelph.
Maltby, J. (2010). An interest in fame: Confirming the measurement and empirical conceptualization of fame interest. *British Journal of Psychology, 101*(3), 411–432.
Mangione-Smith, R., Stivers, T., Elliott, M., McDonald, L., & Heritage, J. (2003). Online commentary during the physical examination: A communication tool for avoiding inappropriate antibiotic prescribing? *Social Science & Medicine, 56*(2), 313–320.

Mayer, R. C., & Davis, J. H. (1999). The effect of the performance appraisal system on trust for management: A field quasi-experiment. *Journal of Applied Psychology, 84*(1), 123–136.

Mayer, R. C., Davis, J. H., & Schoorman, F. D. (1995). An integrative model of organizational trust. *The Academy of Management Review, 20*(3), 709–734.

McClelland, D. C. (1973). Testing for competence rather than for "intelligence". *American Psychologist, 28*(1), 1–14.

McCroskey, J. C. (1968/1982/2001). *An introduction to rhetorical communication.* 1st ed. 1968, Prentice-Hall; 4th ed. 1982, Prentice-Hall; 8th ed. 2001, Allyn & Bacon.

McGuire, W. J. (1961a). The effectiveness of supportive and refutational defenses in immunizing and restoring beliefs against persuasion. *Sociometry, 24*, 184–197.

McGuire, W. J. (1961b). Resistance to persuasion conferred by active and passive prior refutation of the same and alternative counterarguments. *The Journal of Abnormal and Social Psychology, 63*(2), 326–332.

McGuire, W. J. (1964). Inducing resistance to persuasion: Some contemporary approaches. In L. Berkowitz (Ed.), *Advances in experimental social psychology* (Vol. 1, pp. 191–229). Academic Press.

Memon, A., Vrij, A., & Bull, R. (2003). *Psychology and law: Truthfulness, accuracy and credibility* (2nd ed.). John Wiley & Sons Ltd.

Miller, C. R. (2001). Writing in a culture of simulation: Ethos online. In P. Coppock (Ed.), *The semiotics of writing: Transdisciplinary perspectives on the technology of writing* (pp. 253–278). Brepols Publishers.

Miller, W. R., Moyers, T. B., Ernst, D., & Amrhein, P. (2008). *Motivational Interviewing Skill Code (MISC) 2.1.* Center on Alcoholism, Substance Abuse, and Addictions, The University of New Mexico.

Miller, W. R., & Rollnick, S. (2009). Ten things that motivational interviewing is not. *Behavioural and Cognitive Psychotherapy*, *37*(2), 129–140.

Misztal, B. (1995). *Trust in modern societies: The search for the bases of social order.* Polity Press.

Misztal, B. A. (2001). Normality and trust in Goffman's theory of interaction order. *Sociological Theory, 19*(3), 312–324.

Molm, L. D., Schaefer, D. R., & Collett, J. L. (2009). Fragile and resilient trust: Risk and uncertainty in negotiated and reciprocal exchange. *Sociological Theory, 27*(1), 1–32.

Mondada, L. (2011). The management of knowledge discrepancies and of epistemic changes in institutional interactions. In T. Stivers, L. Mondada, & J. Steensig (Eds.), *The morality of knowledge in conversation* (pp. 27–57). Cambridge University Press.

Mondada, L. (2014). The local constitution of multimodal resources for social interaction. *Journal of Pragmatics, 65*, 137–156.

Ng, S. H., & Bradac, J. J. (1993). *Power in language.* SAGE.

Nielsen, A. M. R. (in review). *Measuring in social interaction.* Palgrave.

Nielsen, A. M. R., & Nielsen, M. F. (in review). *"You can't conclude that based on those data!" – improving validity in the social sciences by revisiting trust research.*

Nielsen, M. F. (2000). *Under lup i offentligheden – introduktion til public relations.* Samfundslitteratur.

Nielsen, M. F. (2010a). *Fortolkningsledelse – mellemlederes kommunikative arbejde med værdier og kulturskabelse*. Samfundslitteratur.
Nielsen, M. F. (2010b). *Positionering – mellemlederes kommunikative arbejde med ledelsesrum og ledelsesret*. Samfundslitteratur.
Nielsen, M. F. (2012). Using artifacts in brainstorming sessions to secure participation and decouplesequentiality. *Discourse Studies, 14*(1), 87–109.
Nielsen, M. F. (2014). Sizing up 'the box' in order to fit in. *CoDesign, 10*(2), 112–134.
Nielsen, M. F. (2016a). Tillid i relationer. In *Kommunikation i internationale virksomheder* (Vol. 2, pp. 173–202). Samfundslitteratur. Translated to "Trust in relationships" by Chris Flynn and published 2022 in *The International Business Interaction Series*, SocialFormats Publishing.
Nielsen, M. F. (2016b). Which interactional features may be identified as indicators of achieved mutual trust? Paper presented October 7–8, 2016 at The 6th annual meeting of The Language and Social Interaction Working Group (LANSI), Teachers College, Columbia University, New York City.
Nielsen, M. F. (forthcoming-a). Revisiting authority in social interaction. Draft.
Nielsen, M. F. (forthcoming-b). Indications of trust and mistrust in social interaction. Draft.
Nielsen, M. F., Nielsen, S. B., Gravengaard, G., & Due, B. (2012). Interactional functions of invoking procedure in institutional settings. *Journal of Pragmatics, 44*(11), 1457–1473.
Nielsen, M. F., & Toft, T. L. W. (in review-a). Entitlement to join colleagues' conversations: Spatiality, objects and the moral order of office café areas.
Nielsen, M. F., & Toft, T. L. W. (in review-b). Revisiting the analytical concept 'participant orientation' in ICT-mediated multicommunication.
Nielsen, S. B. (2007). *Udskrevet, men ikke afskrevet. En konversationsanalytisk undersøgelse af magtarbejde indlejret i social handling under geriatriske udskrivningssamtaler* [PhD Dissertation]. Department of Scandinavian Studies and Linguistics, University of Copenhagen.
Oddo, J. (2014). The chief prosecutor and the iraqi regime: Intertextual ethos and transitive chains of authority. In *Intertextuality and the 24-hour news cycle: A day in the rhetorical life of Colin Powell's U.N. address* (pp. 45–76). Michigan State University Press.
Ofshe, R.J., & Leo, R.A. (1997). The decision to confess falsely: Rational choice and irrational action. *Denver University Law Review, 74*, 979–1112.
Ogden, R. (2020). Audibly not saying something with clicks. *Research on Language and Social Interaction, 53*(1), 66–89.
O'Keefe, D. J. (1990). The study of persuasive effects. In D. J. O'Keefe (Ed.), *Persuasion: Theory and research* (pp. 169–213). SAGE.
Ortmann, A., Fitzgerald, J., & Boeing, C. (2000). Trust, reciprocity, and social history: A re-examination. *Experimental Economics, 3*(1), 81.
Parsons, T. (1951). *The social system*. McGraw-Hill.
Peräkylä, A., Henttonen, P., Voutilainen, L., Kahri, M., Stevanovic, M., Sams, M., & Ravaja, N. (2015). Sharing the emotional load: Recipient affiliation calms down the storyteller. *Social Psychology Quarterly, 78*(4), 301–323.
Perelman, C. (1982). *The realm of rhetoric*. University of Notre Dame Press.
Pfau, M., Tusing, K. J., Koerner, A. F., Lee, W., Godbold, L. C., Penaloza L. J., & Hung, Y.-H. (1997). Enriching the inoculation construct: The role of critical

components in the process of resistance. *Human Communication Research, 24*(2), 187–215.
Pomerantz, A. (1978). Attributions of responsibility: Blamings. *Sociology, 12*(1), 115–121.
Pomerantz, A. (1980). Telling my side: 'Limited access' as a 'fishing device'. *Sociological Inquiry, 50*, 186–198.
Pomerantz, A. (1984a). Agreeing and disagreeing with assessments: Some features of preferred/dispreferred turn shaped. In J. M. Atkinson & J. Heritage (Eds.), *Structures of social action* (p. 24). Cambridge University Press.
Pomerantz, A. (1984b). Giving a source or basis: The practice in conversation of telling 'how i know'. *Journal of Pragmatics, 8*, 607–625.
Pomerantz, A. (1986). Extreme case formulations: A way of legitimizing claims. *Human Studies, 9*, 219–229.
Pomerantz, A. (1988/1989). Constructing skepticism: Four devices used to engender the audience's skepticism. *Research on Language and Social Interaction, 22*, 293–314.
Pomerantz, A., & Fehr, B. J. (1997). Conversation analysis: An approach to the study of social action as sense making practices. In T. A. van Dijk (Ed.), *Discourse as social interaction* (pp. 64–91). SAGE.
Pomerantz, A., & Fehr, B. J. (2011). Conversation analysis: An approach to the analysis of social interaction. In T. A. van Dijk (Ed.), *Discourse studies: A multidisciplinary introduction* (2nd ed., pp. 165–190). SAGE.
Potter, J. (1996). *Representing reality: Discourse, rhetoric, and social construction*. SAGE.
Potter, J. (1998). Discursive social psychology: From attitudes to evaluations. *European Review of Social Psychology, 9*, 233–266.
Potter, J. (2004). Discourse analysis as a way of analyzing naturally occurring talk. In D. Silverman (Ed.), *Qualitative research: Theory, method and practice* (2nd ed., pp. 200–221). SAGE.
Potter, J., & Hepburn, A. (2005). Qualitative interviews in psychology: Problems and possibilities. *Qualitative Research in Psychology*, 2(4), 281–307.
Potter, J., & Hepburn, A. (2012). Eight challenges for interview researchers. In J. Gubrium, J. Holstein, A. Marvasti, & K. McKinney, *The SAGE handbook of interview research: The complexity of the craft* (pp. 555–570). SAGE Publications, Inc.
Potter, J., & Wetherell, M. (1987). *Discourse and social psychology: Beyond attitudes and behaviour*. SAGE.
Potter, N. N. (2002). *How can I be trusted?: A virtue theory of trustworthiness*. Rowman & Littlefield.
Preston, L. E., & Sapienza, H. J. (1990). Stakeholder management and corporate performance. *Journal of Behavioral Economics, 19*(4), 361–375.
Psathas, G. (1999). Studying the organization in action: Membership categorization and interaction analysis. *Human Studies*, *22*(2–4), 139–162.
Pudlinski, C. (2005). Doing empathy and sympathy: Caring responses to troubles tellings on a peer support line. *Discourse Studies, 7*(3), 267–288.
Rancière, J. (2002). The aesthetic revolution and its outcomes. *New Left Review, 14*, March-April.
Rankin, N. (2002). Raising performance through people: The ninth competency survey. *Competency and Emotional Intelligence*, 2–21.

Rawls, A. W., & David, G. (2005). Accountably other: Trust, reciprocity and exclusion in a context of situated practice. *Human Studies, 28*(4), 469–497.

Raymond, G. (2003). Grammar and social organization: Yes/no type interrogatives and the structure of responding. *American Sociological Review, 68*, 939–967.

Raymond, G. (2018). Which epistemics? Whose conversation analysis? *Discourse Studies, 20*(1), 57–89.

Raymond, G., & Heritage, J. (2006). The epistemics of social relations: Owning grandchildren. *Language in Society, 35*(5), 677–705.

Raymond, G., & Zimmerman, D. H. (2007). Rights and responsibilities in calls for help: The Case of the mountain glade fire. *Research on Language and Social Interaction, 40*(1), 33–61.

Reiersen, J. (2017). Trust as belief or behavior? *Review of Social Economy, 75*(4), 434–453.

Rempel, J. K., Holmes, J. G., & Zanna, M. P. (1985). Trust in close relationships. *Journal of Personality and Social Psychology, 49*(1), 95–112.

Resnick, S. G., Fontana, A., Lehman, A. F., & Rosenheck, R. A. (2005). An empirical conceptualization of the recovery orientation. *Schizophrenia Research, 75*(1), 119–128.

Richards, I. A. (1930). *Practical criticism: A study of literary judgment.* Kegan Paul, Trench, Tubner & Co.

Romaniuk, T. (2013). Pursuing answers to questions in broadcast journalism. *Research on Language and Social Interaction, 46*(2), 144–164.

Ronald, K. (1990). A reexamination of personal and public discourse in classical rhetoric. *Rhetoric Review, 9*(1), 36–48.

Rose, E. (1992). *The Werald.* The Waiting Room Press.

Roth, A. L. (1998). Who makes the news? Descriptions of television news interviewees' public personae. *Media, Culture & Society, 20*(1), 79–107.

Rotter, J. B. (1980). Interpersonal trust, trustworthiness, and gullibility. *American Psychologist, 35*(1), 1–7.

Rousseau, D. M., Sitkin, S. B., Burt, R. S., & Camerer, C. (1998). Not so different after all: A cross-discipline view of trust. *Academy of Management Review, 23*(3), 393–404.

Russell, B. (1956). On denoting. In: R. C. Marsh (Ed.), *Logic and knowledge* (pp. 39–56). Macmillan. (Original work published 1905)

Ruusuvuori, J. (2005). "Empathy" and "sympathy" in action: Attending to patients' troubles in Finnish homeopathic and general practice consultations. *Social Psychology Quarterly, 68*(3), 204–222.

Sacks, H. (1972a). On the analyzability of stories by children. In J. J. Gumperz & D. Hymes (Eds.), *Directions in sociolinguistics: The ethnography of communication* (pp. 325–345). Holt, Rinehart and Winston.

Sacks, H. (1972b). An initial investigation of the usability of conversational data for doing sociology. In D. Sudnow (Ed.), *Studies in social interaction.* Free Press.

Sacks, H. (1984). On doing 'being ordinary'. In J. M. Atkinson & J. Heritage (Eds.), *Structures of social action: Studies in conversation analysis* (pp. 413–429). Cambridge University Press.

Sacks, H. (1985). The inference-making machine. In T. A. van Dijk (Ed.), *Handbook of discourse analysis* (vol. 3, pp. 13–23). Academic Press.

Sacks, H. (1987). On the preferences for agreement and contiguity in sequences in conversation. In G. Button & J. R. E. Lee (Eds.), *Talk and social organisation* (pp. 54–69). Multilingual Matters.

Sacks, H. (1989). Lecture 6. The M.I.R membership categorization device. *Human Studies*, *12*, 271–281. (Original work published 1964)

Sacks, H. (1992). *Lectures on conversation: Volumes I & II* (G. Jefferson, Ed.; 1. publ. in one paperback volume 1995). Blackwell.

Sacks, H. (1995). *Lectures on conversation*. Blackwell.

Sacks, H., & Schegloff, E. A. (1979). Two preferences in the organization of reference to persons and their interaction. In G. Psathas (Ed.), *Everyday language: Studies in ethnomethodology* (pp. 15–21). Irvington Publishers.

Sacks, H., Schegloff, E. A., & Jefferson, G. (1974). A simplest systematics for the organization of turn-taking in conversation. *Language, 50*(4), 696–735.

Salaman, G. (2004). Competences of managers, competences of leaders'. In J. Storey (Ed.), *Leadership in organizations: Current issues and key trends* (pp. 58–78). Routledge.

Schegloff, E. A. (1968). Sequencing in conversational openings. *Anthropologist, 70*(1), 75–95.

Schegloff, E. A. (1972). Notes on a conversational practice: Formulating place. In D. Sudnow (Ed.), *Studies in social interaction* (pp. 75–119). Free Press.

Schegloff, E. A. (1979). Identification and recognition in telephone conversation openings. 58.

Schegloff, E. A. (1986). The routine as achievement. *Human Studies*, *9*, 111–151.

Schegloff, E. A. (1993). Reflections on quantification in the study of conversation. *Research on Language and Social Interaction*, *26*(1), 99–128.

Schegloff, E. A. (2005). On complainability. *Social Problems, 52*(4), 449–476.

Schegloff, E. A. (2007a). A tutorial on membership categorization. *Journal of Pragmatics, 39*, 462–482.

Schegloff, E. A. (2007b). *Sequence organization in interaction: A primer in conversation analysis*. Cambridge University Press.

Schegloff, E. A., Jefferson, G., & Sacks, H. (1977). The preference for self-correction in the organization of repair in conversation. *Language, 54*(2), 361–382.

Schegloff, E. A., & Sacks, H. (1973). Opening up closings. *Semiotica, 8*, 289–327.

Schenkein, J. N. (1978). Identity negotiations in conversation. In J. N. Schenkein (Ed.), *Studies in the organization of conversational interaction* (pp. 57–78). Academic Press.

Schiemann, S. J., Mühlberger, C., Schoorman, F. D., & Jonas, E. (2019). Trust me, I am a caring coach: The benefits of establishing trustworthiness during coaching by communicating benevolence. *Journal of Trust Research, 9*(2), 164–184.

Schiffrin, D. (1987). *Discourse markers*. Cambridge University Press.

Schoorman, F. D., Mayer, R. C., & Davis, J. H. (2007). An integrative model of organizational trust: Past, present, and future. *Academy of Management Review, 32*(2), 344–354.

Seuren, L. M., Wherton, J., Greenhalgh, T., & Shaw, S. E. (2021). Whose turn is it anyway? Latency and the organization of turn-taking in video-mediated interaction. *Journal of Pragmatics, 172*, 63–78.

Shapin, S. (1994). *A social history of truth: Civility and science in seventeenth-century England*. University of Chicago Press.

Shen, X., & Ferguson, M. J. (2021). How resistant are implicit impressions of facial trustworthiness? When new evidence leads to durable updating. *Journal of Experimental Social Psychology, 97*, 104219.

Sidnell, J. (2012). "Who knows best?" Evidentiality and epistemic asymmetry in conversation. *Pragmatics and Society, 3*(2), 294–320.

Sidnell, J., & Stivers, T. (2012). *The handbook of conversation analysis*. Oxford: Wiley-Blackwell.

Simpson, J. A. (2007). Psychological foundations of trust. *Current Directions in Psychological Science, 16*(5), 264–268.

Smith, D. E. (1978). 'K is Mentally Ill' the anatomy of a factual account. *Sociology, 12*(1), 23–53.

Sparrow, P. (1997). Organisational competencies: Creating a strategic behavioural framework for selection and assessment. In N. Anderson & P. Herriot (Eds.), *International handbook of selection and assessment*. Wiley.

Sperber, D., & Wilson, D. (1986). *Relevance: Communication and cognition*. Blackwell.

Starr, P. (1982). *The social transformation of American medicine*. Basic Books.

Stevanovic, M. (2011). Participants' deontic rights and action formation: The case of declarative requests for action. *InLiSt, 52*, 37.

Stevanovic, M., & Peräkylä, A. (2012). Deontic authority in interaction: The right to announce, propose, and decide. *Research on Language and Social Interaction, 45*(3), 297–321.

Stivers, T. (2005a). Non-antibiotic treatment recommendations: Delivery formats and implications for parent resistance. *Social Science & Medicine, 60*(5), 949–964.

Stivers, T. (2005b). Parent resistance to physicians' treatment recommendations: One resource for initiating a negotiation of the treatment decision. *Health Communication, 18*(1), 41–74.

Stivers, T. (2008). Stance, alignment, and affiliation during storytelling: When nodding is a token of affiliation. *Research on Language and Social Interaction, 41*, 31–57.

Stivers, T. (2015). Coding social interaction: A heretical approach in conversation analysis? *Research on Language and Social Interaction, 48*(1), 1–19.

Stivers, T., Mondada L., & Steensig J. (2011). Knowledge, morality and affiliation in social interaction. In T. Stivers, L. Mondada, & J. Steensig (Eds.), *The morality of knowledge in conversation* (pp. 3–24). Cambridge University Press.

Stokoe, E. (2009). Doing actions with identity categories: Complaints and denials in neighbor disputes. *Text & Talk, 29*(1), 75–97.

Stokoe, E. (2011). Simulated interaction and communication skills training: The 'conversation-analytic role-play method'. In C. Antaki (Ed.), *Applied conversation analysis: Intervention and change in institutional talk* (pp. 119–139). Palgrave Macmillan.

Stokoe, E. (2012). Moving forward with membership categorization analysis: Methods for systematic analysis. *Discourse Studies, 14*(3), 277–303.

Stokoe, E. (2014). The conversation analytic role-play method (CARM): A method for training communication skills as an alternative to simulated role-play. *Research on Language and Social Interaction, 47*(3), 255–265.

Stokoe, E., & Edwards, D. (2009). Accomplishing social action with identity categories: mediating and policing neighbour disputes. In M. Wetherell (Ed.), *Theorizing identities and social action* (pp. 95–115). Palgrave Macmillan UK.

Stokoe, E. H., & Smithson, J. (2001). Making gender relevant: Conversation analysis and gender categories in interaction. *Discourse & Society, 12*(2), 217–244.

Strawson, P. F. (1950). On referring. *Mind, New Series, 53*(235), 320–344.

Suchman, A. L., Markakis, K., Beckman, H. B., & Frankel, R. (1997). A model of empathic communication in the medical interview. *JAMA, 277*(8), 678–682.

Svennevig, J. (2008). Trying the easiest solution first in other-initiation of repair. *Journal of Pragmatics, 40*, 333–348.

Sztompka, P. (1999). *A sociological theory*. Cambridge University Press.

Todorov, A. (2011). Evaluating faces on social dimensions. In A. Todorov, S. T. Fiske, & D. A. Prentice (Eds.), *Social neuroscience: Toward understanding the underpinnings of the social mind* (pp. 54–76). Oxford: Oxford University Press.

Todorov, A., & Oosterhof, N. N. (2011). Modeling social perception of faces. *IEEE Signal Processing Magazine, 28*, 117–122.

Todorov, A., Said, C. P., Engell, A. D., & Oosterhof, N. N. (2008). Understanding evaluation of faces on social dimensions. *Trends in Cognitive Sciences, 12*(12), 455–460.

Tranekjær, L., Nielsen, M. F., & Due, B. (in press). Constructing professional identities by suggesting improvement of professional practices. *Discourse Studies.*

Tsankova, E., Vanman, E. J., & Kappas, A. (2018). Interaction of stereotypical trustworthiness, facial resemblance, and group membership in the perception of trustworthiness and other traits. *Journal of Trust Research, 8*(1), 31–44.

Turowetz, J., & Rawls, A. W. (2020). The development of Garfinkel's 'Trust' argument from 1947 to 1967: Demonstrating how inequality disrupts sense and self-making. *Journal of Classical Sociology, 21*(1), 3–37.

Uslaner, E. M. (2002). *The moral foundations of trust*. Cambridge University Press.

Versteeg, W., & te Molder, H. (2016). What my body tells me about your experience: 'My side' empathy formulations in ADHD coaching sessions. *Journal of Pragmatics, 105*, 74–86.

Vine, M., & Bull, R. (2003). Does facial attractiveness affect judgements of deception? Poster presented at the Annual Conference of the European Association of Psychology and Law, Edinburgh.

Vöge, M. (2010). Local identity processes in business meetings displayed through laughter in complaint sequences. *Journal of Pragmatics, 42*(6), 1556–1576.

Vrij, A. (2000). *Detecting lies and deceit: The psychology of lying and its implications for professional practice*. Wiley.

Vrij, A., & Mann, S. (2001). Telling and detecting lies in a high-stake situation: The case of a convicted murderer. *Applied Cognitive Psychology, 15*(2), 187–203.

Wagner, J., Doehler, S. P., & González-Martínez, E. (2018). Longitudinal research on the organization of social interaction: Current developments and methodological challenges. In S. Pekarek Doehler, J. Wagner, & E. González-Martínez (Eds.), *Longitudinal studies on the organization of social interaction*. Palgrave Macmillan Limited.

Wang, X. (2016). A struggle for trustworthiness: Local officials' discursive behaviour in press conferences handling Tianjin blasts in China. *Discourse & Communication, 10*(4), 412–426.

Warnick, B. (2004). Online ethos: Source credibility in an "authorless" environment. *American Behavioral Scientist, 48*(2), 256–265.
Warnick, B. (2007). *Rhetoric online: Persuasion and politics in the word wide web*. Peter Lang Publishing.
Watson, D. R. (1978). Categorization, authorization and blame—Negotiation in conversation. *Sociology, 12*(1), 105–113.
Watson, D. R. (1983). The presentation of victim and motive in discourse: The case of police interrogations and interviews. *Victimology, 8*, 31–52.
Watson, R. (2009). Constitutive practices and Garfinkel's notion of trust: Revisited. *Journal of Classical Sociology, 9*(4), 475–499.
Weigert, A. J. (2012). Pragmatic trust in a world of strangers: TrustWorthy actions. In M. Sasaki & R. M. Marsh (Eds.), *Trust: Comparative perspectives*. BRILL.
Whalen, M. R., & Zimmerman, D. H. (1990). Describing trouble: Practical epistemology in citizen calls to the police. *Language in Society, 19*, 465–492.
Whitehead, K. A. (2013). Managing self/other relations in complaint sequences: The use of self-deprecating and affiliative racial categorizations. *Research on Language & Social Interaction, 46*(2), 186–203.
Wiggins, S. (2017). *Discursive psychology: Theory, method and applications*. SAGE.
Wilkinson, S., & Kitzinger, C. (2008). Using conversation analysis in feminist and critical research. *Social and Personality Psychology Compass, 2*(2), 555–573.
Willis, J., & Todorov, A. (2006). First impressions: Making up your mind after 100 ms exposure to a face. *Psychological Science, 17*, 592–598.
Wilson, R. K. (2017). *Trust experiments, trust games, and surveys* (E. M. Uslaner, Ed., Vol. 1). Oxford University Press.
Wittgenstein, L. (1958). *Philosophical investigations* (3rd ed., trans. G. E. M. Anscombe). Macmillan.
Wood, A. M., Linley, P. A., Maltby, J., Baliousis, M., & Joseph, S. (2008). The authentic personality: A theoretical and empirical conceptualization and the development of the Authenticity Scale. *Journal of Counseling Psychology, 55*(3), 385–399.
Wooffitt, R. (1991). "I was just doing X . . . when Y": Some inferential properties of a device in accounts of paranormal experiences. *Text, 11*, 267–288.
Wubs-Mrozewicz, J. (2020). The concept of language of trust and trustworthiness: (Why) history matters. *Journal of Trust Research, 10*(1), 91–107.
Zimmerman, D. H. (1992). The interactional organization of calls for emergency assistance. In P. Drew & J. Heritage (Eds.), *Talk at work: Social interaction in institutional settings* (pp. 418–469). Cambridge University Press.
Zimmerman, D. H. (1998). Identity, context and interaction. In C. Antaki & S. Widdicombe (Eds.), *Identities in talk* (pp. 88–106). SAGE.

Index